GEORGE WASHINGTON
A Biography

"One of the best short biographies of Washington in decades. . . . There is a nice balance of public and private, of personal and circumstantial."

—*Kirkus Reviews*

"This biography will be enjoyed by readers interested in American history and by anyone interested in reading about a genuine hero."

—*Baton Rouge Morning Advocate*

"Refreshingly light . . . a wealth of infor... n both personal and professional about a m... has seemingly tended to obscure ... e passage of time."

...bia, S.C.)

"The Washin... ...eadable narrative—an... ...perience behind it."

—*Richmond News-Leader*

"A sound, readable portrait. . . . The narrative is enlivened with interesting tidbits and anecdotes. . . . Alden's study will most likely become the standard 'Washington' for the foreseeable future."

—*Bestsellers*

Other Books by John R. Alden

John Stuart and the Southern Colonial Frontier
General Gage in America
General Charles Lee
The American Revolution, 1775–1783
The South in the Revolution, 1763–1789
The First South
Rise of the American Republic
Pioneer America
A History of the American Revolution
Robert Dinwiddie
Stephen Sayre: American Revolutionary Adventurer

George Washington

A Biography

John R. Alden

A LAUREL BOOK
Published by
Dell Publishing Co., Inc.
1 Dag Hammarskjold Plaza
New York, New York 10017

Louisiana State University Press *Southern Biography Series,*
William J. Cooper, Editor.

Laurel ® TM 674623, Dell Publishing Co., Inc.

ISBN: 0-440-32836-5

Reprinted by arrangement with Louisiana State University Press

Printed in the United States of America
February 1987

10 9 8 7 6 5 4 3 2 1

WFH

Contents

Preface and Acknowledgments

If it be true, as has often been said, that each generation writes its own history, it is also true that each generation produces its own biographies. Such a statement, without qualification, is tinged with cynicism. Every biographer worthy of the name takes what advantage he can of the labors and perceptions of his predecessors. Many lives of George Washington, beginning with the famous one by Parson Weems, have come from the press. Two massive ones, by Douglas S. Freeman and his aides and by James Thomas Flexner, appeared not long ago. They should be consulted by readers who wish to know more about Washington than is chronicled in this book. The Freeman volumes deal with him on almost a day-to-day basis.

We now have a much better understanding of Washington than was available in the past. Scholars have ceased to put gilding upon a wooden hero. It has become clear that he possessed an interesting personality. Thus there can now be no doubt that he was gifted not only with a keen perception of irony but with an earthy sense of humor. Illustrations of the latter are offered herein. Thus the present writer hopes that the decades of study he has spent upon the era of the American Revolution have made it possible to contribute a lucid and balanced account of Washington as a military commander and to assess correctly his role as defender of the American nation during his presidency. There can be no change in the considered verdict of all his worthy biographers and of all those who have read extensively concerning him that he was a great man, a majestic figure, unquestionably the principal, the essential founder and champion of the American republic.

I wish to express my gratitude to a few persons and institutions that have recently given me special assistance—to Kathleen S. Alden; Madaleen S. Thébaud; the staffs of the public libraries of Clearwater, Florida, and Traverse City, Michigan, and of the National Archives; Emerson Ford of the Perkins Library of Duke University; Professor William Cooper of Louisiana State University; and, above all, Professor William Abbot and his colleagues of *The Papers of George Washington,* who saved me from a number of errors. I wish also to acknowledge the unfailing helpfulness and kindness of the staff of the Louisiana State University Press.

I

The Young Virginian

At the end of his own time and for generations thereafter he was acclaimed at home and abroad as the founder of the American nation. He achieved sainthood in the minds of the Americans who came after him. There was a tendency to look upon him as an archangel who possessed the genius of Caesar, the vision of Moses, and the morals of Galahad. A change came. Later Americans gave more and more attention to their rights, less and less to the man who was the principal begetter of those rights. Scholars and teachers in America offered more and more praise to men of the era of the Revolution who talked and wrote in behalf of liberty, to those who labored at European capitals for independence, to those who remodeled American institutions, to Thomas Paine, Thomas Jefferson, Benjamin Franklin, Alexander Hamilton, and James Madison. There was also in the twentieth century a school of biographical "debunkers" who discovered that great men and women, American as well as European, were inconstant and incontinent, addicted to profanity, and menaced by insanity. Among them were writers who sought to destroy the hallowed Washington, to reduce him to mortal or smaller proportions. They found sin in the saint. So doing, they tended to make the Father of His Country into an important scamp. It was often forgotten that the sword can be more potent than the pen, that the bayonet can speak more decisively than the tongue of the diplomat, that Washington was the one man essential to the triumph of the Patriots in the War of Independence, to the creation of the American union, and perhaps even to the success of the democratic revolution throughout the world.

It is no secret that Washington was not born to the imperial purple. Nor was he by birth a member of the First Families of Virginia, the fabled Virginia aristocracy. He opened his eyes without fanfare of trumpets, with modest hereditary prestige, in a brick house near the junction of Pope's Creek with the Potomac River in Westmoreland County, Virginia, at 10 A.M. on February 11, 1732 —a day of the month that became February 22 when Britain and the British empire afterward condescended to strike eleven days from their defective calendar to match it with that of the remainder of the Western world. He was later duly baptized in the Episcopal church. He was not christened after King George III, who came into the world six years later. It has been urged that he was named after a George Eskridge, a benefactor of Washington's mother. It is not unlikely that the parents had King George II in mind.

There was little reason at the time to believe that Washington, that any American subject of the British Crown, would play an important part in the great world. Europeans dominated it. The rulers of all the principal nations of continental Europe were hereditary and virtually absolute. Britain was governed by a king who shared power with great nobles and country gentlemen, but not with masses of common men and women. Attention of writers and historians was concentrated upon the activities of those worthies, together with the achievements of Europeans in the arts and sciences. Merchants on the eastern side of the Atlantic who gained wealth by dealing in raw materials that came from colonies beyond the seas might see growing importance in such possessions. An occasional man of state who peered into the future from London or Paris might foresee riches and power to come from outlying continents, but almost all European men of politics concentrated upon the affairs of their center of the globe. They knew about the foreign policy of the king of Sardinia and the tsar of Russia, the whims of the foreign minister at the Habsburg capital of Vienna, the fancies of the mistress of the French monarch. They assumed that such matters would continue to be of the first importance into the far future. Even in Britain, where royal ministers gave greater heed to things naval and commercial than did their counterparts beyond the Channel, colonies were not commonly in the forefront of official minds. Indeed, it is often said that Britain was pursuing a policy of "salutary neglect" with respect to her American dominions.

Whether British inattention with respect to possessions beyond the Atlantic was healthy may be debated. Certainly it led to a weakening of authority exerted from London in the old thirteen colonies along the western Atlantic seaboard. They were prospering in people and wealth, and their settlements were expanding toward the Appalachian divide. Governors were sent out from the imperial capital. Even when they were supported by appointed members of councils—of upper houses of legislatures—they had lost and were losing power to locally elected lower houses of assembly. Dominance in local affairs was shifting, amidst frequent bickering, to the western side of the ocean. The process led to only occasional thought and to less frequent action in London. There "our colonies" were looked upon primarily as sources of raw materials, including tobacco, rice, and lumber. They must be kept, and even enlarged. Britain was prepared to defend her empire against France and Spain, and to expand it; but it was assumed in the halls of Westminster and the chambers of Whitehall, not without reason, that the inhabitants of Britain's American dominions were culturally inferior, that they would remain subordinate to their superiors.

There was nothing in the heredity of the American infant that pointed toward greatness. He never knew much about his English background. He was told that his ancestors were inhabitants of northern England. His family tree was of "very little moment" to him. Much has been made of his descent from the English Washingtons of Sulgrave Manor, which has become an Anglo-American shrine. This despite the fact that the Washingtons of England were merely gentry rather than nobility. The ancestry of George was indeed very largely English—one of his female forebears came from Belgium—but it was respectable rather than distinguished. The English father of the first Washington to settle in Virginia was a clergyman, an educated man. It may be charitably assumed that he was also devout and benevolent. The Washington who began the American branch of the family was not a very early comer. Nor was he remarkable, so far as records say, for stout allegiance to Christian principles or gentlemanly behavior. He came to Virginia upon a commercial venture and decided to remain in the Old Dominion. Named John, he began to accumulate land and Negro slaves. His son Lawrence and his grandson Augustine similarly sought to collect broad acres and blacks. Augustine also engaged in iron manufacturing, but the high road to wealth and position in Virginia ran through rows of tobacco, and much land and many slaves were needed to produce it in quantities that brought substantial cash or credit when it was sold in Europe. Augustine Washington prospered, but did not amass vast wealth. Dying when approximately fifty years of age, he left behind him more than ten thousand acres, at least forty-nine slaves, a widow, and several offspring.

Not free from hereditary defects nor immune to the blows of Nature, the early Washingtons were sturdy and prolific. By his first wife, Jane Butler, Augustine had four children, including two sons who survived him. After her death, on May 26, 1730, he married again, on March 6, 1731, Mary Ball, a young, orphaned heiress in her middle twenties. She promptly began to produce more progeny for him, the first of her offspring being George. After George came Betty, Samuel, John Augustine, and Charles. Seven of the nine children of Augustine lived beyond infancy, an unusual record. Washington families were quite thick in Virginia in the eighteenth century.

When George was three years of age, his parents moved to a plantation at Little Hunting Creek on the south bank of the Potomac. Later Augustine, his second wife, and his brood settled at Ferry Farm on the north bank of the Rappahannock River opposite Fredericksburg. There Augustine died in 1743, when George was only eleven years of age. He inherited the Ferry Farm, other real estate, and ten slaves. Until he became legally an adult, his mother was his guardian. The consequences were most important for George. His father had sent his two half brothers, Lawrence and Augustine, Jr., to a school in Westmoreland, England. Perhaps Mary Washington lacked ready capital to arrange a similar education for George. It may be that she placed less value upon learning than had her husband. In any event, she kept her oldest son at the Ferry Farm, and he received only local and brief schooling. His formal education may have been even more limited than that obtained by Andrew Jackson and Abraham Lincoln. He acquired none of that classical lore that was driven into boyish heads at Eton, Oxford, Cambridge, Harvard, and Virginia's own College of

William and Mary. George did become familiar with *Don Quixote* and *Tristram Shandy*. His spelling, although it improved with time, remained a bit uncertain to the end of his life. But he profited from his studies. He developed a large, handsome, and most impressive handwriting, became a good draftsman, learned somewhat about mathematics, and gained elementary knowledge of science. He pored over a set of *Rules of Civility and Decent Behavior* with excellent result, developing good manners.

The time came when it seemed necessary to find a vocation for George. He might have been consigned to an obscure life as the owner of the Ferry Farm, which was not fertile. His half brother Lawrence suggested when George was fourteen that he should be sent to sea. However, his mother's half brother, Joseph Ball, like the famous Dr. Samuel Johnson, considered sailing ships to be floating prisons. He advised his sister not to permit the boy to enter either merchant service or the Royal Navy. George would be better off as an apprentice to a tinker than he would be as a common sailor on a merchant vessel, Ball said. Nor was it wise to let him enter the navy, where promotion without the patronage of powerful friends in England was unlikely. His mother adopted the prudent counsel of Joseph Ball, thus preventing George from entering upon a mercantile career and saving him from a frustrating life in the British navy. Instead, continuing to make his home at Ferry Farm until after he had reached maturity, he spent some years as an appraiser of lands rather than of tossing seas. He became the official surveyor of Culpeper County in the valley of the Rappahannock in 1749. In the next few years he earned substantial sums as a measurer of land, and he acquired more than 1,400 acres of land before he reached the age of twenty-one. He might have followed in the footsteps of Peter Jefferson, a surveyor who accumulated handsome holdings for his son Thomas and enabled him to play a great part in the world. Washington, like Peter Jefferson, learned about the values of soil. Eventually he became a very successful land speculator, but he did not confine himself to the collection of fertile soil.

Fortunately for George, Lawrence Washington did not abandon interest in his young half brother. He and George were fond of each other. Lawrence doubtless acquired a measure of polish in school in England and was a likable man. After his return to Virginia he served as a captain in a regiment of regular troops raised in America that participated in an unsuccessful British attack upon

Cartagena on the northern coast of South America during the conflict between Britain and the Bourbon kings of Spain and France known in Europe as the War of the Austrian Succession, sometimes more picturesquely designated the War of Jenkins' Ear. On that ill-fated expedition Lawrence met and came to admire Admiral Edward Vernon. Later settling down at Little Hunting Creek, he assured that officer a measure of immortality beyond his naval exploits by naming the plantation Mount Vernon. Lawrence prospered rather remarkably after a brief military career in the British army. Inheriting Mount Vernon, he was appointed adjutant general of the Virginia militia and elected to the House of Burgesses. Moreover, he married Anne, daughter of Colonel William Fairfax, owner of Belvoir, a commodious house on a plantation near Mount Vernon. He thereby acquired a most valuable connection. Colonel Fairfax was a mature and kind gentleman, a member of the Virginia governor's council. The colonel was also a distant cousin of Lord Fairfax, the owner of a vast property that at an earlier time consisted of more than five million acres of land in the Northern Neck, the region between the Potomac and Rappahannock rivers. George acquired acquaintance with the Fairfaxes through Lawrence, and the colonel became his good friend. George also gained intimacy with George William Fairfax, the colonel's son. He made visits to Mount Vernon, to Belvoir, and to the seat of Lord Fairfax at Greenway Court in the Shenandoah River Valley. Such associations, broadening his horizons and serving to improve his manners, were important to one who had so little formal schooling and who would never have the advantages of a sojourn in Europe. Moreover, the influence of the Fairfaxes would later help George to secure valuable appointments in Virginia.

The affectionate relationship between George and Lawrence and the ties of friendship between George and the Fairfaxes were even more decisive for them than has been indicated, for they offered experiences that counterbalanced those of a boy and young man who spent much of his life among the uneducated rural folk of Virginia and rough frontiersmen. In 1748 George went with George William Fairfax and others on a surveying party across the Blue Ridge into the valley of the Shenandoah. There, meeting a party of Indians en route home from war, the whites supplied liquor that stimulated the braves to do a martial dance over the one scalp that they had secured. George was to make many journeys across the great ridge and would spend several years in public service on the frontiers of Virginia and beyond them in the American wilderness. Romantics have often extolled the ennobling influence of life on the fringes of the new settlements as the whites advanced through and flooded into the territories of the red men. Coarse talk and behavior were also features of pioneer existence. Certainly George heard much earthy and ungrammatical language on the Virginia countryside and also in the western forests. Life for most Virginians was harsh rather than elegant. Crime was frequent, even though punishments were heavy. One Mary McDaniel, convicted of "robing the cloaths of Mr. George Washington when he was washing in the river" in the summer of 1751, was sentenced to suffer fifteen lashes upon her bare back. At Mount Vernon, at Belvoir, and at Greenway, George was exposed to better if not superb English and to superior manners.

Travel is not an indispensable part of a liberal education. There are those who journey widely and learn little; there are those whose jaunts are few and limited, but whose minds are broad and deep. Henry Thoreau tells us that he traveled extensively in the village of Concord—he did see much of the world. So it was with Washington, whose journeys, except for a short visit to the island of Barbados, were confined to the western Atlantic seaboard from Massachusetts to Virginia, with forays west of the Appalachian Mountains, until he was nearly sixty years of age. Only then did he visit northern New England, the Carolinas, and Georgia. But he did make a voyage to the British colony of Barbados in the Caribbean Sea in the fall of 1751 with Lawrence, who suffered from a pulmonary disease, probably tuberculosis, and who hoped that his health would be restored by a visit to the island. The brothers were received in friendly fashion on Barbados by Gedney Clarke, a connection of Colonel Fairfax, and they enjoyed the beauty of the tropical colony and the society of its officials and planters. George had begun to drink wine in Virginia. He danced, went riding on horseback, attended the theatre on Barbados—reared as an Anglican, he was not barred by moral scruples from numerous social pleasures. He would later display a measure of proficiency at billiards and would gamble, not very successfully, at the card table. But his stay on the island was by no means entirely pleasant, for he was stricken by smallpox on November 16 and confined to bed for about three weeks. He recovered, of course, but Lawrence failed to improve. Hoping that Bermuda would be more beneficial, Lawrence made his way to its islands. George sailed directly for Vir-

ginia in the *Industry* on December 21. He was "very sick" two
days later with that malady of the sea that lays low even the strongest of mortals, but he could congratulate himself upon the outcome of his two illnesses. He was able to eat his Christmas dinner.
The mate of the *Industry* was much less fortunate. He was "coop'd
up" in his cabin for a time before Christmas "with a fashionable
disorder" contracted in Barbados. So George wrote in his diary.
The *Industry* put down anchor near the mouth of the York River
on January 27, 1752. George rode to Williamsburg the next day,
presented letters to Robert Dinwiddie, a wealthy Scottish merchant of nearly sixty years who had recently become governor of
Virginia, and was invited to dine. Dinwiddie had traded in the
West Indies, and he had served as British surveyor general of customs there. George made a very favorable impression upon the
governor.

Becoming a legal adult soon after his return from the Caribbean,
Washington acquired full freedom to manage his properties. In the
spring of 1752 he went back into the Shenandoah Valley and resumed his labors as a surveyor. But he soon turned away from
measuring property to other occupation—he had to care for his
lands. Did he also begin to desire a military career? One cannot be
sure, but he did display an interest in soldiering. Learning that
Virginia was to be divided into districts for the purpose of training
militia, he applied to Governor Dinwiddie for an appointment as
adjutant for one of the areas. An adjutant was responsible for enlightening militia officers about things military, and they in turn
were supposed to teach the rank and file. He assured the governor
that it would be "the greatest pleasure" to obey the governor's
commands, that he would do his duties, that he would make himself worthy of the trust reposed in him, that he would by "a constant application" fit himself for the office. No evidence has been
found that Washington had ever had any kind of military training.
Nevertheless, his friend Colonel Fairfax was on the governor's
council, and Dinwiddie eventually assigned Washington to the area
of southern Virginia in December, 1752. Washington received a
salary of one hundred pounds per annum and was given the rank
of major, a bit of a plum for a young man of twenty-one who was a
novice in martial matters. That the rank and the pay were gifts to
one who had a powerful friend is indicated by the sequel. He soon
obtained a transfer to the northern Virginia district, which was
more convenient for him. Moreover, he later managed to make an

arrangement with a deputy according to which the deputy would do whatever had to be done, in return for half the pay of the office. In other words, Washington acquired a sinecure appointment as a major, with an unearned income from the public treasury of approximately fifty pounds per annum. Such sinecures were common in Britain and in the British colonies, and it is obvious that no theoretical objection to the system prevented Washington from seeking, accepting, and savoring the plum. Major Washington had a neat and useful addition to his income.

Too much has been made of the induction of Washington that year into the Masonic order at Fredericksburg—by members of the society and by Europeans who mistakenly believed that the Masons of Britain and America were active in politics, like those of France and Hispanic America. Washington seldom attended Masonic meetings, and there is no reason to believe that the society was important in framing his opinions or in his advance in the world. Much more decisive for him was the continued friendship of Colonel Fairfax and the newly gained goodwill of Governor Dinwiddie. The favor of the owner of Belvoir and the governor was all the more valuable to Washington because Lawrence died in July of 1752. Washington in consequence eventually inherited ownership for life of Mount Vernon. At the time, however, Washington could only mourn the loss of a half brother who had been not only a true brother but had served to a degree as a father. The death of Lawrence especially hurt because relations between Washington and his mother were not affectionate. He was a dutiful rather than an adoring son of a woman who had dutifully reared a brood of children and who believed that her exertions were not fully appreciated.

That year brought still another blow to Washington. He sought to marry, and his advances were rejected, by Betsy, daughter of William Fauntleroy, a prosperous merchant and planter who lived on the south side of the Rappahannock. She was by no means the first girl to whom he paid attention. He had earlier been attracted to several Virginia belles, including, perhaps, a "low land beauty." He had even composed—rather, tried to compose—poetry. His compositions were the feeble lines of an adolescent swain rather than the early outpourings of a Byron or Shelley. He had sighingly tried to address an acrostic in verse to a Frances Alexander. It ran:

From your bright sparking eyes, I was undone;
Rays, you have more transparent than the sun,
Amidst its glory in the rising day,
None can you equal in your bright array;
Constant in your calm and unspotted mind;
Equal to all, but will to none prove kind,
So knowing, seldom one so young, you'l find
Ah! woes me, that I should love and conceal,
Long have I wish'd, but never dare reveal,
Even though severly loves pains I feel;
Xerxes that great, wasn't free from Cupid's dart,
And all the greatest heroes, felt the smart.

He did not finish the effusion. Was his ardor insufficient to complete the poem? Another of his efforts at verse has survived. It reads, in part:

Oh ye gods why should my poor resistless heart
Stand to oppose thy might and power
At last surrender to Cupid's feather'd dart
And now lies bleeding every hour
For her that's pityless of my grief and woes. . . .
In deluding sleepings let my eyelids close
That in an enraptured dream I may
In a soft lulling sleep and gentle repose
Possess those joys denied by day.

It is evident that the admiration expressed by Washington exceeded his command of syntax.*

Betsy Fauntleroy was only fifteen, but quite old enough for matrimony in the Virginia of that time. Washington proposed to her when he was making one of his journeys to the Shenandoah. Allowed by her father to express her preference, she answered the pleas of Washington in the negative. Perhaps her refusal was not very emphatic. After his return from the Valley in the spring of that year Washington was laid "very low" by "a violent pleurisie" —had he been assailed by tuberculosis? Recovering, he made a second effort to win her hand. In May he informed her father that

---

* The two effusions survive in Washington's handwriting in his papers. It is possible that he merely copied them.

he intended, as soon as he regained his strength, to make an appeal to her in person "in hopes of a revocation" of her "former cruel sentence." If Washington did indeed beg Betsy to change her mind, he urged his suit in vain. Evidently she was not overwhelmed by his masculine charms. She was later married twice, to other Virginians. Washington remained single for six more years.

Did Betsy reject Washington because he was not a rich man? Because he was not yet smoothly mannered? Because he was not a handsome man? He had property, he had prospects, and he was physically attractive. Six feet tall, he was lanky, like many another American, like Jefferson and Lincoln.† He had rather long and lean arms and thighs, and he was flat-chested. He had strong but quite regular features, except that the upper part of his nose was unusually broad. His face, like so many countenances of his time, exhibited the marks of smallpox. He had light blue eyes and brown hair and was a vigorous male. A British officer who met Washington some years later reported that he had a dark complexion and a foreign look—which probably means that Washington was tanned at the time, that he had the appearance of an American. Altogether, he was an imposing young man, impressive to his own sex if not to Betsy Fauntleroy. Among the men who discerned superior quality in him was Governor Dinwiddie.

---

† The mature Washington tells us that his height was six feet. He can hardly have made a mistake regarding it. After his death Dr. James Craik measured his corpse and reported that he was exactly 6 feet 3¼ inches. The only explanation this writer can offer for the discrepancy is that the physician made the ludicrous mistake of measuring from head to toe instead of head to heel. By another report of the same time Washington was indeed six feet tall.

II

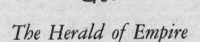

The Herald of Empire

While Washington was beginning his climb to fortune and fame, European rulers and their advisers prepared for armed struggle. The war in which his brother Lawrence took part ended indecisively, a fact recognized in the treaty of peace signed at Aix-la-Chapelle in 1748. Coalitions that had participated in it collapsed, and European nations chose up sides anew for a renewal of hostilities. The Bourbon monarchy of France and the Habsburg empire of Austria had been traditional enemies. Louis XV of France became the ally of Queen Maria Theresa of Austria. They joined the Empress Elizabeth of Russia, the king of Sweden, and various other princes in an effort to reduce the upstart king of Prussia, Frederick the Great, to suitable minor status. Britain resumed hostilities with France, later moved into an alliance with Frederick: Bourbon Spain entered the conflict as an ally of France in 1762. Since formal declarations of intent to use cannon, musketry, and bayonets began in 1756 and peace treaties came in 1763, the conflict is commonly called in Europe the Seven Years' War. In English America it acquired the title of the French and Indian War. The conflict covered much of the globe, and the clash between Britain and France in the New World was only a phase of it, a very important one, to be sure. The shooting commenced in the

forest of the American interior in 1754, and it was Washington
who ordered the first gunfire.

Not that Washington was ultimately responsible for all the
bloodshed of that war or its consequences. France and Britain
drifted almost inexorably into armed struggle. British politicians
saw a balance of power in Europe as an effective protection for
their home islands against French aggression. Moreover, the two
nations were contesting for territory and commerce in India, Af-
rica, the Caribbean Sea, and North America. Tension was severe
between the thirteen colonies and French Canada. As it happened,
the fighting began on a branch of the Ohio River. Occupying the
St. Lawrence Valley, New Orleans, and posts in the region of the
Great Lakes, France grandiosely claimed to own a vast Louisiana,
all of the Mississippi Valley, actually thinly occupied almost entirely by Indians. Except for a few pioneers who had put down in
what is now West Virginia and traders who exchanged guns, rum,
and other goods with the Indians for furs and deerskins, the English colonists were still confined to the Atlantic seaboard. More
modest than the men in power at Paris and Versailles, those who
wielded authority in London contended that the subjects of King
George II could rightfully move into the watershed of the Ohio,
even if as a consequence they drove a wedge between the French
settlements in the St. Lawrence and Mississippi valleys.

Since the French in North America, concentrated in the colony
of Quebec, with a small contingent at New Orleans, numbered
hardly sixty thousand, since there were more than twenty times as
many people in the thirteen colonies, since the British navy was
dominant in the North Atlantic, it may seem that the French flag
must before long be lowered in the fortress of Quebec and the town
of New Orleans. To be sure, the French Canadians were warlike,
and the French were often able to muster Indian allies. Distance,
forests, and waters also served to protect the Bourbon bastions.
The French had another advantage—centralized power in the
Crown. Authority among the English was divided between governments in London and in the thirteen colonies, and it was further
parceled out among royal officials, legislatures elected by the settlers, and in Pennsylvania and Maryland, proprietors and their
agents. Not entirely without reason, advisers of King Louis XV
were confident that they could confine the English east of the Appalachians. Perhaps they did not perceive the full strength of the
English, who tended to move slowly westward by families, with

occasional exertions of force, rather than swiftly by use of over-whelming military power. The French took the offensive in North America almost immediately after the Treaty of Aix-la-Chapelle. In 1749 the Chevalier Céloron de Blainville planted lead plates on the banks of the Ohio that proclaimed the sovereignty of Louis XV over the Beautiful River and the lands it drained. Nor were the French content with symbols and words. In 1752 they drove out English traders who had penetrated far into the region bounded by the Ohio River, the Great Lakes, and the Mississippi River after-ward called the Old Northwest—those traders, bringing guns, tomahawks, blankets, paint, trinkets, and rum to the red men, were able to undersell their French competitors, to offer higher prices for furs and deerskins. Living in the villages of the Indians, inter-marrying with them, French traders made friends for France. En-glish traders performed similarly for Britain. But in 1752 the French used force to drive them away and to suppress Indians in the region who rather favored the English. In the approaching struggle the forces of Louis XV would receive powerful assistance from the aborigines of the area. In the spring of 1753 the French took even more decisive steps. A body of their troops from Quebec appeared on the south shore of Lake Erie. They built a post at Presque Isle, now Erie, Pennsylvania, and another to the south-ward called Fort Le Boeuf.

Would the French advance further? Influential Virginians be-came increasingly concerned. The new Bourbon forts were not on territory usually claimed by the Old Dominion, extensive as that territory was—Virginians were disposed to insist that the south-western part of modern Pennsylvania and the entire region of the Old Northwest were included in their colony in a royal charter granted by King James I in 1609. To them that charter was nearly as sacred as the version of the Holy Scriptures printed under the aegis of that monarch two years later. Alarm arose in Williams-burg. It was not well that the French should use their new bases to challenge the colony of Pennsylvania. What was much worse, they might move into a region that ought to be recognized universally as part of Virginia. Thus they posed a threat to Virginians eager to acquire wealth by occupying new lands, particularly to the Ohio Company, formed in 1747 by leading citizens of the Old Dominion to gain estates and carry on commerce in the Ohio Valley. Law-rence Washington had been a partner in the company, and Gover-nor Dinwiddie was a member of it, along with several Lees, a

Carter, and George Mason. It claimed 500,000 acres on the waters of the upper Ohio, and it had the blessing of the British government. The company had built a store on a branch of the Monongahela River in 1752, and Virginians were meditating the erection of a fort near the strategic point where that river joins the Allegheny to form the Ohio.

Governor Dinwiddie was by no means content to wait for further action by the French. He condemned the advance of their troops in time of peace. Even as they established themselves south of Lake Erie, he proposed that the English colonies raise forces to prevent the French from settling in the Ohio Valley, and he wrote to London to express the hope that Britain would "think it necessary" to stop them. He received instructions from the Earl of Holderness, the British secretary of state in charge of colonial affairs. If either the French or Indians dared to erect a fort or forts "in our province of Virginia," Dinwiddie was to require them to leave. Should they refuse, he was ordered to "drive them off by force of arms." The burden of decision was placed upon the governor. If he resorted to arms with unfortunate results in the western wilderness, in an area he considered to be "in our province of Virginia," he might suffer as a man who had exceeded his authority. He did not ask for more precise orders. He acted.

After securing the advice of his council in a meeting on October 22, 1753, Dinwiddie resolved to send a formal demand to the commander of the French troops on the Ohio that they withdraw from British territory. Learning of the decision doubtless from Colonel Fairfax, Washington asked to be appointed as the bearer of the message. Five days later he was chosen, and on October 31 he was supplied with a commission and instructions. He was, said Dinwiddie in explaining his choice of Washington, "a person of distinction." Washington was only twenty-one and had not yet achieved anything remarkable. The governor presumably intended to say that his emissary was not a mere rough frontiersman or Indian trader. But it is clear enough that Washington, despite his youth, was considered equal to his diplomatic task. Obviously, he was accustomed to travel in wild country, and he was judged to be hardy enough to make the long journey to and from the French post in late fall and early winter. He was ordered, not merely to tell the French to depart, but to ascertain their numbers, the locations of their forts, and their line of communications with Canada. He was supplied with a letter from Dinwiddie to the French officer in command that blandly asserted that the "lands upon the River Ohio" were "in the western parts of the colony of Virginia" and "notoriously known to be the property of the Crown of Great Britain." The troops of Louis XV were building fortresses and forming settlements in the dominions of King George II. They were violating "the laws of nations" and treaties between Britain and France by their invasion. They must depart peaceably. Washington was to secure a reply from their commander, who was asked to treat him with "the candour and politeness natural to your nation." Let it be observed that Fort Le Boeuf, the most advanced French post at the time, was located only fifteen miles south of Lake Erie in the French Creek Valley and on the northern edge of the Ohio River watershed. The incursion of the soldiers of Louis XV into the domains of Virginia—if indeed the territory of Virginia included all of the watershed—was decidedly limited. Evidently Dinwiddie was determined to meet even a potential threat, which did indeed exist, to the English colonies if not to the Old Dominion. Refusal of the French to withdraw would, of course, supply reason for the exertion of force against them.

Washington did not dally. He left Williamsburg immediately after receiving his papers. At Fredericksburg on the following day he prudently employed Jacob Van Braam, a former Dutch army officer who was more or less familiar with French, to accompany him as an interpreter. The two men obtained supplies and equipment in Alexandria and Winchester, and they reached Wills Creek, now Cumberland, Maryland, on November 14. There Washington hired as a guide Christopher Gist, an able and vigorous frontiersman familiar with the Ohio Valley and its copper-skinned inhabitants. The emissary of Virginia also selected four men to assist with horses and supplies, which included meat, bread, and a tent.

The party began its journey through a rough country in which its progress was impeded by newly fallen snow. It found the rivers swollen by rain and melted snow, but managed to reach the point where the Monongahela and Allegheny rivers meet to form the Ohio on November 22. There Washington learned that most of the French troops who had penetrated southward of Lake Erie had retreated toward winter quarters in Canada. More important, he had opportunity to consider the junction of the two streams from a military point of view. The Ohio Company was planning to build a post some distance below the confluence, but Washington saw that a site immediately above it was preferable, that a fort at that place

would have great strategic importance. He and his party moved on
to an Indian village called Logstown, near present-day Ambridge,
Pennsylvania. There on November 25 he acquired information regarding the forces of Louis XV in the middle of the Mississippi
Valley from four French deserters and met the Half-King, a
friendly Seneca chief. The Half-King had visited Fort Le Boeuf,
and he informed Washington of the best route to that place. At
Logstown Washington learned from another Indian that the
French would resume their southward thrust the following spring.

Delaying his departure from Logstown for five days because the
Half-King thought it unwise for him to proceed without a large
escort, Washington finally moved on, with only four Indian friends,
including the Seneca chief. At Venango, where French Creek flows
into the Allegheny, the Virginia envoy and his entourage found
three French officers lodged in a house. The fleur-de-lis flew over
the structure. The senior officer, Captain Philippe Joncaire, politely
invited Washington to supper. Warmed by wine, the Frenchmen
talked about their line of communications with Montreal and informed the Virginian that the Ohio country was and must be recognized as part of the empire of Louis XV. However, they sent him
on to Fort Le Boeuf to see the senior French officer there. Delayed
by rain and snow and forced to make their way through mires and
swamps, Washington and his companions did not reach that place
until December 11. The surveyor and seeker of fertile soil did not
fail to observe that he and his party "pass'd over much good land"
and went "through several extensive & very rich meadows."

Washington and his men received a polite reception at Fort Le
Boeuf from its commandant, Jacques Le Gardeur, Sieur de Saint-
Pierre, an elderly officer with the bearing of a veteran soldier. The
problems posed by Washington were too important to be solved by
a subordinate, and the commandant sent for Louis Le Gardeur de
Repentigny, his superior, who was stationed at Presque Isle. The
senior Le Gardeur promptly appeared on December 12 and began
a private examination with his juniors of the papers presented by
the Virginian. He did not offer a reply until the evening of the
fourteenth. In the meantime Washington examined the fort and
learned that the French were making a fleet of canoes. It was plain
that they would indeed move southward in the spring. Le Gardeur
de Saint-Pierre reported to Dinwiddie that he "made it a particular
duty to receive Mr. Washington with the distinction owing to your
dignity, his position, and his own great merit." He doubtless pro-

vided food and wine that pleased a traveler who had subsisted upon irregular meals formed from aging provisions along with venison and bear meat obtained during his arduous journey. Washington discovered that the French were trying to win over the Half-King, and he was unable to persuade his Indian ally to leave the fort until the sixteenth. Then, having sent forward his weary horses under the care of three white men in his party, Washington set forth in a canoe down French Creek on his return journey with Gist and Van Braam. He took with him a letter from Le Gardeur de Saint-Pierre to Dinwiddie and "a plentiful store of liquor, provisions &c" supplied by the French. A second canoe carried his Indian companions.

The return journey was decidedly adventurous. Passing down French Creek, Washington, Van Braam, and Gist encountered distress and danger. The Indians deserted them on December 18. Because of the low level of the stream the three men were compelled several times to portage through cold water and over ice, but they had the pleasure of seeing a canoe of Frenchmen overturned, with their "brandy and wine floating in the creek." The three Englishmen arrived safely at Venango and met the remainder of their party there on December 22. But new troubles came. As the party moved southward on land, it became apparent that its horses were too weak to carry both riders and baggage. On the day before Christmas, to save the horses Washington put on "Indian walking dress," lifted a pack upon his back, and trudged forward through snow. Gist and Van Braam also moved on afoot. After two days of such travel they found that the horses were still overburdened. Eager to finish his task, Washington determined on the day after Christmas to proceed on foot by an Indian path through the woods west of the Allegheny River, on a shorter route to the Ohio. He gave Van Braam money and provisions, with instructions to lead the animals and their drivers homeward by an easier and longer way. Washington carried a pack, which contained his papers, and a gun. With him went Gist, also bearing a pack and a weapon. Gist accepted the arrangement with reluctance because his superior, accustomed to traveling on horseback, "had never been used to walking before this time." The two men made eighteen miles that day. They were now without the protection of a tent. That night they "lodged at an Indian cabin, and the Major was much fatigued." Gist reported that it was "very cold," that the brooks in their path were frozen, and that "we could hardly get water to drink."

Worse was to come. The two men rose early on the following morning and headed southeastward toward the forks of the Ohio. On a branch of Beaver Creek, about fifteen miles above Logstown, they met Indian trouble. As Washington told the story,

> we fell in with a party of French Indians, which had laid in wait for us, one of them fired at Mr. Gist or me, not 15 steps, but fortunately missed. We took this fellow into custody & kept him 'till about 9 o'clock at night, & then let him go, & walked all the remaining part of the night without making any stop; that we might get the start, so far as to be out of the reach of their pursuit next day, as we were well assur'd they wou'd follow upon our tract as soon as it was light.

Gist offered a different version of the encounter. He specifically mentions only one Indian, who insisted on guiding the two whites, led them in the wrong direction, aroused their suspicion that he was hostile, fired at them, and was then subdued. Gist related that he was disposed to slay the red man but was restrained by Washington. He states that after the departure of the warrior "we set out about half a mile, when we made a fire, set our course, fixed our compass, and travelled all night." Despite the variations in the two accounts, it is clear enough that the Indian did not intend to bestow a blessing upon Washington and Gist.

Nature continued to menace the travelers. They trudged on during the twenty-eighth. They saw some Indian tracks, but they reached the western bank of the Allegheny after dark and felt safe enough to camp and to sleep. There they faced a new problem. They had expected to find the river covered by frozen ice. Instead, the ice extended only fifty yards from each bank, and floes poured down midstream. There was no way to cross except by making a raft. They spent the daylight hours of the twenty-ninth fashioning it "with but one poor hatchet." Finally, after sunset, according to Washington,

> We got it launch'd, & on board of it, & set off; but before we got half over, we were jamed in the ice in such a manner, that we expected every moment our raft would sink, & we perish; I put out my seting pole, to try to stop the raft, that the ice

might pass by, when the rapidity of the stream through it with so much violence against the pole, that it jirk'd me into 10 feet water, but I fortunately saved my self by catching hold of one of the raft logs. Notwithstanding all our efforts we could not get the raft to either shoar, but were oblig'd, as we were pretty near an island, to quit our raft & wade to it. The cold was so extream that Mr. Gist got all his fingers & some of his toes froze, & the water was so shut up that we found no difficulty in getting off the island on the ice in the morning.

If there is anyone who still believes that Washington never erred, that person should note that Gist afterward referred to his frostbitten fingers but, though he was certainly in a position to know the truth, never mentioned damage to his feet.

Washington and Gist walked on up the eastern shore of the Monongahela on December 30 and found refuge with an English trader at Turtle Creek. Their perils had ended. Washington kept his sense of humor. While they tried to secure horses to carry them forward, the two men paid a call upon the Indian queen Alliquippa, who lived nearby. Washington drily reported, "I made her a present of a match coat; & a bottle of rum, which was thought much the best present of the two." Resuming their journey on the first day of 1754, the two men were now able to find shelter for the night. They crossed the Youghiogheny River on the ice on January 2 and arrived at Gist's home. There Washington was able to buy a horse. It rained on January 3, and they rested. The next day they resumed their journey reaching Wills Creek without further event on the sixth. Five days later Washington arrived at Belvoir, where he took another day to relax and undoubtedly spent a bit of time removing traces of travel and changing clothes. He reported to Dinwiddie at Williamsburg on January 16. His journey had taken more than two months.

The governor was eagerly waiting for Washington and welcomed him back from his arduous and dangerous journey. Washington presented to him the letter from Le Gardeur de Saint-Pierre. Its contents could hardly have surprised Dinwiddie. In polite language the French officer refused to abandon his post. It would have been advisable, he wrote, for Dinwiddie to place English pretensions to territory on the Ohio before his superior, the Marquis Duquesne at Quebec, whose orders the commandant must obey. The commandant was not authorized to abandon Fort Le Boeuf. He knew of no act of hostility committed by the French against the English. He had received Mr. Washington "with a distinction suitable to your dignity, as well as his own quality and great merit." He was sure that Washington would so inform Dinwiddie. The governor listened avidly to Washington and asked him to write a report concerning his mission. Using rough notes he had managed to complete during his journey, Washington hastily prepared it, apparently in less than two days, so that it could be formally considered by Dinwiddie and his council. The result was *The Journal of Major George Washington, Sent by the Hon. Robert Dinwiddie . . . to the Commandant of the French Forces in Ohio . . .* soon afterward published at Williamsburg by order of the governor. The *Journal* contained the letters exchanged by Dinwiddie and Le Gardeur de Saint-Pierre, with a succinct account of the adventures of Washington in the western wilderness. He had thus acquired experience in keeping a diary—a type of record that he was to prepare during most of his adult life. The *Journal* was inevitably in rough form, as he explained in a preface to it. But he was able to offer much valuable information, a good map of the Ohio country, and a fascinating narrative.

The *Journal* did not bring instant acclaim to Washington as an author. He would never become a prolific producer of magnificent prose, although he did learn to express himself with great force and clarity. The House of Burgesses was not remarkably impressed by his literary production nor even by his splendid performance on his mission. In February, 1754, that body gave him a mere fifty pounds "to testify our approbation of his proceedings on his journey to the Ohio." However, the *Journal* was reprinted in American newspapers, and copies of it were sent by Dinwiddie to all the colonial governors and to his superiors in England. A large part of it appeared in the popular English *London Magazine* in the following summer. The name of Washington, still only twenty-two years of age, was beginning to circulate in Anglo-America. In time it would become well known indeed.

III

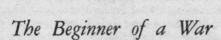

The Beginner of a War

There were at the beginning of the fateful year 1754 informed men in Virginia who believed that Robert Dinwiddie was unwisely aggressive with respect to the French. Were the servants of King Louis XV entirely in the wrong? Was Dinwiddie too solicitous for the welfare of the Ohio Company? He secured from Washington information beyond that contained in the *Journal,* which made it only too clear that the French would move forward in the spring. Fortified by his instructions from London, the governor drove on. Before the end of January he commissioned Washington and William Trent as captains and ordered each of them to raise a force of one hundred men. The Ohio Company was in the process of building a fort on the site at the head of the Ohio River selected by Washington. The governor gave him emphatic orders. He was to complete the post. Much more important, "You are to act on the defensive, but in case any attempts are made to obstruct the works or interrupt any settlements by any persons whatsoever you are to restrain all such offenders; and in case of resistance to make prisoners of or kill and destroy them." Washington obeyed his orders, and as a result it was he who began open hostilities between the armed forces of England and France.

Acceptance of the commission as captain—the highest rank

Dinwiddie could bestow at the moment—was unquestionably a turning point for Washington. His earlier appointments as adjutant and major of militia had not entitled him to command in the field. He now moved toward armed struggle, toward further adventure beyond the Appalachian divide. Perhaps he had long entertained a dream of glory as a soldier. Certainly, as a remarkably sturdy young man accustomed to exercise, horses, hunting, and hardships, he was well qualified physically for martial pursuits. He had displayed courage and resolution. It is to be believed that Dinwiddie, like Le Gardeur de Saint-Pierre, saw other splendid qualities in Washington. To authorize a young man not yet twenty-two years of age to begin firing against the French was to place a heavy responsibility upon him. Empowered soon afterward by the Virginia assembly to raise three hundred men and form them into a regiment, the governor was able to give Washington a higher rank. Dinwiddie appointed as colonel of the regiment Joshua Fry, a mature member of the House of Burgesses who had earlier served in the British forces. Washington applied for the lieutenant colonelcy of the regiment, and Dinwiddie granted his request, this before Washington had departed with his company from the Virginia settlements into the western forests.

Washington and Captain Trent had to collect men and supplies before they could march. They faced many tasks. Virginia was not then richly endowed with a sturdy farm population that would supply large numbers of superior recruits. It was unthinkable that the numerous black slaves in the Old Dominion should be employed. Many of the whites were convicts and indentured servants exported from Britain, and their progeny. To encourage enlistment Dinwiddie announced that 200,000 acres of land in the Ohio Valley would be distributed among those who volunteered. That pledge may have had its effect, for Trent and Washington gradually scraped up their troops. In mid-March Washington, still at Alexandria, was informed by Dinwiddie of renewed reports of French activity beyond the mountains and was urged to hurry forward. Washington set forth from Alexandria with about 140 officers and men at the beginning of April.

In the meantime the French advanced southward in force in the spring of 1754. A body of more than a thousand men with eighteen cannons under Captain Claude Pécaudy de Contrecoeur moved swiftly down the Allegheny River as soon as weather permitted and reached the forks of the Ohio on April 17. Ensign Edward

Ward of Trent's company was there with forty men, trying to build a fort on the site earlier recommended by Washington. Ward began to erect a stockade to check the French, but could not hope to offer a successful resistance. Contrecoeur ordered the Virginians to depart. Faced by overwhelming force, the Virginians agreed to withdraw. Contrecoeur did not push matters to the extreme; he allowed Ward and his men to carry away their arms, tools, and supplies. Then he began to erect Fort Duquesne at the strategic site that had been chosen by the Virginians.

Marching toward the forks, Washington encountered the retreating Virginia detachment under Ward. The young lieutenant colonel was the one who ultimately had to deal with Contrecoeur, for Colonel Fry had not crossed the mountains—he had died after falling from his horse. It was only too plain that the force under Contrecoeur could not be challenged. After a council of war on April 23 Washington began to build a base where Redstone Creek flows into the Monongahela, somewhat less than forty miles south of the forks, and to open a road to the base. He waited for reinforcements known to be on the march from the Virginia settlements.

Without a change in orders from Dinwiddie to Washington, armed clash had now become inevitable, and the lieutenant colonel received no new instructions. Contrecoeur took another forward step that induced Washington to open fire. Contrecoeur was under orders to defend French territory, extending by French definition to the Appalachian Mountains. Learning of Washington's activities, he sent out Ensign Joseph Coulon, Sieur de Jumonville, on May 23, with thirty-three officers and men plus an interpreter, to tell Washington that he and his men must withdraw from the dominions of Louis XV. Jumonville was not to attack the Virginians without cause, but if they remained west of the divide, he was to repulse force by force. His instructions were not quite so forthright as those of Washington, but they were sufficient to warrant an attack against recalcitrant Englishmen who had wantonly invaded the lands of his royal master. Jumonville began his march up the valley of the Monongahela.

Washington was informed in a message from his Indian friend, the Half-King, on the day after Jumonville set out from Fort Duquesne that a French force was moving forward to attack the English. On May 27 Christopher Gist reported to the Virginia commander that fifty Frenchmen were in motion, and the Half-King

sent information that the French soldiers were probably located
near the camp of the chief. Although he was unable to challenge
the full force of Contrecoeur, Washington was strong enough to
attack Jumonville and his men. That night the lieutenant colonel
marched with forty men "along a path scarce broad enough for one
man" in pitch darkness to deal with the Jumonville party. Seven
troopers were lost en route. The remainder of the Virginians met
the Half-King at his camp at sunrise. The French were indeed
located nearby, on Chestnut Ridge, at a point about three miles
north of Summit, Pennsylvania. The Half-King and four or five
other warriors agreed to join Washington in an attack. The Virginians and their redskin allies were almost upon the French, who also
had Indian friends, before they were discovered. Advancing from
all sides, the Virginians were briefly checked by sharp gunfire.
However, during fifteen minutes of fighting, Jumonville and nine of
his men were slain, and the remainder, except for one man who
fled, then surrendered. Washington, reporting his little victory, was
able to say that only one of his own men had been killed and that
only two or three others had suffered injury. His narrative had a
grim note. His "5 or 6 Indians" had chosen "to knock the poor,
unhappy wounded in the head, and bereiv'd them of their scalps."
Washington did not accompany his laconic statement with an expression of regret. He sent the surviving prisoners to Williamsburg
for disposition. He was able to indulge in a bit of youthful brag-
ging, declaring that "I fortunately escaped without any wound, for
the right wing, where I stood, was exposed to and received all the
enemy's fire. . . . I heard the bullets whistle, and, believe me,
there is something charming in the sound." It is said that King
George II, who was a brave soldier if not a brilliant ruler, noted the
gay remark concerning the sound of the bullets and commented,
"He would not say so, if he had been used to hear many." Washington would indeed later display splendid courage in far more
desperate situations without boasting.

   But was the behavior of Washington in that brief engagement
open to far more serious censure? Did he needlessly begin hostilities? One excuses the young Virginian for obeying Dinwiddie,
whose command to fire at the French was in turn more or less
warranted by his instructions from London. But should Washington have parleyed with Jumonville before he began the shooting?
Ought not he have announced his intention to resort to arms? The
victims of a surprise attack, even though it may seem entirely logi-

cal and proper to its perpetrators, are apt to look upon it as un-
sportsmanlike and impolite if not dastardly. The French would find
serious fault in the conduct of Washington. Dinwiddie was pleased
with the performance of the young officer. He promptly gave
Washington the command of the Virginia regiment made vacant by
the death of Joshua Fry and raised Washington to the rank of
colonel. The new colonel was delighted. He wrote joyfully to the
governor, "Believe me, when I assure you my breast is warm'd
with every generous sentiment that your goodness can inspire; I
want nothing but opportunity to testifie my sincere regard for your
person, to whom I stand indebted for so many unmerited favours."

However, the new commander soon encountered reverses. The
French government chose not to make the attack upon the
Jumonville party a reason for a declaration of war against Britain
and sent out instructions to Quebec forbidding reprisals. But its
orders arrived in North America long after its servants there had
sought and secured revenge. Dinwiddie and his masters in London
were not disposed to avoid further conflict. Three companies of
redcoats doing garrison duty in New York City and Charleston,
together with a militia regiment from North Carolina, began to
move to the assistance of the Virginians, but not with speed. In the
meantime, the French commandant at Fort Duquesne acted decisively. He sent forward some four hundred French troops, together
with a body of Indian allies of France, to avenge the defeat of
Jumonville and his men. He chose as commander of the expedition
a captain who was certain to display zeal, Louis Coulon de Villiers
de Jumonville, a brother of the officer slain in the fighting at Little
Meadows. Villiers moved with celerity. He struck before the English could collect their forces.

Colonel Washington and his Virginians were joined by a company of British regulars from Charleston under Captain James
Mackay before Villiers made his appearance. Moreover, Washington was able to build a small post, Fort Necessity, at Chestnut
Ridge in Maryland, near the place where Jumonville fell. But there
were ominous signs for the Virginia colonel and the British captain. It became increasingly clear that they would receive little if
any help from the Indians, indeed that many warriors would assist
the French. The aborigines of the Ohio Valley, observing the advance of the English toward their villages and hunting grounds,
tended to favor the French, who fraternized easily with them and
did not settle upon their lands in large numbers. Washington did

not despise the military prowess of the Indians. He strove to win their help, at least to gain their neutrality, but without success.

Washington, with the Virginians, was moving to erect a second post, beyond Fort Necessity, at Redstone Creek, when he learned of the approach of Villiers. He became aware that he and Mackay would receive little if any assistance from the red men. Mackay was camped at Fort Necessity. After a council of war the two men agreed to concentrate there to meet the expected French attack. As the Virginians fell back, their few Indian friends, including the Half-King, vanished. Concentrating at Fort Necessity on July 1, Washington and Mackay could bring into action more than three hundred men. Had their position been well chosen and fortified, they might have been able to offer a stubborn defense. But the fort was such in little more than name. It was only partly stockaded, and some of the men were sheltered only by earthworks. Moreover, the fort was on low ground, exposing its occupants to gunfire from neighboring heights.

Villiers and his forces appeared outside Fort Necessity about ten o'clock in the morning on July 3 and promptly attacked from all sides. The defenders responded with gunfire until a rainstorm interrupted the action during the afternoon. The shooting resumed as soon as the weather improved, and the losses on both sides mounted. Washington had rum distributed to encourage his men. The Virginians and the British regulars, although their casualties kept increasing, fought on stubbornly as evening approached. By that time a third of the men in the fort had been killed or wounded. In distress, they were rather surprised when Villiers asked for a parley and indicated that he did not require a surrender. The French and their forest comrades also had their slain and injured. Villiers was willing to let his enemies march away southward with their arms after signature of a formal capitulation and evacuation of the fort. His terms seemed generous. Were the defenders to fight as long as they could and be forced at last to surrender themselves and their weapons, they might well be exposed to the tortures and killings in which the Indians habitually indulged themselves after a victory—it was not at all certain that the French could or would restrain their bloodthirsty allies. Washington and Mackay signed the document, and they and their men began retreating on the following day.

Washington, though he had suffered defeat, could assert that he had done everything possible to avert it. However, there was lan-

guage in the capitulation that reflected upon him and that he could
never quite explain away. The document contained a declaration
that the Villiers expedition was solely undertaken to avenge *"l'as-
sassin"* of Jumonville and stipulated that the Frenchmen taken
prisoner "dans l'assassinat" of that officer should be set free. When
the document began to circulate, Washington was condemned in
England and America for cowardice on the ground that he had
confessed to a murder in order to save his own life or to secure his
freedom from captivity. Surely, those who denounced Washington
asserted, he knew that the two French words referred to assassina-
tion. Then had he not confessed to murdering Jumonville? Washington hotly denied that he had intended to admit committing a
crime. The document was written in the French language, and he
was not familiar with it. It had been translated for him by Jacob
Van Braam, whose command of English was uncertain and who
failed to make its meaning clear. Washington claimed that, so far
as he knew, he had merely conceded that Jumonville had been
slain in battle. Let it be observed that Villiers apparently charged
Washington not with a wanton murder, but with a killing of a
political nature, that Villiers made no effort to punish Washington
for his supposed crime. It may be inferred that Villiers in effect
secured an admission that Washington was responsible for the
death of a Frenchman on French soil. It may well be that the
defense of his behavior offered by Washington was quite justified. It
may also be true that after a long battle he was weary and did not
quite understand Van Braam's translation. We do not know how
James Mackay, the British captain, interpreted the words that reflected so seriously upon Washington's conduct. It would be ridicu-
lous to assume that Washington, who displayed splendid courage
on so many occasions, sought to save his life by confessing nakedly
to committing murder.

Washington did not return to Virginia as a conquering hero. He
retreated with his regiment, depleted by battle and desertion, to
Winchester. Leaving the remains of his force there, he went on to
Williamsburg to report upon his failure, thence to Alexandria to
collect recruits to fill the thinned ranks of the regiment. His labors
were interrupted by receipt of bad news. In the autumn Governor
Horatio Sharpe of Maryland, formerly a British army officer, received a commission to lead an army of a thousand British regulars
and provincials against Fort Duquesne. To assist Sharpe with his
plans, Dinwiddie dissolved the Virginia regiment, retaining its

companies in service. He offered Washington a captaincy. The demotion in rank would inevitably be construed by wiseacres as proof that Washington had been punished for failure to do his duty at Fort Necessity. The young colonel rejected the offer with disdain. Then it was proposed that he retain his rank as colonel, but that he have only the pay and authority of a captain. He was not mollified. He wrote to a friend, "If you think me capable of holding a commission that has neither rank nor emolument annexed to it, you must entertain a very contemptible opinion of my weakness, and believe me more empty than the commission itself." The arrangement was all the worse in that Sharpe was to have captains from the British regulars who could and very likely would insist that they were the superiors of Washington in rank. Disgusted, Washington resigned from the Virginia regiment, and his military career came to a halt in the autumn of 1754. But only temporarily. Sharpe did not take the field. He was replaced by a senior British officer, for the struggle between Britain and France was widening and intensifying.

Was Washington engaged in a civilian campaign at Alexandria in the late summer of 1754? On September 5 William La Péronie, a Frenchman who had served as adjutant under Washington, wrote to him from Williamsburg, "As I imagine you by this time plung'd in the midst of delight heaven can afford: & enchanted by charms even stranger to the Cyprian dame I thought I would contribute a litle to the variety of yours amusement to send you a few lines to peruse." La Péronie linked with the Cyprian dame the name "M's Nel," presumably a Nell who had the habits of a courtesan or prostitute. Nothing more can be learned about Nell. Was Washington engaged in an affair with her? Was La Péronie misinformed? Was he merely having a bit of fun? In behalf of the idea that Washington was involved with Nell, it can be said that he was a vigorous young man. The La Péronie reference remains a minor mystery. But the Frenchman was not the only friend who wrote to the young Washington regarding female charms. In 1757 George Mercer, also a Virginia officer, informed him that South Carolina girls lacked "those enticing, heaving, throbbing, alluring plump breasts common with our northern belles." It may safely be concluded that the effusions of La Péronie and Mercer were not by their nature offensive to Washington, who would later indulge in masculine ribaldry.

IV

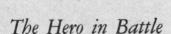

The Hero in Battle

Neither Britain nor France was willing to abandon the contest begun by the attack upon Jumonville. The French arranged to send additional troops across the Atlantic. Men in power in London were equally determined to assert the pretensions of Britain. British warships intercepted some of the French regulars on the Atlantic, extending the undeclared war to the oceans. Hostilities on the Ohio widened into bloody conflict on several fronts. Forces of British and American troops took the field in Nova Scotia, New York, and Virginia to drive the French back. Major General Edward Braddock, a veteran British officer, came to Virginia as commander in chief in the thirteen colonies with the 44th and 48th regiments of redcoats and instructions to drive the French from Fort Duquesne, to replace it with a strong British post, and thence to march to Niagara, where additional forces of George II would establish a link with him. Washington went off to war again in the spring of 1755. He became, as he keenly desired to be, an authentic hero.

Let it not be thought that the mind of young Washington was entirely occupied by thoughts of glorious deeds on the field of battle. He harbored a desire to voyage across the Atlantic and to see London, the metropolis of his world, the wonders of which had been described to him by relatives. Moreover, he was busy establishing himself as a planter when news of the approach of Braddock reached him. In December, 1754, he leased Mount Vernon, with about two thousand acres of land and eighteen slaves, from the widow of Lawrence Washington, agreeing to pay for it each year fifteen thousand pounds of tobacco or the equivalent in cash. Thereafter he was master of his own household, for his mother continued to live at the Ferry Farm, an arrangement that was specially pleasing for him, since he and his mother shared a strength of will that tended to reduce affection between them. He was so much occupied with establishing the plantation at Mount Vernon that he was reluctant to leave it. In the end, he risked losses by placing it in the care of his younger brother, John Augustine, while he was away on campaign.

Washington ardently sought to serve again and not merely because he lusted for military fame. He was patriotic—loyal to Britain and keen to take part in efforts to injure and humiliate her traditional and detested French enemies. He was not yet ready to settle down to the quiet life of a Virginia landowner. Indeed, combining patriotism and martial ambition, he wished to embark upon a career as an officer in the British army. He sent a welcoming message to General Braddock, soon after that officer landed in Virginia, late in February, 1755, and he let it be known that he desired to join the expedition that would march into the western wilderness. At first he hoped to secure from Braddock a commission in the British army. Apparently he sought appointment as a major, a rank that would give him precedence over British captains, such as James Mackay, who refused to acknowledge any Virginia officer as their superior. At that time British officers normally paid for commissions up to the colonelcy, the cost rising from rank to rank. Such commissions were valuable pieces of property, entitling their holders to retirement upon half pay. Except for men who belonged to powerful families in Britain, promotion was slow and earned by long years of service. Washington did not offer to pay for a commission, and he sought one that he had not earned by seniority or valor.

Learning that Braddock could appoint no officer above the rank of captain by brevet—higher ranks were filled in London—the Virginian asked to be allowed to act as a volunteer on the general's staff. His request was readily granted, for he could supply much valuable information to the general. "It's true," wrote Washington,

"I have been importuned to make this campaign by Gen. Braddock in his family who I suppose, imagined that the small knowledge I have had an opportunity of acquiring of the country, Indians, etc. worthy of his notice; and therefore thought I might become useful to him in the progress of his expedition." There may have been a trifle of boasting in the word "importuned." His mother was unhappy, fearing she would lose her son. She urged him not to serve, but he refused to heed her pleas. He had obtained a splendid opportunity to take part in an important campaign, and he would not let it pass. His appointment was one of dignity—he would even be able to carry orders from Braddock to British colonels and majors —and he might well gain glory and preferment by superior performance. "I have now a good opportunity," he wrote to John Augustine, "and shall not neglect it, of forming an acquaintance, which may be serviceable hereafter, if I can find it worthwhile pushing my fortune in the military way."

There was a bustle of activity in preparation for the expedition. The two regiments of British infantry arrived in Chesapeake Bay. Four colonial governors met with Dinwiddie at Alexandria to adopt measures in support of Braddock. Dinwiddie moved with zeal and energy. He raised eight companies of Virginians, and he collected large quantities of food for the army. Maryland and North Carolina each supplied a company of provincial troops. Braddock also commanded the three independent companies of redcoats he found in America upon his arrival. He had brought with him some artillerymen, and he borrowed guns and thirty British sailors to work them from the fleet that had brought the two regiments from Britain. Despite vexing problems and all sorts of delays, Braddock had ready for duty by early June 1,760 British regulars and 463 provincials, together with men to fire his cannon. There was one seemingly small defect in the arrangements. Considering that the French would have the help of Indians of the Ohio Valley, few of whom were now inclined to help the English, Dinwiddie tried to secure the services of Cherokee and Catawba tribesmen friendly to Britain who lived on the western borders of the Carolinas. They might have served as a counterweight to the allies of the French and could have insured Braddock against a surprise attack. The Cherokee and Catawba warriors did not appear—Governor James Glen of South Carolina invited them to a conference with him at the very time they would have been valuable to Braddock. Presents were always distributed to Indians at

such gatherings, and the Cherokee and Catawba preferred to talk
with Glen rather than fight for Braddock. At the time the failure to
secure their help seemed of no great importance, since by all appearances the British general already had forces ample for his first
and major task, the capture of Fort Duquesne. He had had little
experience in combat, but there was no reason to question his courage or his determination to succeed.

Washington found Braddock and his "family," that is, his staff,
entirely congenial, and they gave him both respect and liking. He
joined them at Frederick, Maryland, about the beginning of May
and traveled with them as far as Wills Creek. The army was moving up toward the Appalachian divide. Its progress was retarded by
lack of horses, forage, and wagons. Washington expected further
delay, for it would be necessary to carry Braddock's artillery over
the mountains, but he was confident of the success of the expedition. He foresaw "no danger from the enemy," for the French
would be compelled to employ a large part of their forces to check
English onslaughts in northern and western New York. Sent back
by Braddock to Williamsburg to secure money to pay the troops,
he rejoined the army at Wills Creek. There he found Braddock in a
quite understandable fret. The general was a friendly man, but a
plain-spoken soldier. Angered because colonial officials and contractors had failed to meet the needs of the army, he condemned
them, not merely as individuals but as Americans. Washington
boldly engaged in warm debate with the general, defending his
fellow Americans—it was unfair, he said, to condemn all of them
because of the shortcomings of a few delinquents. Perhaps Braddock, who was tolerant if not talented, saw that he had erred. He
held no grudge against the forthright Virginian. The debate may
have left an anti-British residue in Washington. He had not forgotten the refusal of British officers to recognize the right of a Virginia
colonel to command. Was there hostility among the British, not
only toward him, but toward all Americans?

For the moment jealousy of the British was submerged in Washington. Wagons, horses, and equipment appeared, in part through
the activity of Benjamin Franklin, another American who would
learn that there was a careless disposition among the British to
look down upon mere colonials. Difficulties in transport continued,
but the expedition moved slowly forward. The vanguard left Wills
Creek in early June, though it was soon necessary to send some of
the cannon back for lack of horses to pull them. Officers similarly

reduced their baggage. The pace of the expedition did not improve. It moved about two miles per day. Washington was especially unhappy because of the slow progress of the army, for he was compelled to deal with a private enemy as well as the public one. He was suffering from headaches and fever, accompanied by the "bloody flux" that was so prevalent in his time. He had become a victim of malaria or a similar malady.

Unable to stay on his horse, Washington was compelled to seek the permission of Braddock to ride in a covered wagon. But on June 16 he had to leave that vehicle to give advice to the general. There was concern among the staff lest the army be so long delayed that Fort Duquesne would be strongly reinforced before the arrival there of the English. Rumors had it that French forces were moving southward from the Great Lakes. Braddock sought the opinion of Washington, who urged that the army be organized into two divisions to secure more rapid advance. The first of these, less encumbered by military gear, should push on as swiftly as possible. It could reach its destination before French reinforcements, who would have difficulty traversing French Creek, the waters of which were probably very low because of a drought. The first division would have ample strength to overwhelm the existing garrison. The second contingent could follow at a slower pace. Washington was confident that his plan would bring success. Braddock was impressed by the arguments of the Virginian and took his advice, to the great pleasure of its giver. He must have been remarkably persuasive. It was extraordinary that a veteran British commander should accept the argument of a young man whose martial experience was so limited, particularly because it was contrary to all professional military precepts to divide an army as it approached a hostile force. Was the feverish Washington more emphatic than he should have been? Did he lust for action? There was merit in the traditional practice. Perhaps he should have suggested that there was no need to set it aside, that there was no compelling argument for haste. Weather would not require speed—winter, with its crippling effect upon campaigning, was far off. There was a second reason to anticipate that the French would have difficulty in reinforcing the fort, for they were under pressure by British forces to the north. Still another factor to be considered was the behavior of the Indian allies of the Bourbon monarch. Would they take the field against a powerful army?

In any event, the army proceeded in accordance with the thinking of Washington. The first column, containing somewhat more than 1,300 men, under Colonel Sir Peter Halkett, with ten cannon and plenty of ammunition for the infantry, pushed forward on June 18. Braddock rode with that column. Washington was so ill five days later that he could not accompany it. He was eager to "be in on the kill," to take part in any fighting that might occur, and to ride triumphantly into Fort Duquesne with the victors. But he was forced to remain in his wagon, trundling along bumpily and unhappily with the second division, under Colonel Thomas Dunbar, day after trying day. His servant, John Alton, attended briefly to his wants, but Alton also fell ill. A physician tried unsuccessfully to restore Washington to health. Nevertheless the Virginian seems to have wanted to leave his sickbed to join the first division. But Braddock was much concerned for the welfare of his volunteer aide. He ordered Washington not to leave his bed, assuring him that he would be permitted to move forward as soon as his condition improved. The general also ordered the physician to treat the sick man with the powder of Dr. Robert James, a panacea of the time for fever. The powder was probably not effective, but Washington believed that it was a genuine remedy, for his fever and other complaints ameliorated within four days. By June 28 he fancied that he was on the way to recovery. He would have paid five hundred pounds rather than miss his chance to join in the capture of the fort, and by July 4 he was en route in his wagon toward the first division. He was apparently almost fully recovered, though doubtless still weak, when he caught up with the Halkett contingent on July 8.

In the meantime, on July 3, Braddock reconsidered his plan of approach. One of his officers, Sir John St. Clair, proposed that the first division halt until the second one, now many miles in the rear, could come up. To Braddock, it seemed unnecessary and perhaps unwise to wait for Dunbar and his men. The scanty information available to the general suggested that Fort Duquesne was not strongly held. He determined to proceed without the second division. A few Indians who had joined him had departed because their women had attracted excessive attention from the soldiers. The services of the red men as scouts had been lost. A few stragglers had fallen into the hands of hostile warriors, and it was evident that the French were informed regarding the advance of the army. There was some uneasiness among the redcoats concerning conflict with enemy Indians, whose behavior in war had been described for them by provincial troops. Minor hardships vexed Halkett's men. Still, there seemed to be no good reason to fear that the French and their allies could offer a stubborn resistance. Washington joined a confident force under a confident Braddock.

It became increasingly evident that all was well. About two o'clock in the morning on July 9 the first column began its final approach toward the fort. An advance guard under Colonel Thomas Gage of the 44th Regiment led the way. Moving forward to cross the Monongahela River to its western bank, Gage and his men saw about thirty hostile warriors, who scampered off. The column followed the advance guard without incident. Moreover, Gage encountered no opposition when he and his men waded through the river back to its eastern bank at a second ford, although orthodox tactics dictated that the enemy would make a stand there if the French chose to come forth from their fort. The column followed Gage a second time across the stream, again without untoward result beyond wet feet. Before midafternoon the column was over the river and moving forward through rather open woods. It was within seven miles of the fort, and there was no great natural obstacle in its path. A night of rest, and it would be at the fort the next day. Strung out in a long line, it was suddenly attacked. Washington, barely able to mount a horse, was with Braddock and the main body, again serving as an aide to the general. He heard the now familiar rattle of gunfire at the head of the column.

Had all of the army been with Braddock, the French at Fort Duquesne would hardly have ventured to fight. They had not received much assistance from Canada. Indeed, prudence indicated that the garrison should evacuate rather than try to defend the post. Was it feasible first to strike a blow and then flee quickly if English resistance was stubborn? Captain Daniel Liénard Beaujeu could muster at Duquesne fewer than 250 French regulars and Canadian militiamen, but there were at the fort more than 600 Indian allies of France from villages north of the Ohio. Beaujeu resolved to attack rather than await almost certain defeat. He knew that he would not be forced to face the entire British army. His Indian friends were reluctant, but he persuaded them to take the field.

Advancing through the woods, Beaujeu and his people were almost upon the British advance guard before they were seen. Gage's men opened up with their muskets, checking the attack. But the

French and their warriors then divided into two parts, one moving
forward along the southern side of the British column, the other
along its northern one. There were ravines on both British flanks
that added to the cover supplied by trees and brush. Slipping
through the ravines, the French and Indians began to pour a heavy
fire from both sides of the column. Chilling war whoops resounded
through the forest. The British in their red coats, especially the
officers, were easy targets and began to fall to the ground. Musket
fire from the column against enemies who could hardly be seen and
who used trees and brush for cover had little effect. The attackers
occupied a hill north of the central part of Braddock's army and
sent a hail of bullets from it. The redcoats fell into confusion. Their
cannon could not be used, and their officers tried in vain to rally
them. Lieutenant Colonel Ralph Burton of the 44th, acting upon
orders from Braddock, collected men for a counterthrust up the
hill. If successful, Burton could have disrupted the attack. He fell
wounded, and his men retreated. Gunsmoke floated over the battlefield, accompanied by the groans of those struck by enemy bullets. The troops refused to charge into the forest. Remaining in
column, they fired their muskets almost at random, even slaying
and wounding their comrades. The flanking French and Indians
were not checked until they approached the rear of the column,
where they were driven back by a company of redcoats or provincials who had had time to prepare for the onslaught. The provincials behaved better than the regulars. The main body of the column stood its ground for hours. The redcoats, though they refused
to take the offensive, would not run. Many of their officers were
killed or wounded. Braddock was mortally wounded by a musket
ball. At last the carnage and confusion were so great that flesh and
blood could stand no more, and the entire column fled in wild
disorder. Cannon and provisions were left behind. Colonel Gage
bravely rallied about eighty men to supply a measure of cover for
the dreadful retreat. A few pursuing Indians slew some survivors
as they tried to ford the Monongahela. Weary, most of the French
and Indians did not pursue. The remains of the shattered army
finally found refuge with Dunbar's force, far from the scene of
battle. Its casualties were almost unbelievable—about two-thirds of
the men with Braddock were either slain or wounded. The attackers suffered relatively few losses. Returning to Fort Duquesne in
triumph, the warrior allies of the French celebrated it in their cus-

tomary way. They tortured and killed the handful of prisoners they had taken.

It is evident that various untoward circumstances, together with inferior tactics, contributed to the disaster. Long afterward, Washington declared that he had urged Braddock to order his men to take cover and fight the French and Indians in their own way but that the general had declined to accept his advice. It would hardly have been possible for redcoats trained for formal combat quickly to adopt such tactics. If the advice of Washington, followed by Braddock, to divide the army was dubious, there is no doubt that the Virginian covered himself with glory in the battle. Despite his recent illness, he acted with enormous energy and courage as aide to the general. Two other aides were wounded early in the battle, and he had to do far more than normal duty as a member of the staff. Carrying orders from Braddock here, there, and everywhere, he was a target for various enemy muskets. Four bullets went through his coat, and two horses were shot down under him, but almost miraculously, he was unharmed. Sent by Braddock to inform Dunbar of the disaster and ask him to furnish reinforcements and wagons, he rode all night through the darkness to the camp of Dunbar, arriving there during the morning of the tenth in a state of exhaustion with his tale of dreadful defeat. He remained at the camp for three days.

Dunbar had advanced only a few miles beyond the Great Meadows. The news brought by Washington created a near panic, but Dunbar was able to restore order and even to send forward two companies of troops. The troops were not needed, and they returned. With them on the eleventh came more of the army, mostly fugitives in utter disarray except for the contingent led by Gage that had provided cover for the retreat. Braddock, near death, was carried into Dunbar's camp. The general issued orders for a retreat of the army and for the destruction of ammunition, cannon, wagons, and provisions that were to be left behind and that might fall into the hands of the enemy. More fugitives from the battle appeared. On the thirteenth the beaten army moved back toward the Great Meadows. As darkness approached, Braddock died. Attending him to the end, Washington arranged for a funeral service on the following morning. The general was buried in the road followed by the army. Washington sent wagons over the grave to obliterate signs of burial so that the corpse could not be found by Indian marauders. The army moved on, with Colonel Dunbar now in command. It was not molested by the victors. Two days later it began to gather at Wills Creek. Recuperating there, Washington was able on July 18 to send descriptions of the defeat to his mother, Governor Dinwiddie, and his brother John Augustine.

Washington placed the blame for the disastrous defeat chiefly upon the British soldiers. Their officers had displayed "incomparable bravery," but the redcoats had succumbed to "a deadly panick." On the other hand, he reported, with a certain grim satisfaction, the Virginians "behav'd like men and died like soldiers." At that time he believed that the frightful casualties suffered by the army were inflicted by "our own cowardly, English soldiers who gather'd themselves in a body contrary to orders 10 or 12 deep, wou'd then level, fire and shoot down the men before them." He wrote that "the dastardly behavior of the English soldiers expos'd all those who were inclined to do their duty to almost certain death" and that at length the British, "in despight of every effort to the contrary, broke and run as sheep before the hounds." He reported that "when we endeavour'd to rally them . . . it was with as much success as if we had attempted to have stop'd the wild bears of the mountains." Afterward he was inclined to find fault with Braddock, who had indeed displayed a lack of imagination and had suffered from *rigor Martis*.

Whatever responsibility rested upon Washington for the outcome of the advance under Braddock, he had naught to do with planning for the immediate use of the remaining British troops. Colonel Dunbar, gathering advice from other officers, concluded that it was impossible to resume the attack against Fort Duquesne before winter came. The morale of the army was low, and supplies were lacking. Artillery to break down the walls of the fort was not to be had. A siege might be protracted, might continue until weather forced the British to abandon it. Dunbar resolved to continue the retreat begun by Braddock and take the remains of the redcoats to Philadelphia, where they would come under the control of General William Shirley, successor to Braddock as commander in chief. Washington saw merit in the argument respecting cannon. He could not approve a decision that took the redcoats to Philadelphia, where they could accomplish nothing during 1755, away from the frontiers of Virginia and Maryland, where they were badly needed. In any event, the death of Braddock put an end to any possible obligation on his part to serve further with them. Very gradually gaining strength, he was able to set forth for home. Still weak from his illness and exertions, he arrived at Mount Vernon on July 26. He continued to recuperate there in peace and quiet. As news of the battle of July 9 spread, he acquired true heroic stature. No one could afterward doubt his utter courage. He had also given proof of physical endurance far beyond the ordinary. He had become a man marked for splendid performance in time of great trial.

The ghastly defeat saddened and alarmed the Virginians. Governor Dinwiddie, receiving a garbled report of it, could not give it credence. Then, given an only too true account of the disaster, he wept. He desperately sought to collect more men and to resume the advance toward Fort Duquesne. There was still time for taking the post before winter set in. He begged Dunbar to remain at Fort Cumberland, recently erected at Wills Creek, and to prepare for a second expedition, but Dunbar insisted that nothing could be done to retrieve the disaster. Nor would General Shirley listen to a plea from Dinwiddie for renewed action. Dunbar went off to Philadelphia, taking with him not only the remains of the 44th and 48th regiments but also the three independent companies of redcoats that had been stationed in Virginia before the coming of the troops from Europe. Virginia now had less protection than before the arrival of Braddock. Moreover, it was to be expected that hostile Indians would be emboldened by the defeat of his army and that they would pour down upon the undefended frontiers of Maryland and Virginia. Indeed, a few ravaging bands appeared almost immediately. Dinwiddie called up militia and rangers for temporary service and sought a more effective means to guard the western settlements of the Old Dominion. Almost inevitably he and members of the House of Burgesses, in session in August, decided to revive the Virginia regiment and ask Washington to lead it.

On August 2, still in such poor condition that he found it difficult to ride about his plantation, Washington considered his situation. He knew that the emergency would bring forth plans for employing him. His half brother Augustine, a member of the Burgesses, suggested that he travel to Williamsburg to consult. Washington declined to visit the capital. He excused himself upon the score of continuing fatigue, but also informed Augustine that he was not "dispirited at what has happen'd," that he was "always ready and always willing, to do my country any service that I am capable off." Well, not quite; for he added, "but, never upon the terms I have done, having suffer'd much in my private fortune, besides impairing one of the best of constitution's." He complained that "I was employ'd to go a journey in the winter (when I believe few or none wou'd have undertaken it) and what did I get by it? My expenses borne! I then was appointed with trifling pay to conduct a handful of men to the Ohio. What did I get by this? Why, after putting myself to a considerable expense in equipping and providing necessarys for the campaigne I went out, was soundly beaten, lost them all—came in, and had my commission taken from me or, in other words . . . reduced under pretence of an order from home." Was he accusing his sponsor, Dinwiddie, of failing to recognize his merits? He continued, "I then went out a volunteer with Genl. Braddock and lost all my horses and many other things. . . . I have been on the loosing order ever since I enter'd the service." Accordingly, he was disposed to refuse to take the field again without assurance against further losses. Twelve days later he was "weak and feeble," but virtually recovered and more disposed to resume soldiering. He said, "I never will quit my family, injure my fortune, and (above all) impair my health to run the risque of such changes and vicissitudes as I have done" without "something certain" in the way of reward. Also, he would insist upon having a voice in choosing officers who would serve under him. At first he had believed that he would receive censure rather than credit for further service. But now he was willing to be persuaded to take up arms once more. His mother again urged him to abandon military life. He told her that honor would force him to accept a command if it were tendered with suitable terms.

The offer came, and it was handsome enough. He was in very high favor in Williamsburg. Everyone was talking about his display of courage and resolution. Colonel Fairfax assured him that his "safe return gives an uncommon joy to us and will no doubt be sympathiz'd by all true lovers of heroic virtue." The Burgesses voted him three hundred pounds in recompense for his losses in the recent campaign. Governor Dinwiddie and the Burgesses undertook to form a new Virginia regiment of one thousand men to protect the frontiers of the colony. Washington was asked to serve as its commander with his old rank of colonel, to assume leadership of all the forces of Virginia. Learning that he was indeed being urged to take the field again, he went to Williamsburg to consult. Informed that the governor had already appointed captains to serve under him, Washington rejected the appointment. At length, by permitting him to select his immediate subordinates, the governor secured the consent of the young colonel. It was not gladly given. A year later Washington wrote, "I have long been satisfied of the impossibility of continuing in this service, without loss of honor. Indeed, I was fully convinced of it before I accepted the command the second time (seeing the cloudy prospect that stood before me;) and did for this reason reject the offer, (until I was ashamed any longer to refuse), not caring to expose my character to public censure." His reluctance undoubtedly proceeded more from a realization that he could hardly gain great glory from executing his new duties, useful as his services might be, rather than from the terms of his appointment.

It is evident also that Washington was now held in high esteem by the Burgesses. But he had begun to lose favor with Dinwiddie. After Washington had accepted the command, Dinwiddie urged his superiors in London to grant a British army commission to Washington, "who was one of General Braddock's aids-de-camp, and I think a man of great merit and resolution. . . . I am convinced," he wrote, "if General Braddock had survived, he would have recommended Mr. Washington to the royal favor." Dinwiddie would continue to press for such a commission, but with decreasing zeal. He seems to have concluded that Washington set a high price upon his services. The friendship between the two men was cooling, in part, no doubt, because Washington was increasingly associated with leaders of the House of Burgesses politically hostile to Dinwiddie, including John Robinson, who was the Speaker, and Landon Carter. In colonial times a British governor, defending British authority, almost inevitably offended Americans elected to legislative office. Relations between Dinwiddie and the majority of the burgesses were tense. He was condemned because he had twice been forced by orders from London, against his will, to spend Virginia tax money without the consent of the Burgesses. He was unpopular also because he had tried to exact a neat fee for himself from land grants. Virginians holding and seeking such grants as a way to wealth were not at all fond of fees or taxes. Nor did the governor win friends because he had become wealthy through trade. Men whose property was derived from land and from increasing numbers of slaves—not a few of them threatened with insolvency because of their extravagant way of life—tended to frown upon a canny Scot who accumulated more and more pounds and shillings. The Burgesses had seized control of public money, and Washington was compelled to do military business directly with them. They increasingly rallied to the support of a fellow Virginian and encouraged him to quarrel with the governor. Washington could hardly have failed to swell from unstinted praise such as he received from Landon Carter, a man not given to flattery. "Tread the same path that you first cut out to your own glory, that your country may in the end feel the good effects that she promises herself from your singular virtues and fortune." There were troubles ahead for the twenty-three-year-old colonel and commander in chief, and all of them were not caused by the French and Indians.

V

The Frontier Commander

The extraordinary young Colonel Washington continued to be extraordinary. He was to spend three more years in service on the Virginia frontier. He continued to lust for the red coat of an officer of King George II, and he learned much about the art of warfare as it was waged in North America.

It was clear enough to all perceptive Virginians when Washington resumed command that Fort Duquesne not only barred advance into the Ohio Valley but served as a base for attacks upon Virginia frontiers by Shawnees and other red men who lived in villages north of the Ohio River. If the fort were taken, the hostile Indians, far more dangerous to outlying farmers and villagers than the French, could be brought to heel. The aborigines, learning to use muskets and hatchets supplied by whites, were no longer able to hunt with the primitive weapons they had employed before the coming of the whites. But they had not learned how to make or repair muskets or to fashion bullets or gunpowder. Thus they must yield to the whites who controlled the source and replenishing of their new weapons. From Fort Duquesne the French distributed muskets, powder, and lead along with liquor and propaganda. If the post were seized, the neighboring Indians must bend the knee to governing Englishmen. Unfortunately, the Virginians were un-

willing, even with help from Maryland, to make the great effort
necessary to take the fort—they sought but could secure little assistance from Pennsylvania, dominated by pacifistic Quakers until
1757. Relief could also have come from a successful English advance into the St. Lawrence Valley that would cut off reinforcements and supplies from the fort. But such help did not soon come.
In consequence, Virginia was reduced to a wretched defensive.

Had devotion to duty by Washington been the key to protection
of Virginia, all would have been well. He quickly began his labors,
appointing officers, collecting recruits, securing clothing for his
men, and seeking reliable sources of supply of provisions. Hastily
riding westward to put things in order on the frontier, he went
through Williamsburg and Alexandria to Wills Creek, where he
assumed command of nearly two hundred Virginians stationed at
Fort Cumberland, newly erected there. He found that drunkenness
and profanity were rife among the troops, and he ordered that
soldiers guilty of such misconduct be punished. Announcing the
names of the officers of the regiment, including some excellent
ones, such as Lieutenant Colonel Adam Stephen and Major Andrew Lewis, he sought to give them a measure of dignity. Each
officer was to wear a suit of regimentals of good blue cloth, a coat
faced and cuffed with scarlet and trimmed with silver, a scarlet
waistcoat with silver lace, blue breeches, and a silver-laced hat. For
duty in the woods they were to put on the dress of the common
soldiers—they being clothed in inconspicuous garb—in order to
deprive hostile Indians of conspicuous targets.

The Indian menace was real. Before he reached Fort Cumberland, red-skinned raiders attacked a pioneer settlement on the
Greenbrier River, beyond the Appalachian divide. They created
havoc, killing several backwoodsmen, carrying off two girls, and
seizing horses and cattle before the approach of troops under Major Lewis induced them to flee into the woods. It became apparent
to Washington after a tour of the Virginia frontier that settlers west
of the Shenandoah Valley could not be protected and that those
who lived in the Valley were threatened. He gathered recruits at
Fredericksburg, hurrying them forward "to repel those barbarous
and insolent invaders, of our country." He wished to "make the
savages and French (who are no better) pay for their presump-
tion."

Riding toward Williamsburg, Washington received another dis-
turbing report from Winchester in a letter from Adam Stephen

that asserted that Fort Cumberland was cut off by the Indians. "They go about and commit their outrages at all hours of the day, and nothing is to be seen or heard of, but desolation and murder heightened with all barbarous circumstances, and unheard of instances of cruelty." Stephen declared luridly, "They spare the lives of the young women, and carry them away to gratify the brutal passions of lawless savages. The smoke of the burning plantations darken the day, and hide the neighboring mountains from our sight." Washington hastened to Winchester. There he found everything in wild confusion. Fleeing families of backwoodsmen were flocking into the village for safety. Its inhabitants were fleeing eastward for the same reason. Washington tried to call up men for militia service. They refused to serve, saying that they preferred to die with their families rather than that they and their families should be slain separately. Soldiers in his regiment deserted and were sheltered by civilians. He was compelled to impress a blacksmith to repair guns—the smith proposed to solve the emergency by going to Pennsylvania. In the name of liberty, men defied the colonel and threatened "to blow out my brains." His commands were disobeyed unless they were enforced by a squad of troops or by his drawn sword. He became thoroughly disgusted. He concluded that laws to restrain irresponsible individuals were needed more in new America than they were in old Europe. Writing almost as if he were the British military officer he desired to be, he told Dinwiddie he could not carry on unless Virginia put teeth into its military laws. He did do his duty. He ordered recent recruits and militia from the older counties of Virginia to come to his assistance. Reports reached him that a band of savages were attacking near Winchester, and he went with a detachment to deal with it. He had been misled by a false alarm. Troops and militia at last came to join him, but they were too late. The Shawnee and Delaware warriors who had created the havoc had vanished. There had been only a few score of them. They had slain perhaps seventy Virginians. Washington arranged to build and garrison small posts in the Valley in an effort to check future raiders.

Returning to Williamsburg late in October to report to Dinwiddie, Washington learned that the Virginia assembly had acted to increase his authority. He could use flogging to maintain discipline in his regiment; he could even, with the consent of the governor, impose the death penalty upon deserters. His new powers were of little immediate value. Winter was approaching. He made a final

tour of inspection on the frontier, consigning its defense to his
senior officers for many weeks. Except for Major Andrew Lewis,
they were not active. With 230 mounted men and 80 Cherokee
warriors enlisted through the efforts of Dinwiddie, Lewis went on a
raid toward the Shawnee villages across the Ohio. He and his men
suffered from rain, snow, and cold. They did not reach their goal;
they captured one French civilian. In the meantime, Washington
aimed at another objective, that prized British commission, going
to Boston to seek it.

Washington now sought nothing less than a colonelcy in the
British army. He and his officers had heard a rumor that General
Shirley, who was also governor of Massachusetts, had power to
give the Virginia regiment royal status. His officers were, of course,
as eager as he to secure the change. Washington had been given a
special argument for the much desired transfer. Captain John
Dagworthy, who commanded a few Marylanders at Fort Cumberland, was insisting that he was superior in rank to all Virginia
officers on the specious ground that he had once held a royal commission, even though his authority under that document had long
since expired. Since the fort was located in Maryland, he had asserted authority over the many Virginians stationed there. The
situation was intolerable, and Washington was prepared to resign if
it were not remedied. He had another reason for traveling to Boston. It was possible that the pleas sent to London in his behalf had
borne fruit and that Shirley had been authorized to grant him,
though not his subordinates, a suitable royal rank. Dinwiddie
doubted that Shirley had the right to act in behalf of the Virginians, but he renewed his efforts to secure promotion for Washington and urged Shirley, if he could, to give all the Virginia officers
temporary commissions under the Crown—they might later be
made permanent by action from the imperial capital. Washington
had met Shirley in Alexandria before the Braddock campaign and
had found him to be a "gentleman and great politician." Washington could lose nothing by seeking out the general. He might gain
much. In any event, a journey northward through the colonies
might be pleasant and informative.

The colonel set out early in February, 1756, accompanied by two
aides, Captain George Mercer and Captain Robert Stewart, and
two servants. The party stopped at Philadelphia for a few days.
There Washington saw a city for the first time, Philadelphia being
then and for several decades thereafter the largest in North Amer-

ica. He bought some new clothes to make a favorable impression upon Shirley. Passing on through New Jersey, the party ferried from Perth Amboy to Brooklyn and thence to Manhattan, arriving there on February 15. Washington and his entourage lingered in New York City for five days. He was entertained by Beverley Robinson, a son of Speaker John Robinson who had married a New York heiress, Susannah Philipse. The colonel met Mary Eliza, a younger sister of Susannah. He was obviously a catch. Afterward a rumor spread of a match between Washington and Mary Eliza. The report apparently had little substance. He was with her on social occasions. He went to see public entertainments, and he lost a little money playing cards. More was spent upon a purchase of shoes. He hastened on by land and sea to Boston, reaching that place on February 27.

The Virginian was welcomed at the Massachusetts capital. The Boston *Gazette* announced the arrival of "the Hon. Col. Washington, a gentleman who had deservedly a high reputation for military skill and valor, though success has not always attended his undertakings." He bought a new hat, some silver lace, and two pairs of gloves. He saw the sights of the city. As befitted a military man, he visited Castle William, the fort in Boston harbor. Playing at whist or loo, he lost a bit more money. Putting down political cards, he lost again.

Listening to Washington, Shirley was polite. He had not received authority from London to do anything in behalf of the Virginia officers in general or for its leader in particular. He could and would restrain the troublesome Captain Dagworthy. That man was only an officer of Maryland, and he should obey the orders of his Virginia superiors in rank. Washington left without substantial gain.

The disappointed colonel spent another four days in New York City. It is not recorded that he saw Mary Eliza Philipse there. Then he rode on southward through Philadelphia. His progress was delayed by illness, but he reached Annapolis on March 23, delivered letters to Governor Sharpe from Shirley, and proceeded rapidly to Williamsburg. Before he reached that place, he learned about the plans of Shirley for the approaching campaign. The French were still in firm control of the St. Lawrence Valley. British power must be concentrated in New York for thrusts into Canada. Accordingly, there was to be only a secondary drive toward the forks of the Ohio, with Sharpe in command. There was no important role for Washington in the plans. Moreover, he was informed that Dagworthy was boasting of his influence with Sharpe, that Dagworthy was saying that he would put the Virginians in their place (though as it turned out, that obstreperous man was put in *his* place). In pique Washington resolved to resign his colonelcy.

Washington changed his mind. At Williamsburg he learned that the Indians were again on the rampage. He therefore set out quickly for the frontier. En route he resolved to seek what he might well attain, an appointment as second in command to Sharpe. He asked for it in letters to Sharpe and Shirley. They were agreeable, and Shirley recommended it to the Earl of Loudoun, a Scottish officer sent out from London in 1756 to serve as commander in chief. As it happened, there was no expedition to the Ohio either in that year or in the following one. Washington did receive one favor. An order came from London that colonial field officers were to rank above British captains.

The war went badly for the British in the North. Fort Oswego on Lake Ontario fell to a French army under the redoubtable Marquis de Montcalm in 1756. The English fared even worse in the next campaign. They suffered a disastrous defeat at Fort William Henry in New York, and Loudoun failed to mount a projected attack upon the French fortress at Louisbourg on Cape Breton Island. There was general agreement in Virginia that without cannon to break down the walls of Fort Duquesne and without potent Indian allies, the colony must remain on the defensive. Washington shared that opinion, galling as it was to carry on an inglorious defense rather than carry the war to the enemy.

The story of conflict on the Virginia frontier in 1756 was a sequel to that of the autumn of the preceding year. Its vexations were enough to try Washington's soul. French and Indian raiders appeared from the forests with the coming of spring. One party of them was engaged and checked by frontiersman Richard Pearis and other borderers. Its French leader was slain, and his scalp was sent to Williamsburg to secure the reward that Virginia paid for such items. Other marauders ranged from Fort Cumberland through the Shenandoah Valley. Assuming command at Winchester in the first week of April, Washington was plunged into difficulties. The raiders seemed to be everywhere. It was difficult for him even to communicate with the garrison at Fort Cumberland. The Indians attacked this family and that log fort. Panic spread, and settlers again fled over the Blue Ridge to safety. In one clash seventeen men of Washington's regiment were slain. The colonel called up recruits for his troops, urged militia to come forward. They were slow to respond, quick to desert. By the time he had accumulated enough force to deal with the invaders, toward the end of April, they had finished their cruel work and had fled through distant woods to safety.

The colonel complained about his harsh lot. The militia were unreliable. "I never know any yet to appear in ten days after they were expected," he wrote. Moreover, they compensated for late arrivals by early departures. The men in his regiment performed better, but they were often of inferior quality. It was possible to draft men into it, but Virginia law was drawn in such fashion that many men other than indentured servants and vagrants were exempt. He told Dinwiddie and leaders of the House of Burgesses that he was not given men and means to meet his exasperating responsibilities. He did not mince words. When he received word of Williamsburg gossip that there was disorder, drunkenness, and profanity in his regiment—apparently in the garrison at Fort Cumberland—he became furious. He assumed that the censure was directed against him. It was too much that gentlemen safe at the capital should condemn a man exerting himself to the utmost in almost desperate circumstances. He was soothed by letters from Williamsburg. "Our hopes, dear George," wrote John Robinson, "are all fixed on you." Robinson was praying for his safety. Hearing talk that Washington was threatening to resign, Landon Carter urged him not to abandon his command. "Sir, merit begets envy, and should such a thing happen at this hour, it must glut the malice of those who wish you ill." If Washington resigned, his critics would contend that he did so because of cowardice. Charles Carter informed the colonel that "you have never in the least been reflected upon, you are too much affected." He said that the talk was not directed against Washington, that the colonel continued to be in high favor in the House of Burgesses.

Washington was indeed popular at Williamsburg. It seemed that he, if not his officers, would be put upon the British establishment. Informing Washington of the coming of General Loudoun, Dinwiddie confidently told him, "I doubt not you will be taken care of." The Burgesses sent a petition to London asking that the Virginia regiment be placed upon the royal payroll. Dinwiddie believed that Loudoun might act in behalf of the colonel before there could be a response to the plea of the Burgesses. Washington asked the governor to recommend him to the new commander in chief. Learning that Loudoun would recruit Americans in British regiments, Dinwiddie once more urged that Washington receive special reward. The governor did not know Loudoun, but he was acquainted with General James Abercromby, who was to serve as second in rank to Loudoun. Accordingly he begged Abercromby to use his influence with Loudoun for appointment to one of the new regiments of "Colonel George Washington, who, I will venture to say, is a very deserving gentleman, and has from the beginning commanded the forces of this dominion." Dinwiddie asserted that Braddock, had he lived long enough, "would have provided handsomely" for the Virginian. The governor added that Washington "is a person much beloved here and has gone through many hardships in the service, and I really think he has great merit, and believe he can raise more men here than any one present that I know. If his Lordship will be so kind as to promote him in the British establishment I think he will answer my recommendation." Nothing happened. The officers of the Virginia regiment sent a petition to London asking for incorporation into the British army. Washington conveyed a copy of it to Beverley Robinson for presentation to Loudoun. Nothing happened. To the dismay of Dinwiddie the commander in chief brought over British and foreign officers to recruit and lead a battalion of four regiments of colonists to be known as the Royal Americans.

Continuing to hope for that coveted British appointment, Washington devoted himself to his tasks on the frontier. The French and Indians were less active in the summer of 1756, and he had time to put his troops in order. The colonel imposed discipline, ordering the execution of one man who had twice deserted as an example for others who might think of absconding. He demanded that his officers do their full duty and that they cease to rob the public. In their returns captains were telling him that they had fewer men than they reported to government for allowances. Why? He secured a raise in pay for his men. Demanding that everyone under him must do his duty, he won the respect and admiration of his officers and of at least some of his men. But old problems persisted, and new ones appeared. What should he do about Quaker draftees who refused to perform any act of military usefulness? Dinwiddie advised him to put the Quakers on a diet of bread and water until they saw the error of their ways, then counseled him to let the Quakers go. The difficulty vanished. Others were not so easy to solve. Where should posts of defense against the enemy be placed? He wished to evacuate the Virginians from Fort Cumberland. Dinwiddie, responding to a request from General Loudoun, insisted that they remain there. Relations between Washington and Dinwiddie began to deteriorate. The governor was in failing health. Washington was constantly vexed, and he did not hesitate to voice his grievances. A note of irritation crept into their correspondence. By August, Washington was captiously telling John Robinson that "in all important matters" he was directed by Dinwiddie in an "ambiguous and uncertain way."

In the autumn the French and Indians resumed their incursions. On a tour of inspection in southwestern Virginia, Washington himself, unguarded, narrowly escaped attack by raiders. However, the sharpest thrusts of the invaders were aimed at the outlying parts of Maryland and Pennsylvania. Many of those areas were devastated. Washington was not responsible for the troubles of those colonies, but he offered a remedy to John Robinson. Virginia ought to join them in the spring of 1757 in a joint expedition against Fort Duquesne, he suggested. Cannon would be needed. Help should be secured from Cherokee and Catawba warriors who could assist in taking the war into the country of the enemy. The best defense was to go on the offensive. It was risky to employ Indian allies. He had learned that the red men were often difficult to please, that they were fickle in their allegiances to whites, that Indian friends could easily and swiftly become enemies. But he advised that the risk that the Cherokee and Catawba might turn against the English should be taken. He did not expect that his strategy would be executed. It had appeal for Dinwiddie, who was in the process of enlisting the Cherokee and Catawba. It did not stimulate all the executives and lawmakers of the three colonies to unite in action for the common good. Washington must again, against his wishes, act on the harassing defensive.

The problems of the colonel were enough to exasperate a saint. In September a Williamsburg newspaper published an essay entitled "The Virginia Centinel No. X" by an unknown author or authors that nastily and wittily censured the Virginia regiment. The essay claimed that the regiment's officers were incompetent and brutal and that it was composed of "dastardly debauchees" who spent their time "skulking in forts." The regiment was actually in much better order than it had been, and, doing arduous duty from which no glory would come, it had suffered dozens of casualties. Washington and his officers were infuriated. In private letters he threatened to resign unless there was redress. His half brother Augustine assured him that he was "in as great esteem as ever" with Dinwiddie and "especially" with the Burgesses. Was Washington jealous of Colonel James Innes, a Scot who had formerly served in the British army and who had commanded at Fort Cumberland? Augustine warned that Dinwiddie might replace George with a fellow Scot. In November the officers of the regiment, on the dubious ground that the governor and the House of Burgesses had not officially defended them against "The Virginia Centinel," formally threatened to resign as a body. John Robinson urged Washington not to leave the service because of an attack by a "vile and ignorant scribbler." The storm blew over. Richard Bland told Washington that he ought not blame Dinwiddie for his troubles—they should be laid at the door of the House of Burgesses, which had failed to supply enough money for the war effort. But the colonel continued to censure the governor. In a letter to Robinson he said, "My orders are dark, doubtful, and uncertain; *to-day approved, to-morrow condemned!*" He was "left to act and proceed at hazard, accountable for the consequence, and blamed without the benefit of defence!" He was unfair to the governor, who was also sorely tried.

The hullabaloo created by "The Virginia Centinel" diminished. Washington and his subordinates continued to hope that they would receive royal commissions. The home government might still respond. It was believed that General Loudoun would come to Virginia. He might be persuaded to act. Toiling until winter was well under way to put everything on the frontier in good order, Washington and his officers learned that Loudoun would not appear in Virginia. Late in January, 1757, the officers endorsed a memorial to the earl for royal establishment, undoubtedly prepared by Washington, and he wrote a special appeal in his own behalf. He sent the two papers to Captain James Cuningham, the chief aide of the general, and he asked permission from Dinwiddie to go northward to present in person the arguments for himself and his officers. The governor was doubtless aware that the colonel had turned against him and also that another approach to the general would be useless, but he gave his consent.

The two documents are remarkable. Washington condemned the House of Burgesses because it had provided only for defense and inadequately even for that. He did not spare Dinwiddie. He did not mention the many favors given him by the governor, saying now that it was the Burgesses rather than Dinwiddie who had supported his claims to favor. He asserted, "The orders I receive are full of ambiguity. I am left, like a wanderer in the wilderness, to proceed at hazard. I am answerable for consequences, and blamed, without the privilege of defence." He had done his full duty. The regiment had performed better than could have been expected. It had suffered one hundred casualties in the preceding campaign, and it ought to be made part of the British army, Washington said. He offered fulsome praise to the general. Learning of the appointment of Loudoun as commander in chief, he recalled that he had "fondly pronounced your Lordship our patron." The name of Loudoun was familiar to him "on account of the important services performed to his Majesty in other parts of the world" by the general. The earl was actually a short, fat, unimpressive man who owned his prominence to the fact that he was a close relative of the duke of Argyll, a rich Scottish nobleman and a most influential British politician. Leading British troops against Bonnie Prince Charlie in Scotland in the rebellion of 1745, Loudoun had won no laurels. Nevertheless, Washington wrote, "Do not think, my Lord, that I am going to flatter; notwithstanding I have exalted sentiments of your Lordship's character and respect your rank, it is not my intention to adulate. My nature is open and honest and free from guile!" Washington laid it on thick. He said that he offered "no misrepresentations, nor aggravated relation of facts, nor unjust reflections." But was he inaccurate as well as unjust to Dinwiddie? "With regard to myself," he declared, "I cannot forbear adding that, had his Excellency General Braddock survived his unfortunate defeat, I should have met with preferment agreeable to my wishes. I had his promise to that purpose. . . . General Shirley was not unkind in his promises, but he has gone to England." Loudoun read the two papers, and Cuningham wrote to Washington on February 27 that though the general was too busy to reply, he seemed to be "very much pleased with the accounts you have given him of the situation of our affairs to the south'ard." Several friends of the Virginian recommended him to the general. Riding northward, Washington secured an interview with Loudoun at Philadelphia on March 20. He received no satisfaction from it. The general would not put the Virginia regiment on the royal payroll. He was committed to employment of British and foreign officers for the Royal Americans. He had nothing to offer Washington. In fact, Loudoun undertook, with the consent of Dinwiddie, to reduce the importance of Washington's command.

Dinwiddie was in Philadelphia at the time, conferring with the general and other governors regarding plans for the approaching campaign. Did one Scot, Loudoun or Cuningham, tell another Scot, Dinwiddie, that he had been attacked by Washington? In any event someone informed him, and he could hardly fail to be resentful, the more so because he had a special relationship with the general. Although Dinwiddie acted as the chief executive of Virginia, Loudoun held the title of governor as a perquisite. Dinwiddie was legally a lieutenant governor. The two men split the salary and fees of office between them. Loudoun could make the situation of Dinwiddie very uncomfortable, could even arrange for his dismissal. Did an angry Dinwiddie speak to the general without enthusiasm about Washington? No answer to that question has been found. But Loudoun decided, with the approval of Dinwiddie and the other governors, that the duties of the Virginia regiment on the frontier would be reduced, that its importance and that of Washington would be lessened. As protection against raids from Fort Duquesne the general decided to place some royal troops in Pennsylvania, to require Maryland to defend Fort Cumberland, and to propose sending part of the Virginia regiment to Charleston to help defend that city against a possible attack by the French. Washington and the remainder of his regiment were confined to duty in the Valley. The colonel was not aware of those decisions when he left Philadelphia. He learned about them after his return to Virginia early in April, but he must have sensed that all was not well.

Dinwiddie struck back at his aggressive subordinate. It would not do to remove Washington from command, for he retained his popularity in the House of Burgesses. But the governor undertook to bring the colonel to heel. Dinwiddie wielded larger authority than he had had in the past. Before the campaign of 1757 he regained the authority over expenditures that he had earlier lost to the Burgesses. He hastened the departure of the contingent of the Virginia regiment assigned to duty in Charleston. He used the diminished duties and size of the regiment as reasons for reducing several of its captains to lieutenant. He declined to appoint as supply officers friends of Washington recommended by the colonel. He closely inspected accounts submitted by Washington. The colonel had received insufficient and contradictory orders from him? Dinwiddie proceeded to give him clear and specific instructions, telling him precisely where to locate forts and men in the Valley. The long campaign of Washington for advancement ended in loss of importance. It was useless to protest.

Washington might have resigned, but he realized only gradually that Dinwiddie was striking back at him. The colonel, as usual, did his duty in the campaign. His problems were fewer and less worrisome than they had earlier been. The Virginia frontier was relatively quiet. Although the British forces under Loudoun failed dismally to the north, they occupied the French to such an extent that the garrison of Fort Duquesne could not be reinforced. There was a rumor in the summer that a large Franco-Indian force was approaching Fort Cumberland, but it proved to be false. Small bodies of warriors committed their customary depredations in the backwoods. Washington and his men were able to retaliate. The long-sought help from the Cherokee and Catawba was beginning to appear. The colonel sent out some of them with parties of his men on raids toward the Ohio. His Indian allies brought back a few scalps, for which they were duly paid by Virginia. Washington found it difficult to deal with the Indians to the south. They were capricious, unreliable, suspicious, and eager for largesse. He received no help from Edmund Atkin, a South Carolinian who had received a royal appointment as superintendent for all the Indians on the borders of the southern colonies. Atkin appeared at Winchester, spent a good deal of money, and vexed rather than pleased the Cherokee before he departed southward. Later, as Washington feared, the new intimacy between Virginia and the Cherokee led to strife and ultimately to war with them, in 1760. He would not be involved in that struggle. He continued to face disobedience and desertion in his regiment. He had two deserters hanged as a lesson for his troops, for he had learned that discipline enormously increased the power of an armed force.

The frontier was sufficiently quiet that Washington was able to leave it in August and again in September, first to care for his property and then to attend the funeral of his good friend Colonel Fairfax. But his health was not good, and his relationship with Dinwiddie deteriorated. He began to suffer again from dysentery, and his "bloody flux" gradually grew worse. Incensed by a scandalous rumor that he had lied about the Indian menance in the spring of 1756 in order to get more men and money from the Burgesses, he wrote to ask Dinwiddie whether the governor knew the source of the canard. He assured Dinwiddie that he did not

believe the governor was responsible for it. But why had Dinwiddie
turned against him? He had always done his full duty. He received
a reply that must have given him pause. The governor advised him
"not to credit every idle story you hear" and then added, "My
conduct to you from the beginning was always friendly, but you
know I had good reason to suspect you of ingratitude, which I am
convinced your own conscience and reflection must allow I had
reason to be angry. . . . However as I've his Majesty's leave to go
for England, propose leaving this November, and I wish my successor may show you as much friendship as I've done." If Washington had not earlier realized that his censure of Dinwiddie had
rebounded, that gentlemanly rebuke should have informed him of
the fact. Washington nevertheless rejoined, "I do not know that I
ever gave your Honor cause to suspect me of ingratitude, a crime I
detest and would most carefully avoid. If an open, disinterested
behavior carries offence, I may have offended, because I have always laid it down as a maxim to represent facts freely and impar-
tially, but no more to others than I have to you, sir." Washington
had not yet learned that remorseless telling of the truth is a vicious
virtue, or a virtuous vice. Almost admitting that he had criticized
the governor to others, he asked Dinwiddie to give evidence of
ingratitude. Did Washington think that his condemnation of the
behavior of another man, whether it proved to be just or unjust,
ought not be resented? In the same letter the colonel requested
leave to go from Winchester to Williamsburg to settle accounts
with the governor. But Dinwiddie did not wish to see him. He
refused permission, saying that the journey was unnecessary, that
Washington had had enough leave for the year, that he was needed
on the frontier. There, by no means to the credit of Washington,
the dispute ended. His behavior toward its close may be excused in
part because his dysentery had become alarming. Upon the advice
of his physician, without permission, he went home to Mount
Vernon. Dinwiddie, also ailing and preparing to leave for England,
heard the news. The Scot conducted himself like a gentleman. He
had not known about Washington's illness. He wrote to Captain
Robert Stewart, from whom he had learned about "the violent
complaint" from which Washington suffered, that it gave him
"great concern, it was unknown to me or he shou'd have had leave
of absence sooner, & I am very glad he did not delay following the
Doctrs. advice, to try a change of air. I sincerely wish him a speedy
recovery."

If Dinwiddie was not fond of Washington, he nevertheless retained respect for him at the troubled end of their close relationship, a remarkable tribute to the colonel. We do not know what Washington thought in tranquillity and perspective about the man who had started him up the ladder to fame.

VI

The Triumphs of the Colonel

Washington was indeed in sad condition at the end of the campaign of 1757, but he regained his health and at last rode into Fort Duquesne as a victor, more than four years after he began the war against the French. Then, still troubled by dysentery, he abjured the battlefield and retired to a happy life as a married man and a planter. He had achieved more than enough to be recognized as the first among American military men. He would not be forgotten when his fellow colonials were in dire need of a commander.

Establishing himself for the winter at Mount Vernon after hostilities ended in 1757, the colonel sought help for his malarial complaint and the "bloody flux." Again he suffered from pain and fever. An unbalanced and irregular military diet doubtless added to his difficulties. He had another trouble—his teeth were deteriorating. He had been forced to have one removed while he was still in the Valley. He consulted the Reverend Charles Green of Alexandria, who ministered to the body as well as the soul. Green could not offer a solution to the dental difficulty. Washington evidently suffered from pyorrhea, and neither Green nor anyone else at that time knew what to do about it except to extract teeth as they became too loose for comfort. Green advised the colonel to cure the dysentery by avoiding flesh and eating only "jellies and such kinds of food." Hannah Bushrod Washington, wife of the colonel's brother Jack, who normally would have prepared the vegetarian food, was absent. Accordingly, Washington sought help at Belvoir. The master of that place was now George William Fairfax, son of Washington's deceased benefactor, and its mistress was the wife of George William, Sarah Cary Fairfax. The colonel had long known the younger Fairfax and was friendly, even intimate with him. He liked Sarah, commonly known as Sally, very much. She saw to it that he was supplied with the sort of nourishment prescribed by the clergyman. The diet did not cure his dysentery, although he painstakingly followed directions. Moreover, riding frequently that winter downriver to Belvoir, he enjoyed his visits more than ever. They were the happier because George William Fairfax was absent in England. Washington had long been an admirer of Mrs. Fairfax, and she was kind to him. She flirted with him, discreetly. So he fell in love with a married woman. In fact, he became so much attached to her that he would risk his reputation and public career for her.

In February, 1758, military business called Washington imperatively to Williamsburg. He set out for that place, but was forced to turn back. His "fever and pain" increased as he rode, and physicians warned him that the journey might endanger his life. Returning to Mount Vernon, he continued to suffer. In early March he wrote, "At certain periods I have been reduced to great extremity, and have now much reason to apprehend an approaching decay, being visited with several symptoms of such a disease." He said that his constitution was "certainly greatly impaired," and he thought it might be necessary to resign his command. However, he was soon well enough to go to Williamsburg to seek better medical advice. He apparently received it and followed it. He was in sufficiently good condition before spring to display interest in a recent widow and heiress, Mrs. Daniel Parke Custis. He called upon her at her plantation on the Pamunkey River. Early in April he rode westward once more to duty in the Shenandoah Valley. The following summer he ordered a ring from Philadelphia. It is likely that the ring was intended to grace a finger of the widow, though he had had little time to pay court to the lady in person. He was compelled to continue his suit by correspondence.

Washington took up arms again under very changed circumstances. The great William Pitt had emerged as the dominant figure in the British cabinet, and Britain was beginning under his leadership to wage war with energy and determination. Giving Frederick the Great of Prussia sufficient help so that he could hold off the enemies of Britain and Prussia on the European continent, the imperious Pitt brought forward new and younger commanders and demanded victory from them. He used naval power to prevent France from sending reinforcements and supplies overseas. Hemming in the French colonies, he sent fresh British troops across the Atlantic. Moreover, he stimulated the British colonies in North America to renew and to increase their efforts, promising to repay them for additional expenditures in the common cause. American colonials were delighted by a new arrangement regarding military command. Henceforth their officers were to take precedence over all British ones in lower ranks—an American colonel would not be required to yield to a British captain or major. Ever larger British and American forces moved forward, against Louisbourg, in northern and western New York, and in Pennsylvania. A formidable army gathered at Raystown, now Bedford, Pennsylvania, to march against Fort Duquesne. Washington eagerly sought to take part in that offensive, and he had his wish. Virginia undertook to raise a second regiment under Colonel William Byrd and ordered both Washington and Byrd, with most of their men, to serve under General John Forbes, a veteran Scottish officer who led the forces that collected at Raystown. Washington was delighted. He continued to be commander in chief of the Virginians. He was not satisfied, however, to be only one of many American officers who joined Forbes. He urged Colonel Gage and General John Stanwix to recommend to Forbes that he be given special status. He had abandoned thought of wearing a red coat. There is no doubt that Gage did what he could for Washington. The British colonel had learned to like him and recognized his remarkable qualities. He wrote to Washington in 1757, "I think your welfare will contribute to that of your country." He also asserted, "I shall always be glad to hear of your health, happiness & success." If Washington no longer sought a British commission, he still wished to be "distinguished in some measure from the *common run* of provincial officers, as I understand there will be a motley herd of us." If it seems immodest of him to have asked for such treatment, one must also recall that he had undoubtedly earned it by long, faithful, and arduous service. He received it.

But not immediately. The army at Raystown gathered very

slowly. In the meantime Washington performed his last military duties in the Valley. They were not onerous or dangerous, at least so far as relations with the French were concerned. They and their red-skinned allies did not appear in force. He fretted and worried about Indians, but those about whom he was concerned were friends of King George II. Bands of Cherokee and Catawba warriors came northward to fight for him, remained briefly, and went home. He was annoyed because they were of little military use, but he was alarmed lest they become bitter and dangerous enemies. The Catawba were few and not formidable, but the Cherokee could muster as many as 2,500 warriors from their villages near the Appalachian divide. French agents were seeking to turn the Cherokee against the English, not without success. Perhaps 700 of them came north in the spring and summer of 1758, but only a handful joined General Forbes. What was far worse, contact between Cherokee braves and frontiersmen led to clashes that ended with casualties among both parties. Washington was well aware that the Indians were often childlike, that they demanded from their enemies a tooth for a tooth, a life for a life. He was only too familiar with the prowess of the Indians in forest warfare. He recognized that in such fighting one Indian was superior to one white man—a fact that does not imply inferiority of a body of well disciplined and well armed whites accustomed to such conflict to an equal number of warriors. Washington feared that the Cherokee would turn against all the English because of the clashes between them and the backwoods people, that they would seek revenge for their losses. His judgment was only too well founded. They took the warpath against the English in 1760—after he had ceased to be directly responsible for the defense of western Virginia.

Washington was indeed distinguished from the *"common run"* of American officers by General Forbes, but not with unalloyed pleasure on either his own part or that of the general. The Scottish commander in chief had, of course, heard about the Virginian before Forbes left England, and he let it be known soon after his arrival in America that he desired the services of Washington. The colonel assured the general in flattering language that he would gladly do duty under him. "I have no higher ambition than to act my part well, during the campaign," he wrote, "and if I should *thereby* merit your approbation, it would be the most pleasing reward, for the toils I shall undergo. . . . It gives me no small pleasure that an officer of your experience, abilities, and good character, should be appointed to command the expedition, and it is with equal satisfaction I congratulate you upon the promising appearance of a glorious campaign." But the relationship that began so suitably became sour with the passage of time. Collecting most of his men at Fort Cumberland, Washington remained there for many weeks, awaiting orders to march. During that time he became a harsh critic of Forbes, condemning him for failure to move more rapidly and especially for his choice of a line of march toward Fort Duquesne.

Forbes, with some 1,600 British troops and a train of artillery, landed at Philadelphia rather than at a port on the Chesapeake. Moving westward toward a base already established in the Quaker commonwealth, Forbes and his second-in-command, Colonel Henry Bouquet, a veteran and able officer of Swiss birth, were inclined to push on as directly as possible from Raystown to their goal. There was a serious disadvantage in following that route, which required the crossing of high hills and the building of a road through forests and over the heights. However, it was the shortest route, and use of it would permit the army to approach the fort without crossing the Youghiogheny River. They tended to prefer it to making use of the road that had been cut by Braddock, which required passage over that river. There was the possibility that the French would be able to offer a strong defense behind the Youghiogheny, especially if the stream happened to be swollen by rain. Besides, to make use of the old road from Raystown via Fort Cumberland would lengthen the march of the army by as much as eighty-six or ninety-six miles, Forbes believed.

Virginians, including Colonel William Byrd and Washington, began to protest against abandoning the Braddock approach. From Fort Cumberland, Washington denounced the Pennsylvania route in letters to his friend Major Francis Halkett, who was at Raystown, and to Colonel Bouquet, who was making advance arrangements for Forbes. He asserted that in championing the road from Fort Cumberland he had no "private interest," that he sought only "the general good." He said that it was impossible to build a new road, even one fit for packhorses, in time to reach Fort Duquesne before winter forced the army to halt. Were it attempted, "all is lost by Heavens! Our enterprise ruin'd; and we stop'd at the Laurel Hill this winter." He pooh-poohed the danger that might be met at the crossing of the Youghiogheny. He claimed that the army, by marching to the southward from Raystown to Fort Cumberland, would travel only nineteen miles farther than it would by making its way across Pennsylvania. Surely, using a road already cut through the wilderness, it would reach the fort much earlier than if it forced a path through the woods and over the hills of Pennsylvania. His estimate of the additional mileage via the Braddock road was too low; that of Forbes was too high. But Washington was somewhat nearer to the fact than was the general. Whose judgment was correct? Probably that of the Virginian.

But was Washington, as he claimed, moved only by military considerations? It has been argued that he was swayed by greed and also by a desire to promote the prosperity and expansion of Virginia. If the Braddock road remained the sole avenue from the Atlantic seaboard to the Ohio Valley, though only for a short time, would not increased use of it augment the value of his Bullskin plantation, so near to that route? Not much. Would not trade develop more rapidly along that road, to the benefit of Virginia? Would not the claim of the Old Dominion to the forks of the Ohio and lands beyond—it was not known whether Virginia or Pennsylvania had the better claim to the forks—be strengthened? Would not Washington have a better opportunity to secure good land in that region in consequence of his service in the first Virginia regiment if Virginia triumphed over Pennsylvania? Such a contingent argument is strained indeed. Washington did seek to advance the interests of Virginia. Nevertheless he could assert that they were not paramount in his mind, that they happened to coincide with sound military thought.

The thinking of Forbes and Bouquet was otherwise. They were told by Major George Armstrong, a Pennsylvanian, that the Pennsylvania route was practicable; they questioned the motives of Washington; and Forbes decided to move forward through the Quaker colony. He had overwhelming force at his command, more than eight thousand men, including redcoats, Pennsylvanians, Marylanders, and Virginians, but his advance was very slow. Watching from Fort Cumberland the difficult progress of the main body of the army, Washington continued to predict disastrous failure in letters to Bouquet, to Governor Francis Fauquier of Virginia, and to Speaker John Robinson. In consequence men at Williamsburg acted meanly and provincially. They decided to recall the Virginia troops from the army unless Fort Duquesne was taken by December 1. Then, on second thought, they reversed that decision.

In the meantime the army suffered a defeat that fortified the pessimism of Washington. On September 14 Major James Grant, a British officer leading an advance contingent of regulars and Americans, attacked a body of French and Indians sent forward from Fort Duquesne. The result was disconcerting. The force under Grant was driven back and suffered more than three hundred casualties. Grant and others with him became prisoners. Enemy losses were small. The outcome of the engagement might have been even more damaging had not Virginians with Grant covered the retreat. The defeat, however, was not too serious, since Forbes continued to have the advantage of overwhelming strength. His army plodded on.

Washington first met Forbes, in accordance with an order from the general, on September 16. The interview took place at Raystown, for the westward progress of the commander in chief had been delayed by an attack of dysentery. The two men were not congenial, for Forbes had concluded that there was a Virginia "scheme against this new road" and that it was "a shame for any officer to be concerned" in it. He later said that Washington's "behaviour about the roads was no ways like a soldier." Instructed by the general to join him at Raystown with his Virginians, Washington brought them into camp there six days later. There he and his men remained until after the middle of October while other parts of the army inched forward, piece by piece. Then Washington led a contingent of Virginians, Marylanders, and North Carolinians westward, joining the vanguard at the Loyalhanna River where Bedford now stands. The bulk of the army collected there soon afterward. Although it included only a few Cherokee who served as scouts, it was well prepared against a surprise attack.

But Washington remained pessimistic. From the Loyalhanna he wrote to Governor Fauquier on October 30 that "the weather growing very inclement, must I apprehend terminate our expedition for this year, at this place." Its "affairs are now drawing to a crisis." On November 5, expecting that Forbes, who was so ill with dysentery that he had to be carried in a litter, would soon order resumption of the march toward Fort Duquesne, still fifty miles away, Washington again predicted failure of the expedition in a report to the governor. Hardships, want of clothing, shortage of food, and physical obstacles declared against moving on toward the fort as winter approached. "But it is no longer a time for pointing out difficulties," he added. He would unquestionably do his full duty.

Washington was not the only officer in the army who was discouraged. Forbes held a council of war on November 11 with his eight colonels, and it was agreed that the army should abandon its advance. Then, on the next day, came good news. A party of scouts sent out by Washington brought in three prisoners. They gave reliable information that the French garrison was weak and that it would have the help of only a few Indians—Friedrich Post, a Pennsylvania missionary, had exerted his influence among the Delaware and Shawnee tribesmen, and most of them had decided to remain neutral. Rejoicing, Forbes ordered the discard of heavy baggage and a rapid march toward the fort. Colonel Armstrong led the way. Washington followed with Virginians using axes to clear away trees and brush. His mind was not entirely on his work. Even as he and his men cleared the road, he told Forbes that it would remain inferior to the Braddock route for communication with a British post at the forks of the Ohio—if one was established to replace the French fort. He was still seeking advantage for Virginia against Pennsylvania. But he and the army persevered and moved on. The French commander, François Marchand de Ligneris, had no more than five hundred men, probably many fewer, and a small body of Indians to defend Fort Duquesne. He stood his ground until the army was within a day's march. Then, recognizing the impossibility of successful resistance, he set fire to the post and fled far down the Ohio River. The army marched into its remains without resistance on November 25. Forbes undertook to replace it with a new structure named Fort Pitt, and he supplied a garrison. Most of his army disbanded and went home. Among those who departed was Washington. He rode back to the camp at the Loyalhanna, thence to Winchester, on to Mount Vernon, and at length to Williamsburg, which he reached before the end of December.

Washington had had enough of soldiering to last him for many years. He was once more troubled by dysentery, "an inveterate disorder in his bowels," as he afterward described it. At Williamsburg, perhaps before he reached that place, he submitted his resignation as colonel and commander in chief of the Virginia forces. He was given a vote of thanks by the House of Burgesses. More important, he received an address signed by most of the officers of his regiment that expressed their sorrow for the departure of "such an excellent commander, such a sincere friend, and so affable a companion." It proclaimed "adieu to that happy union and harmony which has been our principle cement!" The officers asserted that "our unhappy country will receive a loss, no less irreparable." One suspects that Adam Stephen was displaying his addiction to rhetorical phrases. But it is not to be doubted that the attachment of the officers to their retiring leader was sincere and deep.

Washington was in youth no brilliant forest Napoleon; he would not become in maturity an American Julius Caesar. His prediction that a smaller force moving swiftly would take Fort Duquesne went awry; his prophecy that a large and slowly advancing army would fail to take it was also erroneous. He had displayed no remarkable ability in maneuvering troops in battle. He had offered fulsome and insincere flattery to British generals in vain attempts to win great favor. He had been youthfully arrogant. He had been jealous of competitors, tactless, and ungrateful. But there was a power within him. He had also given proof of remarkable physical and moral courage. Complaining frequently about his burdens, he had never shirked them. Dealing sternly with vicious troops who deserted, gently with good ones who happened to misbehave, he won the respect of private soldiers as well as officers. He acquired valuable experience in leading his regiment and militia and in his association with British officers and armies. That experience would afterward be most useful to him and to his fellow Americans.

Washington resigned long before the end of the Seven Years' War, but he did not return to service. The struggle continued for more than four additional years and ended with stunning triumphs for Britain, including the spectacular capture of Quebec and the conquest of Canada. He watched its progress with interest; he did not seek military employment of any kind. His physical condition was in itself sufficient reason for returning to a quieter life. Another attack of the "bloody flux" might well lead to his death—General Forbes, an older man, to be sure, died from that sickness after the capture of Fort Duquesne. The dream of a career in the British army that Washington cherished so long had come to an end. Men in power in London ignored his contributions to the empire; British commanders in North America did not beg him to take up arms again. He had done enough, had suffered enough. He had had the moderate satisfaction of riding into the French post as one of the victors. It may safely be inferred that his devotion to the Mother Country, which must have been enhanced by British recognition and rewards for his services, had actually diminished. One may speculate about the consequences, had he become a British army officer. It is doubtful that he would have been available afterward to command American forces struggling for independence and to lead in the creation of the American republic. The failure of British leaders to reward the young colonial for his achievements, to enlist his services, may have been costly indeed to the empire that they ruled.

Washington had not turned violently against Britain; he had not become utterly American. He retained an affection for Virginia. Duty and desire no longer drew him toward the battlefield. Moreover, a prospect of a good life as a civilian was opening before him. Recognition of his merits was not confined to Virginians who gathered at Williamsburg. It had spread among plain as well as not-so-plain citizens. He had taken advantage of his popularity to seek election to the House of Burgesses, membership in which brought possible power in addition to social prestige. He considered campaigning in his home county of Fairfax in 1755, but refrained when he discovered that he could not win. Instead he contested in Frederick County in the Valley and was defeated. Three years later, however, the men of Frederick gave him an easy victory. Absent with Forbes, he had pleased them with gifts of sixty-six gallons and ten bowls of rice punch, fifty-eight gallons of beer, thirty-five gallons of wine, eight quarts of hard cider, and three and one-half pints of brandy. He continued to represent Frederick at Williamsburg for seven years. Washington could well afford to entertain thirsty citizens of Frederick, for he was prospering financially as well as politically. He was about to marry an heiress, achieve wealth, and become a principal planter of Virginia. He did not marry without pangs of disappointment.

VII

The Colonel, Sally Fairfax, and Martha Custis

Washington was almost twenty-seven years of age when he married. He was a lusty young male, and one is tempted to infer that he had long been deeply interested in women, in legal or illegal unions with them. Moreover, despite his devotion to war, he had had time in which to pursue attractive ladies in the older settlements of Virginia and less sophisticated girls in the Valley. There were camp women who followed the soldiers in his campaigns. One may speculate that his unsuccessful courtship of Betsy Fauntleroy was accompanied by other, less formal enterprises in which he did not fail to achieve success. It may well be, however, that he was shy, that he avoided entanglements with available and coarse women. Certainly, in his midtwenties he gave his heart to a refined lady, before he married Martha Dandridge Custis, once thought to be the great—indeed the only—love of his life.

On March 30, 1877, the New York *Herald* printed a letter of September 12, 1758, from George Washington to Sally Fairfax. The centennial celebration of the birth of the nation had ended only three months earlier. The Americans had not failed to pay appropriate tribute to the dauntless hero of the Revolution, the progenitor of the Republic, the possessor of all the virtues, the man with-

out a flaw. At the Philadelphia Exposition, arranged to remind
citizens of their glorious heritage, they had bought thousands of
reprints of the issue of the Ulster County, New York, *Gazette* that
mournfully announced the death of the greatest of the Founding
Fathers. The publication of the letter gave a shock. Writing from
Fort Cumberland, Washington indicated that he was not really
very fond of Mrs. Custis, that he sought the favor of the wife of an
absent friend. He had paid court to Mrs. Custis, and his later
marriage to her had always been considered an ideal one. But had
he actually deceived her and also tried to corrupt a married
woman, as the letter suggested? Was the sainted Washington attempting a base seduction?

The famous letter was of the someone-loves-someone-you-know-
who variety, a letter befitting a lovesick youth of sixteen or seventeen rather than a man of Washington's age. It was obviously written in such fashion as to avert censure in the event that it fell into
the hands of a curious third person. "Dear Madam," it began,
"Yesterday I was honourd with your short but very agreable fa-
vour of the first instt. .—how joyfully I catch at the happy occasion
of renewing a corrispondance which I feard was dis-relished on
your part, I leave to time, that never failing expositor of all things
—and to a monitor equally as faithful in my own breast, to testifie.
—In silence I now express my joy—silence which in some cases—I
wish the present—speaks more intelligably than the sweetest elo-
quence." But he certainly did not fail to try to voice his sentiments.
The letter proceeded to announce that the writer extended his affection to its recipient rather than to Martha Custis.

If you allow that any honour can be derivd from my opposition to our present system of management, you destroy the
merit of it entirely in me by attributing my anxiety to the
annimating prospect of possessing Mrs. Custis.—When—I
need not name it.—guess yourself.—Shoud not my own honour and country's welfare be the excitement? 'Tis true, I pro-
fess myself a votary to love. I acknowledge that a lady is in the
case—and further I confess, that this lady is known to you.—
Yes Madam, as well as she is to one who is too sensible of her
charms to deny the power, whose influence he feels and must
ever submit to. I feel the force of her amiable beauties in the
recollection of a thousand tender passages that I could wish to
obliterate, till I am bid to revive them.—but experience, alas!

sadly reminds me how impossible this is.—and evinces an
opinion which I have long entertained, that there is a destiny,
which has the sovereign controul of our actions—not to be
resisted by the strongest efforts of human nature.

She did indeed contribute to the making of his destiny. She was not
overswayed by another paragraph in which he declared again that
she was the object of his affections.

You have drawn me my dear Madam, or rather have I
drawn myself, into an honest confession of a simple fact—
misconstrue not my meaning.—'tis obvious—doubt in [it] not,
nor expose it,—the world has no business to know the object
of my love,—declard in this manner to—you, when I want to
conceal it—One thing, above all things in this world I wish to
know, and only one person of your acquaintance can solve me
that, or guess my meaning.—but adieu to this, till happier
times, if I ever shall see them.—the hours at present are melancholy full.—neither the rugged toils of war, nor the gentler
conflict of A—— B——s is my choice.—I dare believe you
are as happy as you say—I wish I was happy also. Mirth,
good humor, ease of mind and.—what else? cannot fail to
render you so, and consummate your wishes.—

He went on to more prosaic matters, and to a request for a reply.

If one agreeable lady coud almost wish herself a fine gentleman for the sake of another; I apprehend, that many fine
gentlemen will wish themselves finer, e'er Mrs. Spotswood is
possest.—She has already become a reigning toast in this
camp; and many there are in it, who intend—(fortune favour-
ing)—to make honourable scar's speak the fulness of their
merit, and be a messenger of their love to her.
I cannot easily forgive the unseasonable haste of my last
express, if he deprivd me thereby of a single word you intended to add.—the time of the present messenger is, as the
last might have been, entirely at your disposal.—I cant expect
to hear from my friends more than this once, before the fate of
the expedition will, some how or other be determind, I therefore beg to know when you set out for Hampton, & when you
expect to return to Belvoir again—and I shoud be glad to hear

also of your speedy departure, as I shall thereby hope for your return before I get down; the disappointment of seeing your family woud give me much concern.—From any thing I can yet see 'tis hardly possible to say when we shall finish. I don't think there is a probability of it till the middle of November. —Your letter to Captn. Gist I forwarded by a safe hand the moment it came to me.—his answer shall be carefully transmitted.

Colo. Mercer to whom I delivered your message and compliments, joins me very heartily in wishing you and the ladies of Belvoir the perfect enjoyment of every happiness this world affords. Be assurd that I am D Madam with the most unfeigned regard,

> Yr. Most Obedient
> & Most Obligd Hble Servt
> Go Washington

N.B.—Many accidents happening (to use a vulgar saying) between the cup and the lip, I choose to make the exchange of carpets myself—since I find you will not do me the honour to accept of mine.

Readers of the letter, among them sober scholars familiar with the life of Washington, were aghast. The learned Worthington C. Ford, who began to publish an edition of the writings of Washington in 1889, included it. The erudite John C. Fitzpatrick, whose collection of Washington writings came from the press in and after 1931, also reprinted it. Neither Ford nor Fitzpatrick was willing to say that the letter was authentic, and presumably profound biographers of the creator of the nation asserted flatly that it must be a forgery. They pointed out that it was available only in newspaper form. Where was the original letter? It has not been brought forward for examination; it could not be produced, they argued, because it did not exist. Washington could not possibly have indited such a message. Moreover, was there not solid evidence that their American Galahad was indeed in love with Mrs. Custis and therefore not interested in any other woman? They pointed to a letter from Washington to her of July 20, 1758, obviously written at Fort Cumberland, printed by both Ford and Fitzpatrick. It reads: "We have begun our march for the Ohio. A courier is starting for Williamsburg, and I embrace the opportunity to send a few words to one whose life is now inseparable from mine. Since that happy hour when we made our pledges to each other, my thoughts have been continually going to you as another self. That an all-powerful Providence may keep us both in safety is the prayer of your ever faithful and affectionate friend." How could anyone question such a noble and moving expression of love and fidelity?

Alas, it is quite clear that Washington did not write that splendid and touching message of July 20. Its language was beyond the literary powers of the young Washington, who had difficulty with spelling, grammar, and syntax. It is doubtful that he could have framed such a letter even in his maturity, although he acquired facility in writing with experience and the passing of time. The letter made its appearance in print after the publication of the one in which he declared his affection for Sally Fairfax. The original in Washington's handwriting has not been found, and it is safe to conclude that it cannot be produced. One infers that it was composed by a fluent admirer of Washington who was convinced that he was in love with Mrs. Custis, that he should have sent her such a message, that he must have done it, that it was a service to morality, if not to scholarship, to supply the letter. It probably did not occur to the forger that establishment of the authenticity of the letter to Sally Fairfax, together with acceptance of the forgery, would put Washington in a very bad light indeed, as a man who both played fast and loose with Mrs. Custis and paid improper attention to Mrs. Fairfax. And the letter to Mrs. Fairfax was authentic. It is preserved in the original in the Harvard College Library, and other letters from Washington to Mrs. Fairfax are available. We know from other sources that he did visit Mrs. Custis, recently widowed, at her home on the Pamunkey River before the campaign of 1758. She was wealthy and a catch. There are good reasons to believe that he was seriously considering a proposal of marriage to her, including that order of a ring from Philadelphia that was doubtless intended for the third finger of her left hand. His denial to Mrs. Fairfax in September, 1758, that he was absolutely committed to Mrs. Custis should be taken at face value. But his connection with her was unquestionably developing, presumably by correspondence that has been lost. On campaign, he did not see her for many months. He married her immediately after returning home.

Just what was the relationship between Washington and Mrs. Fairfax? It can be described with some certainty. Born Sarah Cary in Virginia, she had been a wife for ten years. She was apparently not a beauty, but she was intelligent, amusing, and charming. Visiting the Fairfax home at Belvoir frequently, Washington came to know her very well. There can be no question that he found her enormously attractive. He began to try to establish a correspondence with her as early as 1755. She liked him, and she did not consistently refuse to answer his letters. It is reasonable to infer that she was flattered by his attentions. But she did not express an affection for him beyond that of friendship or a flirtation that must be kept within bounds. Apparently she pretended in her reply to his long love letter that she did not understand his message. Washington wrote again to her, thirteen days after penning that letter, "Do we still misunderstand the true meaning of each other's letters? I think it must appear so, tho' I would feign hope the contrary as I cannot speak plainer without, but I'll say no more, and leave you to guess the rest." But then he did say more, again asserting his love for her in indirect language that probably would not be correctly construed by the prying eyes of a third person. Both he and she were familiar with the plot of *Cato*, the popular play by Joseph Addison, which was performed at Williamsburg by students of the College of William and Mary as early as 1736. She had referred to a scheme for a private performance of the play. He declared, "I should think my time more agreeable spent believe me, in playing a part in Cato, with the company you mention, and myself doubly happy in being the Juba to such a Marcia, as you must make." In the play the North African Prince Juba and Marcia, the daughter of Roman Cato the Younger, were lovers. In the drama Juba, an ally of Cato in the last struggle of the Roman republicans against Julius Caesar, saved Marcia from the clutches of a villainous Sempronius and won her affection. But Cato refused consent to a marriage of his aristocratic Roman daughter to a mere North African prince so long as the republic endured. Committing suicide after the final triumph of Caesar in the battle of Thapsus, Cato withdrew his opposition to the union. The play ended with Juba and Marcia free to marry. Washington could hardly have hoped that he would enjoy the fortune of Juba. His Marcia continued to fend him off.

At last Washington was compelled to recognize that his passion for Sally Fairfax was hopeless. He did the sensible and practical thing. In the end the brave man favored Fortune. After his return home from the capture of Fort Duquesne he quickly married the likable and wealthy Mrs. Custis, on January 6, 1759, and brought her to Mount Vernon. The Washingtons and the Fairfaxes lived thereafter on very friendly terms. There is no evidence that Martha was unhappy because she was second in the affections of her husband. If Sally's husband knew of the love that Washington expressed for his wife, evidence has not been found that he voiced resentment. Perhaps he did know about it. Perhaps, being confident that he possessed the affection of his wife, he was somewhat amused. Washington continued to visit Belvoir, with his wife. Temporarily in England soon after the marriage of the Washingtons, the Fairfaxes urged them to cross the Atlantic for a visit. They did not accept the invitation, but there was no hostility between the two couples. Belvoir and Sally Fairfax continued to have a special place in Washington's heart so long as he lived. Belvoir burned down in 1773. Twelve years after the final departure of the Fairfaxes for England, after the close of the War of Independence, Washington rode down the banks of the Potomac to see its remains. A part of the walls and the chimney still stood. He gazed sadly at the remains. Soon there would be only "a heap of ruins." He mournfully recorded that "when I considered that the happiest moments of my life had been spent there; when I could not trace a room in the house (now all rubbish) that did not bring to my mind the recollection of pleasing scenes, I was obliged to fly from them with painful sensations, and sorrowing for the contrast." Much later, looking back from the serenity and weariness of approaching old age, he again declared that the youthful years in which he was a constant visitor at Belvoir were the happiest in his life. There can be no doubt that Sally Fairfax always retained a special place in his heart.

Which does not mean that there was a lack of fondness between George and Martha Washington. It may safely be concluded that she found the martial idol of Virginia a most attractive suitor. Nor need one doubt that he courted a woman whom he liked—everyone liked Martha Custis Washington—although he obviously was not utterly entranced by her charms. She was barely literate. Nor was she a beauty. Only five feet tall, she was plump. She had an aquiline nose and large eyes. Had she been of loftier stature and of an imperious nature, she might have been considered imposing, if not handsome. But she was modest and sweet-tempered, a lady in manners and in conduct about whom there was never a word of scandal. She was about nine months older than Washington. She had a special attraction for him in that she was wealthy. Born Martha Dandridge into a family of no great importance, she had married Daniel Parke Custis, a rich planter who had recently died young, leaving her with two small children, John Parke and Martha Parke, commonly known as Jack and Patsy. She had borne two other children who died in infancy. Her share in the estate of her first husband has been estimated to be as much as £23,000, and her offspring also inherited valuable properties. She was one of the richest women in Virginia, a financial catch. Her property immediately passed, in accordance with law, into Washington's hands. Added to his own growing accumulations, it changed him from a rising young soldier and planter into one of the few really wealthy men of Virginia.

Afterward Washington defended the sort of marriage he had made. It had been "most conducive to happiness." He advised a stepgranddaughter not to expect unalloyed felicity in marriage. She must not expect to bathe "in an ocean of love. . . . Love is a mighty pretty thing, but, like all other delicious things, it is cloying." He assured her that "the first transports of passion would subside," that "love is too dainty a food to live on *alone,*" and that "it ought not to be considered further than as a necessary ingredient for that matrimonial happiness which results from a combination of causes." A marriage partner ought to "possess good sense, a good disposition, and the means of supporting you in the way you have been brought up. Such qualifications cannot fail to attract (after marriage) your esteem and regard into which or into disgust, sooner or later love naturally resolves itself." Experience would "convince you that there is no truth more certain than that all our enjoyments fall short of our expectations, and to none does it apply with more force than to the gratification of the passions."

Upon a time Washington had been more or less willing to sacrifice the respect of society, even to abandon a promising career, to possess Sally Fairfax. He could not have carried on a liaison with her without heavy cost to him and to her. It pleased her to be the object of his attentions, but she kept him at arm's length. He suffered because she made him keep his distance. In the end, however much she may have encouraged his addresses, she saved him from disgrace and preserved a great future for him.

VIII

The Magnate of Mount Vernon

Washington became, by marrying Martha Custis, a patrician, a member of the fabled FFV, the First Families of Virginia. For sixteen years he lived like an affluent aristocrat. He used the coat of arms of the English Washingtons and their motto, *Exitus acta probat,* which has been translated as "The end justifies the means," but which actually declares, "At the end of life my deeds will be approved." Like an English squire he served on the vestry of his Episcopal church and attended it without undue zeal but with regularity. He became a justice of the peace in his county, Fairfax, one of the men who governed it. Continuing to sit in the House of Burgesses, he was elected in Fairfax in 1765 and chosen again four years later, the second time without opposition. At first a planter, he became a farmer. He was also a land speculator and a man of business. Unlike many Virginia patricians of his time he was able both to live elegantly and to preserve his property. Indeed, he increased rather than dissipated his wealth. He owned Mount Vernon only for life, but he bought land in its vicinity until he presided over some seven thousand acres adjacent to the Potomac, together with smaller pieces elsewhere in the settled parts of Virginia. The slaves he acquired by his marriage, perhaps one hundred in number, burgeoned in numbers and value through propagation. He purchased more. He was, like many men of means in his time, a speculator in lands beyond the Appalachian Mountains. Unlike most of them, he was successful, obtaining cheaply many thousands of acres. He was an honest and shrewd businessman. He gained additional wealth, perhaps eight thousand pounds, when his stepdaughter died in 1773. Washington was a man of substance in civil as well as military life.

Washington also gained in health. In the summer of 1761 he was again suffering from recurrent fever and pain. He reported that he was apparently "very near my last gasp," that he fell into "a very low and dangerous state." He feared that "the grim King would certainly master my utmost efforts and that I must sink in spite of a noble struggle." In desperation he went to the Berkeley Springs to take the waters in the hope that they would be beneficial. The ride to that place in the heat of summer fatigued him. He found about two hundred people with various complaints seeking relief at the springs. He had to buy a tent and marquee for shelter. The mineral waters, exercise, and mountain air were apparently of some avail. His fevers abated, although his pains grew worse and his sleep continued to be disturbed. However, after his return home, he was able to say, in the autumn, "Thank God I have now got the better of my disorder and shall soon be restord I hope to perfect health again." It would appear that he had had his last major attack of his malarial complaint and dysentery. Those troubles at least eventually ceased to worry him. He gained the vigor of his early years.

Although not deliriously happy, Washington was contented at Mount Vernon. He and his wife were well matched. They became remarkably congenial, and he was faithful to her. It was not uncommon for a planter to produce a child by a slave, and there is a tendency to find such offspring for any prominent man who owned blacks. However, the many blacks who have borne the name of Washington are not descended from the Father of His Country, if in fact from any white Washington. Except by metaphor the great man of the Washingtons was childless. His wife gave birth four times in her first marriage, never in her second one. In consequence it has been suggested that the master of Mount Vernon may have been sterile. He was certainly not impotent. A fertile husband and a fertile wife not uncommonly fail to add to the population. Moreover, it is possible that Martha was no longer capable of bearing a child. Like most men, Washington desired to have a son, but he encountered disappointment. He was a good father to the young Custises who accompanied Martha to her new home and who became his wards.

Those who bestow black progeny upon southern planters are also inclined to think of them as hot-blooded men who settled serious disputes by resort to swords or pistols on the dueling ground. Washington took lessons in fencing when he was on duty in the Valley, and he became familiar, of course, with guns, including the pistol, the musket, the fowling piece, and the rifle. He inevitably had his quarrels with other men, but he never engaged in personal combat with weapons. He stoutly defended his interests. However, like Thomas Jefferson, James Madison, and other prominent Virginians of the era of the Revolution, he did not seek to assert them by means of steel or gunfire at ten paces at dawn. He was slow to anger, although his rage could be immense when aroused. It is to be assumed that he was too formidable to be lightly challenged. There was another reason for his failure to take part in a duel. He was concerned about proper deportment in youth, and his manners improved with the years. His behavior was undoubtedly softened by his intimacy with the gentle Martha. He consorted more and more with polite ladies and men at Mount Vernon, Williamsburg, and elsewhere in Virginia and Maryland rather than with rough soldiers and frontiersmen. At Williamsburg he spent much time with the most sophisticated Virginians. There he met royal governors Francis Fauquier and Lord Botetourt, men notable for gracious deportment. He exchanged ideas with fellow members of the House of Burgesses. He went to the theater, danced at assemblies, drank tea, and played cards with gentlemen, becoming distinguished for his courtesy.

It is not meant to suggest that Washington acquired brilliance. He never became an eloquent orator; nor did he shine with clever aphorisms in ordinary conversation. His mind was clear and logical, but his thinking was deliberate rather than rapid. He remained modest about his intellectual powers. They were greater than he realized, and they were brought forth by his experiences as a soldier, planter, businessman, and lawmaker. He learned more about his fellow men, acquired knowledge of the ways in which laws are made, and became proficient in the uses of money. He developed a cool and discriminating judgment and with it a remarkable ability to take advantage of the insights of other men. He learned to express himself clearly. His spelling, grammar, and syntax improved

somewhat, and the power of his personality shone through his less
than graceful compositions. His very handwriting suggests large-
ness and staunchness of spirit.

Washington lived very well in the style of a Virginia grandee. He
renovated Mount Vernon. The house, with its siding covered so as
to simulate stone, with its pillars, with its noble prospect of the
Potomac and the distant shore of Maryland, became a landmark.
Keeping a stable of horses, he maintained a coach for the use of his
family. He also had a boat on the river. Through friends and especially through merchants in London, he procured new furniture,
draperies, carpets, china, and silverware. His stepdaughter, Martha
Parke Custis, had to have a spinet. His stepson, John Parke Custis,
must have books. Washington ordered through the same channels
farm implements, guns, the best Madeira wine, and Bibles. His
coach came from London. It may have been a secondhand one, for
he ordered a sound one, stipulating that it need not be new. He
obtained everyday and elegant clothing in quantity for himself,
Martha, and her children. The results of purchasing by mail were
not always happy, partly because the specifications that he sent to
London were not sufficiently precise, partly because of the careless-
ness of his agents. He asked for two whipsaws and received two
dozen of them. Gowns were too large, clothing for the males was
too small, shoes pinched the feet of both sexes. Washington added
to such discomforts by purchasing thin black breeches for summer
wear, breeches that must have become hot under the Virginia sun.
Even so, he and his family dressed and lived as handsomely as their
time and location permitted. They had the services, of course, of
slaves who performed household duties.

Upon a time, as the begetter of the American nation, Washington was also supplied with a stuffed shirt. Historians deprived him
of even minor vices. But he drank wine; he played billiards; he
gambled for small sums at cards, losing more than he gained; he
attended cockfights; his language was not unfailingly chaste. He
had a sense of humor. On occasion he resorted to irony, especially
concerning the behavior of others. He could be facetious. In a
letter of 1762 to his good friend Colonel Burwell Bassett, who had
married Anna Maria Dandridge, a sister of Martha, Washington
wrote:

I was favoured with your epistle wrote on a certain 25th of
July when you ought to have been at church, praying as be-

comes every good Christian man who has as much to answer for as you have; strange it is that you will be so blind to truth that the enlightning sounds of the Gospel cannot reach your ear, nor no examples awaken you to a sense of goodness; could you but behold with what religious zeal I hye me to church on every Lords day, it would do your heart good, and fill it I hope with equal fervency.

The arrival of a baby Bassett furnished additional cause for humorous remarks.

I am told you have lately introduced into your family, a certain production which you are lost in admiration of, and spend so much time in contemplating the just proportion of its parts, the ease, and conveniences with which it abounds, that it is thought you will have little time to animadvert upon the prospect of your crops &c; pray how will this be reconciled to that anxious care and vigilance, which is so escencially necessary at a time when our growing property, meaning the tobacco, is assailed by every villainous worm that has had an existence since the days of Noah (how unkind it was of Noah now that I have mentioned his name to suffer such a brood of vermin to get a birth in the Ark).

As befitted a man who spent much of his life among country folk, on the frontier, in military camps, and with gay men of the world rather than in the pulpit, Washington indulged in earthier humor, much of which has been lost. He could be clever and witty. In 1784, learning that Colonel Joseph Ward, one of his former officers, had married a younger woman, Washington—demonstrating that he was familiar with the name of the fair lady of Don Quixote—wrote to the Reverend William Gordon, who must have been a worldly man as well as a clergyman and historian:

I am glad to hear that my old acquaintance Colo. Ward is yet under the influence of vigorous passions. I will not ascribe the intrepidity of his late enterprize to a mere *flash* of desires, because, in his military career he would have learnt how to distinguish between false alarms and a serious movement. Charity therefore induces me to suppose that like a prudent general, he had reviewed his *strength,* his arms, and ammuni-

tion before he got involved in an action. But if these have been
neglected, and he has been precipitated into the measure, let
me advise him to make the *first* onset upon his fair del Toboso,
with vigor, that the impression may be deep, if it cannot be
lasting, or frequently renewed.

Washington had other amusements. He was a superb horseman.
At Mount Vernon he rode out almost every day when the weather
permitted to inspect his property. He went fox hunting with his
neighbors and used a fine fowling piece in search of other game. He
also enjoyed fishing. He loved Mount Vernon and never lost his
affection for the country life that he led there.

The learned and witty contemporary of Washington, Dr. Samuel
Johnson, immortalized by his biographer, James Boswell, read literature extensively in youth, only occasionally in later life. Washington perused very little in the way of classical or liberal learning
at any time in his life. He did not have access to many books when
young; he was constantly busy in maturity. He had no Latin or
Greek, those staples of scholarship in his time. He did buy books
for himself, but they dealt chiefly with things military, farming,
and the raising of horses—with practical matters. He must have
had a measure of familiarity with the King James Version of the
Holy Scriptures, for he attended the Episcopal church quite regularly. He was not hostile to schooling or to the liberal arts—he
would later become their champion. He had the task of overseeing
the education of his stepson, "Jacky" Custis, as well as care of the
boy's property. When Jacky was almost seven years of age, Washington hired for him a tutor, Walter Magowan, who lived at Mount
Vernon until young Custis was thirteen. Presumably Magowan
taught his charge to read and write English. Certainly the tutor
tried to induct Jacky into the mysteries of the Roman language.
Washington sent to London for a Latin-English dictionary; Latin
grammars; a book of fables; the writings of the historian Sallust,
the poet Horace, and the playwright Terence; and other tomes.
When the boy was about eleven years of age, he began the study of
Virgil and of Greek in the Scriptures. He continued to plow into
Latin, not very deeply, under the tutorship of the Reverend Jonathan Boucher, an Episcopal clergyman who ran a school for boys,
first in Virginia and later at Annapolis, and carried on the process
of polishing the youth begun by Magowan. Boucher proposed to

push Master Custis further into Greek. Washington began to give serious thought to education.

Was it desirable that his stepson should concentrate so heavily upon things classical? Politely declaring that he would yield to the superior knowledge of Boucher, Washington suggested that almost exclusive emphasis upon the translation and reading of Latin and Greek literature was not appropriate for a person of wealth who would be a Virginia planter. Washington wished to make young Custis "fit for more useful purposes, than a horse racer," but not for a professorship or the pulpit. Might it not be well for him to learn French, the international language of polite society? To acquire proficiency in mathematics and surveying? Boucher took the hint. The student continued with Latin, but Washington undertook to supply him with books of philosophy, theology, science, history, English poetry, travels, and arithmetic. Washington also arranged dancing lessons for Jacky, who apparently had no great desire for intellectual attainment, who was pleased with himself because he learned to "write as good English & spell as well as most people." As the youth grew toward manhood and became Jack, he supplied another problem. Boucher reported that he had never known any young fellow "so exceedingly indolent, or so surprisingly voluptuous." One might suppose, the astonished clergyman informed Washington, that "Nature had intended him for some Asiatic Prince," presumably a sultan or nabob with a harem, for "Jack has a propensity to the Sex, which I am at a loss how to judge of, much more how to describe." What Washington did about that difficulty, faced in greater or lesser degree by innumerable worried parents, remains unknown.

As Jack grew to maturity, his stepfather had to consider the matter of advanced education. Jack and Boucher urged that the young man should go abroad, to England and Europe, to acquire polish from travel, in the fashion that English gentlemen were then accustomed to make the Grand Tour after leaving school. Those who are familiar with the diaries and journals of James Boswell will recall his erotic adventures and dissipations in London in the 1760s. Washington knew nothing regarding the behavior of Boswell; but he suspected that his ward, if without a guide and mentor, might spend much time in places of amusement, innocent and otherwise, rather than in the contemplation of Gothic churches and works of art, that he would consort more often with courtesans than with cultivated and virtuous ladies. Boucher was prepared, if paid sufficiently, to accompany his student. Martha gave her consent. Boucher asked for pay equal to one-half of the income of his charge. Washington pondered. He concluded—to the disappointment of Boucher, who as an Englishman afterward said that the American patriot was mean with respect to money—that it would be better and cheaper for Jack to go to college, in America, where vice was less prevalent, where well behaved clergymen did most of the teaching, where Jack might add further to his stock of learning. Accordingly, an appropriate college had to be found.

Choosing an institution of higher learning for Jack did not plunge Washington into the plethora of catalogs and advertisements that confronted parents with a similar problem two centuries later. There was no American university in the eighteenth century, and there were only seven colleges to be considered. There were no standard tests for admission that might bar Jack, and there was no lack of money to pay his tuition and other expenses. All of the colleges were small, almost all of them eager to add to their meager student population and to their income. The recently founded Dartmouth College was as yet intended for Indians rather than young men of European ancestry who desire a career in business, who cannot make their way through the entrance doors of Harvard and Yale. Brown, then the College of Rhode Island, was new, Baptist, and distant. Harvard and Yale, also far away, were Congregationalist and afflicted by Puritanism. Rutgers had just begun to appear and had a Calvinist background. The College of New Jersey, afterward Princeton, though Presbyterian, had appeal for Washington, as it had then and later for many in the South. He also rather approved of the College of Philadelphia, which was to grow into the University of Pennsylvania. Boucher, however, urged that his charge should attend an Episcopalian institution, and Washington, as a good member of the Anglican church, agreed. The choice then lay between the College of William and Mary and King's College, afterward Columbia University. Washington had a low opinion of the faculty of the Virginia school. Accordingly, Mr. Custis, when he was about eighteen years of age, became a student in New York City.

It was doubtful from the beginning that Custis would long continue at King's College. While Washington and Boucher were discussing his future, he became engaged to Eleanor Calvert, a granddaughter of the fifth Lord Baltimore. Although her father, Benedict Calvert, was illegitimate, she was descended from the distinguished family of the proprietors of Maryland. It may be inferred that Jack was eager to marry. Moreover, it is to be feared that he was spoiled, too well aware that at his majority he would inherit fifteen thousand acres of land, most of it near Williamsburg, some lots in that village, more than two hundred slaves, and at least eight thousand pounds in cash and investments. His ego was not reduced by his journey to New York City late in the spring of 1773. Washington undertook to escort him to that place. The two rode northward in the company of William Alexander, a prosperous New Jersey merchant who claimed to be the earl of Stirling and was recognized as such in America but not in Britain. The three were handsomely entertained en route. They were the guests of Governor Robert Eden of Maryland, Governor Richard Penn of Pennsylvania, and Peter Kemble, a prominent New Jerseyman who was the father-in-law of General Thomas Gage, Washington's acquaintance from the days of the Braddock campaign. Gage had been commander in chief of the British army in North America for a decade, directing it from his headquarters in New York City. There Washington attended a formal public dinner in honor of Gage, who was about to go to England upon leave of absence. He was also the guest of General and Mrs. Gage at a private repast before returning to Virginia. Custis entered upon studies in languages, mathematics, philosophy, and science. Surprisingly, his teachers reported that he was diligent. He was snobbish. He had with him a servant as well as a horse, dwelled in a suite of three rooms, and had the special and dubious privilege of dining with the professors. He assured his mother and stepfather that his mentors were not in "the least remiss in their duty" toward him, that they made "as much distinction" between him and "the other students as can be expected." He remained at King's College only until September. Washington had smoothed the way for the marriage of his charge. He had done what he could to secure a substantial dowry for his stepson, but had been compelled to accept a promise from Benedict Calvert, not a man of opulence, that his daughter would share equally in his estate with his other nine children. Returning home from college, Custis persuaded his mother to allow an early marriage. Washington reluctantly gave his consent, and Custis forsook academic halls for the life of a planter. Washington sent an apologetic explanation for his ward's withdrawal from King's, arranged to pay Jack's bills, and offered a gift of money to soothe the wounded feelings of the professors. They may have had more than one reason to rejoice over his permanent departure.

It is apparent that Washington, not formally educated, was, with due regard for the vocational needs of his stepson, friendly toward liberal learning, that his approach to advanced studies for men was more generous, and more enlightened, than that of Boucher. Even if Washington was in the pattern of the self-made man—no one makes the mold for himself—he did not despise academic knowledge. Suspecting that his good friend William Ramsay, a merchant of Alexandria who had married one of the Ball family connections, wished to send one of his sons to the College of New Jersey, Washington offered to make arrangements to provide twenty-five pounds per annum in Virginia money for the boy so long as he was at school, since the youth seemed to be "fond of study and instruction, and disposed to a sedentary studious life" in which he might "not only promote his own happiness, but the future welfare of others."

One of the great qualities of Washington was his capacity to grow. Sobering with the years, his displayed willingness in maturity to listen to better-informed persons, to consider their views, and accordingly to change his own. Having been fortunate enough to survive an attack of smallpox and to escape the serious disfigurement that sometimes afflicted those who recovered from the disease, Washington undertook to protect Jack Custis against it. Vaccination was still unknown, but it had become possible to inoculate a person so that he would have a mild attack of the malady and gain safety from a major one. Occasionally, however, inoculation was fatal. Washington arranged it for Custis while he was still at school in Annapolis, not telling Martha about the gamble until it proved successful—the patient's face was almost untouched by pocks.*

It is to be believed that Washington would have given attention to a proposal that Patsy Custis, of whom he was fond, should receive at least some of the benefits of a liberal education. But no such suggestion was offered. There was no institution of higher or even medium learning for females in America. A girl might learn to read and write. If she was reared in a family of some means in Virginia, she would receive instruction regarding manners and dancing and perhaps acquire some proficiency in singing or at the

---

* George III lost a son in a similar gamble.

piano. Ordering many books from London for her brother, Washington asked that a Bible, a prayer book, and a volume of sacred music be sent across the ocean for the growing Patsy. He hoped that Patsy would be the attractive and dutiful wife of a planter and would bear children. Providence ruled otherwise. When she was about twelve years of age, she had an attack of epilepsy. Several fits of "the falling disease" followed. There was no cure for it. For lack of a more effective remedy Washington and her mother took the girl to the Berkeley Springs in the summer of 1769. They tried useless panaceas, among them bleeding, for physicians still believed that the flow of blood from the body would carry away harmful elements. The seizures became more frequent. On June 19, 1773, Washington wrote in his diary, "At home all day. About five o'clock poor Patsy Custis died suddenly." Next day he sent the sad news to the Burwell Bassetts that their niece, "the sweet innocent girl," had "entered into a more happy and peaceful abode than any she has met with in the afflicted path she hitherto has trod." He reported that "she rose from dinner about four o'clock in better health and spirits than she appeared to have been in for some time; soon after which she was seized with one of her usual fits, and expired in it, in less than two minutes without uttering a word, a groan, or scarce a sigh." Mrs. Washington was prostrated, and Washington thoughtfully tried to soothe her by bringing her mother, Mrs. Dandridge, to Mount Vernon. Life had to go on.

It was a busy life. There were planters who neglected their lands, assumed that their fields of tobacco would enable them to live in luxury, dissipated their property, and lost it. Sending their smokeweed to merchants in Britain, they were tempted to spend as if they would consistently be able to sell an abundant crop at a high price. When their tobacco did not bring in enough money to pay for goods and luxuries ordered from Britain, the merchants gave them credit, but charged interest, which added to the troubles of the improvident. At Mount Vernon, Washington was at first only a planter. He, too, became indebted to a firm of London merchants, although he wisely turned himself into a busy farmer by 1766. He remained solvent—even so, he owed his London creditors well above eight hundred pounds seven years later, when the money he received from the estate of Patsy Custis put his accounts in England in the black. Perceiving that dependence upon the culture of tobacco injured both land and purse, he turned to the growing of wheat. Indeed, he experimented with an almost astonishing variety of products, including oats, corn, alfalfa, timothy, clover, flax, hemp, peaches, apples, and cherries. He kept sheep, cows, pigs, and horses, ran two flour mills, made whiskey, and engaged commercially in a herring fishery on the Potomac. He maintained a dairy. It would appear that some of his many ventures were stimulated as much by curiosity as they were by hope of gain. Supervising the labors of many slaves and also of white artisans, he was a very busy man. He enjoyed his work on the land as well as social activities in Virginia and neighboring Maryland. He later derived pleasure from interbreeding asses and mares, even though the project was not profitable. "I make a miserable hand at breeding mules," he confessed.

Engaging in trade as well as agriculture, Washington was also a very active speculator. He was a member of a syndicate formed to secure a large quantity of fertile soil by draining the Great Dismal Swamp and of another that sought to secure wide lands north of the Ohio River. He was at one time eager to obtain a grant of as much as twenty-five thousand acres in the Yazoo country or the vicinity of Mobile, in the new British colony of West Florida. Nothing came of those ventures. He was interested in a scheme to circumvent the falls of the Potomac so that traffic could move up the river to Fort Cumberland, and he continued to champion Braddock's road to the Ohio River, in the hope of opening up a water-and-land route that would permit Virginians and Marylanders to carry on a lucrative trade beyond the Appalachians. Primarily, however, he sought to acquire new lands for himself in southwestern Pennsylvania and in the area that is now West Virginia that would increase in value as settlers moved into those regions. He visited them in the autumn of 1770, traveling as far westward as the mouth of the Kanawha River. He bought one tract in Pennsylvania through a distributing office of that colony. It will be recalled that Governor Dinwiddie promised lands in the West to those Virginians who volunteered for service at the beginning of the Seven Years' War. Washington exerted influence at Williamsburg and saw to it that the pledge was kept. He thus secured several thousand acres, partly on the basis of his own service, partly by purchasing the rights of some of his officers and men. He also took advantage of the famous royal Proclamation of 1763 which contained an offer by the British of rewards in land to all those who had served in the war. He bought the rights of Captain John Posey obtained in accordance with the proclamation. One way and another he eventually accumulated more than thirty thousand acres, the majority of them beyond the mountains, which cost him little in money, much in care and effort. Although he failed to people one of his grants in Pennsylvania immediately before the War of Independence, he was ultimately the most successful land speculator of his time. There is a temptation to assume that a speculator is dishonest, at least unscrupulous. It was urged that Washington took unfair advantage of the Virginians who had served under him by sending out his friend William Crawford to select the best lands for him before his comrades-in-arms could see the tracts allotted to the group. Washington hotly denied that he had behaved improperly. He pointed out that he had obtained, with "the cream of the crop," as much poor land. He could also have said that his fellow officers and men would have received nothing whatever had he not importuned the government in their behalf. It may be concluded that he did indeed see nothing wrong in his conduct, that he had made efficient use of his economic power, and that he was not unduly generous to his former officers and troops.

There can be no question regarding the fundamental honesty of Washington. He paid his debts. He energetically defended his interests. Had he been asked why he did so, he would undoubtedly have replied that it was necessary—which it often was—if he was not to be bilked. Like many an American man of business afterward accused of sharpness with respect to money, he was generous to friends and others in economic distress. No one ever went away hungry from Mount Vernon. It is a tribute to his integrity, knowledge, and fair-mindedness that he was often asked to manage the affairs of friends and to render an impartial opinion regarding conflicting claims to property.

As the War of Independence approached, Washington was known throughout the American colonies for his courage and military exploits. In Virginia he had established a reputation as the possessor of sound judgment, as a man of principle who could be trusted. And his name was spreading through the Old Dominion and the colonies in general as that of a firm champion of American rights in the British empire.

IX

The Champion of American Rights

*T*oward the end of May, 1765, the House of Burgesses was still in session, although it had finished almost all of its business. The majority of its members had left Williamsburg. The news came that the British Parliament had passed the Stamp Act. It was evident that Britain was committed to a new policy that included both taxation of the colonists in North America for revenue and firmer imposition of British authority upon them. Driven on by the passionate orator Patrick Henry, the remnant of the Burgesses declared that the stamp duties violated the rights of the Virginians. Such taxes were unconstitutional, could not be levied upon Virginians possessing the rights of Englishmen without the consent of their representatives in the House of Burgesses, they said. Its members adopted resolutions calling for American resistance, and they circulated throughout the colonies.

A crisis in relations between America and Britain followed. Washington had apparently departed from Williamsburg. He endorsed the resolutions, although he did not employ the extreme language used by Henry. Describing the situation in America to Francis Dandridge, an uncle of his wife's in England, Washington said that the Stamp Act "engrosses the conversation of the speculative part of the colonists, who look upon this unconstitutional

method of taxation as a direful attack upon their liberties." Moreover, Britain had adopted "some other (I think I may add) ill
judgd measures." He reported that the colonists could not pay the
stamp duties, even if they wished to do so, for they did not have the
necessary cash. He observed that the Americans were reducing
their orders for British goods, that they were neglecting to pay
their debts to British merchants in order to punctuate a demand
for repeal of the duties. His language was cautious, devoid of the
vehemence employed by Patrick Henry. Moreover, Washington
continued to extend his friendship to George Mercer, the officer in
the Virginia regiment who had secured appointment as the distrib-
utor of stamps in the Old Dominion. Mercer had been forced by
public opinion to resign his post and had even been threatened
with physical violence by angry planters. Was Washington disposed
to be remarkably careful in what he said and did? Not at all. But
he would not say more than he was prepared to support by deeds.
He believed that in the very nature of things a Parliament in which
there were no Americans lacked the right to tax them for revenue.
The Stamp Act Congress, forthrightly speaking for all of the thirteen colonies, similarly declared the duties to be unconstitutional.

Parliament repealed the detested Stamp Act in March, 1766.
Washington was not entirely satisfied. He was concerned because
other colonial grievances remained—Britain continued to regulate
American maritime commerce by means of duties and by other
methods that were burdensome and largely unnecessary. He doubtless had in mind, among other restrictions, the British requirement
that tobacco intended for northern European markets must be sold
in Britain and taxed as it was landed. He said, correctly, that such
channeling of American products was not needed, since the colonists would in any event send things agricultural across the ocean
to Britain and buy manufactured articles from Britain. His argument held true until the Americans turned energetically toward
industry, much later. Quite humanly, he was not hostile to an
economic regulation from which he might profit. At that time Britain offered subsidies to Americans who would grow indigo and
hemp. The former was much needed for making dyes; the latter
was in demand not for marijuana but for production of rope, indispensable to navy and merchant vessels. He tried to grow hemp,
without much success.

The Stamp Act was repealed in the spring of 1766, but Britain
undertook in the following year, under the leadership of Chancel-

lor of the Exchequer Charles Townshend, to increase rather than remove the trammels upon the Americans and also to extract revenue from them by means of import duties. There was doubt in London regarding the colonial argument against the Stamp Act—had it been directed only against "internal" taxes, inland levies as opposed to duties collected at the ports? Parliament passed the Townshend Acts, which imposed duties upon tea, lead, glass, paper, and paints entering American harbors. Other cramping measures followed. In the royal Proclamation of October 7, 1763, Britain had forbidden white settlements beyond the Appalachian divide, presumably to protect the lands of the Indians. In 1768 the cabinet began to frame a new and more permanent boundary, running southward from Lake Erie to Fort Pitt, thence down the Ohio to the mouth of the Kanawha River, and on southward.

A second Anglo-American crisis developed. Cautious colonists, fearing turmoil and interruption of trade, were reluctant to resume the contest with Britain, but the majority were disposed to resist. If Washington was not remarkably ardent in defense of American liberties in the first crisis, he was zealous in the second one. The cynical will suspect that he was primarily swayed by crass economic motives. Such was not the case. There probably was a residue within him of resentment against Britain because of the rejection of his efforts as a young officer to secure a royal commission. Doubtless he was also offended by the limits placed upon expansion beyond the mountains, where he was in the process of securing thousands of acres of land. But he believed that the Indian boundary of 1763 would soon be breached, and almost all of his claims were located east of the line of 1768. His relatively inexpensive ventures, directed toward eventual rather than quick rewards, did not appear to be seriously affected. Still, his dealings with British merchants continued to offer vexations. On occasion he was charged more for goods than they cost in Virginia, and sometimes they were of inferior quality. He observed that Robert Cary and Company, with which he did most of his business, charged him 5 percent on his debts but paid only 4 percent on moneys of Jack Custis in its hands. Naturally he would have liked to be free to sell his products without British restraints. But though there was some self-interest involved, the stand he took was based essentially upon his situation as a colonial, as an American who sincerely and deeply resented all British infringements, whether or not they affected him directly. Grievances of Massachusetts farmers and New

York merchants, as well as his own, angered Washington. In his sober judgment the new British measures were proof that the men dominant in London were determined to have their iniquitous way with America, and he was prepared to risk his property and his person in defense of American rights.

Accordingly, Washington, with his friend and neighbor George Mason, took a principal part in framing and putting into execution a nonimportation agreement in Virginia. Since, Washington wrote to Mason in April, 1769, "our lordly masters in Great Britain will be satisfied with nothing less than the deprication of American freedom, it seems highly necessary that some thing shou'd be done to avert the stroke and maintain the liberty which we have derived from our ancestors." He asserted that "no man shou'd scruple, or hesitate a moment to use arms in defence of so valuable a blessing, on which all the good and evil of life depends; yet arms I wou'd beg leave to add, should be the last resource, the dernier resort." It was therefore prudent to try the economic weapon first. With Mason and Washington leading the way, most of the members of the House of Burgesses gathered unofficially in Williamsburg soon afterward and established an association for the purpose. Its clauses were less drastic than Washington desired, but the Virginians did establish a boycott upon Townshend-taxed goods and other British products. It was to endure until the duties were rescinded. There were Virginians who wished to add a provision for nonpayment of private debts to British merchants to the agreement for association. Washington opposed such an addition, because of its injustice to private British persons, and it was not adopted. He lived up to the agreement.

The second Anglo-American crisis passed. Britain gave way again before the storm of American protest, again grudgingly, offering a compromise that was pregnant with future troubles. Government announced in the spring of 1769 that there would be no more British taxes for revenue and that the Townshend duties would be repealed except for the tax on tea. The American boycott then collapsed except for a rather ineffective attempt to continue it with respect to tea. The majority of the colonists turned to cheaper Dutch tea smuggled in from abroad. Others carelessly used the leaves to make their comforting beverage without troubling to find out whether they had passed through an American customhouse. The great constitutional issue seemed in practice to have ended in a compromise. Once more Britain and America entered upon a period of relative quiet.

Washington shared in the general relaxation. Fond of tea, he may have pleasantly imbibed brews made from Townshend-taxed stuff. Certainly he saw nothing wrong in hobnobbing with British officials who defended the authority of the Mother Country. In the spring of 1773 he planned to travel out to the Ohio Valley with John Murray, the Earl of Dunmore, who had become governor of Virginia and who shared the interest of Washington in speculation in western lands—Dunmore had five children for whom he wished to build estates. The scheme fell through, but not because of politics. Washington was a guest of the governor's for dinner a year later, also for breakfast. The cordial relation between Washington and Thomas Gage established during the Braddock campaign had waned for lack of contact. Becoming a general and commander in chief of the British army in North America, Gage was now commonly portrayed by American propagandists as a wicked tool of tyrannical Britain because he held the supreme command over troops who had been sent to Boston in 1768, who had committed "murder" in the "massacre" there in 1770. Washington would also later come to think of Gage as an arbitrary minion of an overbearing Britain, but in the spring of 1773 he still looked upon Gage as a friend. It will be recalled that the Virginian attended a public farewell dinner for the general and also accepted an invitation from him to a private repast in the spring of 1773.

Strife between Britain and America was renewed in that year, primarily because of the famous Tea Act devised by the prime minister, Lord North. The law extended favors to the East India Company that enabled it to undersell smuggled Dutch tea, thus tempting the colonists to buy the English product and pay substantial Townshend duties. Samuel Adams and other men in Boston who were especially gifted in perception of British tyranny took action. Three East Indiamen carrying company tea cast anchor in Boston harbor in the later months of 1773. A band of irate men dressed like Mohawk Indians boarded the ships on December 16 and destroyed the tea by tossing it into the harbor. Later consignments from across the ocean were sent away, sequestered, or ruined by angry citizens in other ports.

The violent destruction of private property in the "Boston Tea Party" was widely condemned, not only by men averse to challenging British authority but by firm defenders of American rights, including Washington, who contended that the East India Company ought to be reimbursed. Swift and vigorous response in London to the Boston frolic prevented an accommodation. George III, Lord North, and a large majority in Parliament decided that Boston and Massachusetts must be brought to heel. The colonists in general must learn by example that Britain was not to be defied with impunity. On leave of absence in England, Gage was appointed governor of Massachusetts and sent to Boston to establish order. He was authorized to put four regiments, or more, of his troops in the city. Parliament passed a series of Coercive Acts that closed the port of Boston until payment was made for the tea destroyed there and remodeled the government of Massachusetts to bolster royal authority.

The crisis deepened. Boston and Massachusetts did not yield. They had new grievances. The closing of Boston harbor created unemployment, the presence of more and more troops in the city fostered discontent, and the remodeling of the government supplied both cause and means to defy Britain. Royal authority outside Boston collapsed. In the autumn of 1774 the Massachusetts House of Representatives changed into a revolutionary provincial congress. It became evident that Massachusetts, indeed New England, would revolt rather than obey. Governor Gage somberly warned his superiors that the Yankees were ready to fight and that they would fight very well. The provincial congress, meeting outside the city, prepared for armed struggle. Bringing in more and more troops, Gage kept his men in order and asked for new instructions from London. It was only too apparent that Boston had become a tinderbox.

Nor did the Americans generally bend before the display of British authority. They rallied to the support of Massachusetts. They found additional evidence of British tyranny in the Quebec Act of 1774, which extended the boundaries of the Canadian colony to the Ohio and Mississippi rivers and granted freedom of worship to its Roman Catholics. Did Britain intend to use Quebec to bar the westward expansion of her old and Protestant subjects? There were those in Virginia who were inclined to submit or to temporize, among them Bryan Fairfax, a friend of Washington's and a brother-in-law of Sally's. Fairfax urged in letters to Washington in the summer of 1774 that the colonists should avoid extreme measures, should ask for redress. Washington responded in the most emphatic language that the cause of Massachusetts was the cause of America. He saw little advantage in petitioning. He perceived a persistent attempt on the part of Britain to tax for revenue. "I think the Parliament of Great Britain hath no more right to put their hands in my pocket, without my consent, than I have to put my hands into yours for money." He defended that conclusion on broad grounds, including "an innate spirit of freedom." He had become convinced that such taxation was "not only repugnant to natural right, but subversive of the laws and constitution of Great Britain itself." The Coercive Acts violated the rights of the citizens of Massachusetts. General Gage was acting like "a Turkish bashaw" and had given "an unexampled testimony of the most despotic system of tyranny, that ever was practised in a free government. . . . Shall we, after this, whine and cry for relief, when we have already tried it in vain? Or shall we supinely sit and see one province after another fall a prey to despotism?" The Americans must not submit to acts of tyranny "till custom and use shall make us as tame and abject slaves, as the blacks we rule over with such arbitrary sway"—he recognized that slavery deprived the blacks of their natural rights, though he did not urge immediate freedom for them. But white-skinned Americans must stand forth at all costs in defense of their rights and must adopt a thoroughgoing boycott of British goods as a countermeasure. Taking that stand, he was not an extremist. Other Virginians were clamoring for both nonimportation of British goods and nonexportation of American products to Britain, even for nonpayment of debts to British merchants. Washington would not go so far, but he was not lagging far behind Patrick Henry and Richard Henry Lee, the most aggressive Virginia leaders.

To establish the boycott it was obviously desirable to arrange for another gathering such as the Stamp Act Congress that could not only take up economic weapons but speak for all the colonies. Virginia led the way. Governor Dunmore tried to prevent the Old Dominion from acting by putting an end to a meeting of the House of Burgesses. Its members then formed a convention and urged all the colonies to send delegates. Shortly afterward, the Massachusetts House of Representatives issued a similar invitation. Except in thinly settled Georgia, where royal governor Sir James Wright was very influential, all of the colonies responded, using conventions rather than legislative bodies wherever necessary for the purpose. The result was the convening of the First Continental Congress in Philadelphia on September 5, 1774. Among the seven delegates chosen by the Virginia convention in August was Washington. Peyton Randolph, Speaker of the House of Burgesses and leader of the numerous Randolph clan, received the most votes in the convention. Washington, increasingly recognized as an able, devoted, and courageous champion of American rights, stood second or third in the poll. Other men selected were Richard Henry Lee, Patrick Henry, Richard Bland, Benjamin Harrison, and Edmund Pendleton. Virginia sent northward a remarkably gifted delegation.

X

The Commander in Chief

Never *addicted to* oratory, always too modest regarding his intellectual abilities, Washington came forth in the First Continental Congress neither as a debater nor as a framer of state papers. Nor did he shine in speeches or in the making of policy in the Second Continental Congress. There was an ample supply of political and philosophical talent and genius in those assemblages. Even so, he came to the fore. Fellow delegates from nearly all parts of America had an opportunity to inspect him. As the third Anglo-American crisis deepened, as resort to arms became ever more likely, they learned that he was a man to be trusted with power. After the outbreak of hostilities in the battle of Lexington and Concord on April 19, 1775, they chose him to lead the American forces. They did not make a mistake.

Riding to Philadelphia with Patrick Henry and Edmund Pendleton, the one distinguished for emotional speeches, the other for legal expertise, Washington arrived at the meeting place of the Congress the day before it convened. He faithfully attended sessions of the Congress. Finding lodging in a tavern, he was also very active socially. He dined out almost every day, drank tea in company, played cards, and spent evenings over glasses of wine and punch with fellow delegates. He became acquainted with the redoubtable Adams cousins, Samuel and John, from Massachusetts, who were in the forefront of the struggle against Britain; with John Dickinson of Pennsylvania, a wealthy gentleman disposed to be more cautious than the Adamses; with Joseph Galloway of Pennsylvania, who was eager for an accommodation with the Mother Country. The delegates inspected the Virginian, the well-mannered, quiet, and impressive man with the military bearing. He would be useful indeed if words became blows. Delegate Silas Deane of Connecticut wrote to his wife, "Colonel Washington is nearly as tall a man as Colonel Fitch, and almost as hard a countenance; yet with a very young look, and an easy, soldier like air and gesture." The very presence of Washington encouraged his fellow delegates to act vigorously.

The Congress did not fail to challenge the powers that were in London. Ignoring Parliament, petitioning George III for redress, and asking the British people for support, the Congress adopted a Declaration of Rights that demanded recognition by Britain of American liberties based upon "the immutable laws of nature, the principles of the English constitution," and charter rights; repeal of the many obnoxious measures adopted by Parliament after 1763; and withdrawal of the British army from the Atlantic seaboard. A minority would have gone so far as to deny Britain the power to regulate American maritime commerce. Toward compelling Britain to yield, the Congress asserted that there must be importation neither of goods nor of slaves from British sources after December 1, 1774. If redress failed to appear before September 10, 1775, almost all exports to Britain and the British West Indies were to cease. An Association of committees along the seaboard was to enforce the rules. Quebec was invited to join in forming a continental front. Most important of all, in the event, the Congress let it be known that an attack against the Patriots of Massachusetts by the army under Gage would be considered as an offensive against America.

The situation was ominous. Logic declared that Britain would likely resort to the use of military force. There were delegates from the middle and southern colonies who were reluctant to promise assistance to the Yankees. It was suspected that their leaders were aiming at nothing less than independence—certainly Samuel Adams was not horrified by the thought of separation from the empire. Washington did not share the fears of those who hesitated to support the Congress. Although the economic weapons taken up by the Congress were somewhat heavier than those he had earlier supported, he firmly endorsed its actions. During its sessions there was an attempt, perhaps inspired by General Gage, to wean him away from the defenders of liberty in Massachusetts. He received a letter from Robert Mackenzie, an old friend, once an officer in the Virginia regiment, who was serving as a captain in the British forces at Boston. Mackenzie made much of mob action against friends of Britain in Massachusetts and asserted that there was a "fixed aim at total independence" in the province. Replying, Washington excused the rioters because they were "every day receiving fresh proofs of a systematic assertion of an arbitrary power." He was sure that it was not "the wish or interest" of the people of Massachusetts or any other colony, "separately or collectively, to set up for independency." But—the Americans would never "submit to the loss of those valuable rights and privileges which are essential to the happiness of every free state, and without which life, liberty and property are rendered totally insecure." He was prepared to fight in behalf of those rights and privileges. He assured Mackenzie that "more blood will be spilt . . . if the ministry are determined to push matters to extremity than history has ever yet furnished instances of in the annals of North America." He had become an American utterly devoted to freedom within the British empire. And if it could not be secured within the empire . . ?

The First Continental Congress adjourned on October 26, after arranging for a meeting of the Second Continental Congress in Philadelphia on May 10, 1775, to consider further action, and Washington went home. Nearly six months passed before Britain responded to the challenge posed by the colonists. During that time Gage continued to bring troops into Boston, collecting about four thousand men in the city. A British fleet gathered in the harbor to assist him. He fortified the isthmus that then connected Boston with the mainland. Massachusetts Patriots amassed arms and ammunition against the time when blows might follow angry words. The Association rigidly enforced the boycott throughout the colonies, and units of militia drilled more zealously than in the past. Mob violence against men who declined to take a stand against the Mother Country became frequent. Here and there tar and feathering of such men made its ugly appearance. There had been from the beginning of the troubles those who would be loyal to Britain in any case. They were now joined by others who feared the consequences of a struggle with Britain that might bring political upheaval and social leveling in the event of a Patriot triumph. A Loyalist party emerged, including something like one-fourth or one-fifth of the white colonists. A body of neutrals also made its appearance. But the majority of the Americans pressed on. Occasionally a Patriot writer pseudonymously suggested that an independent American republic was desirable.

At home again, Washington put his private affairs in as good order as possible and joined other Virginia leaders in preparing for armed conflict. For a time there was a belief among Americans in London and at home that the boycott would again compel Britain to draw back. The British decision did not reach America until April. In the meantime, Washington and many other Virginians made it clear that they would, if necessary, take the field. Washington sponsored an independent company of young men of Alexandria who were making ready. He drilled it, and he procured gunpowder for it from Philadelphia. In January, with George Mason, he led a drive to collect money in Fairfax County toward arming and drilling the militia, ostensibly to "relieve our mother country from any expense in our protection and defence." Chosen again as a delegate to a Virginia convention that met on March 20 at the village of Richmond, well beyond the reach of Governor Dunmore, he again toiled for military preparedness. The convention resolved that the colony should be put "into a posture of defence" and undertook to raise and train troops. The convention also chose as delegates to the Second Continental Congress the seven men who had attended the first one. Washington stood second in the poll, behind Peyton Randolph, chairman of the convention. The soldier was coming to the fore. There could be no doubt that Washington would, as he informed his brother Jack, execute his "full intention to devote my life and fortune in the cause we are engaged in, if need be."

The Earl of Dunmore, alarmed by the preparations of the Virginia Patriots for war, struck back as best he might. He aimed a blow at Washington and other members of the old Virginia regiment who had received land grants beyond the mountains. He declared that surveys made for Washington by William Crawford were illegal because Crawford had not legally qualified as a surveyor. On the basis of a technicality that at an earlier time would have been overlooked, the governor cast doubt upon the ownership by Washington of twenty-three thousand acres on the far side of the Appalachians. Washington protested, in vain. He was given new reason to detest British authority. During the period April 16 to 20 he had as his guest as Mount Vernon Colonel Charles Lee, a British officer who had cast his lot with the Patriots. Young Henry Lee of the Virginia Lees and George Mason also visited Mount Vernon at that time. The likelihood of armed hostilities must have been discussed, especially between the host and Charles Lee, who was ready to fight against his native country.

The War of Independence was at hand. Dunmore moved against the Virginians. HMS *Fowey* lay at anchor in the James River. The governor arranged to have a squad of British marines seize about twenty barrels of gunpowder kept in a public magazine at Williamsburg and to carry them off to the ship. As the news spread, Virginians marched toward the capital to retrieve the property of the colony. It was needed, some of their leaders disingenuously said, for use in the event of a slave uprising. Dunmore offered an equally dishonest excuse for his action that the Patriots accepted— he said that the powder had been removed to a safe place because he had been informed that such a revolt was imminent, and he gave his word of honor that the powder would be returned to Williamsburg when the danger passed. The war did not begin in Virginia. Shooting began in Massachusetts on April 19. Washington received the news of it about eight days after the event.

George III and his cabinet considered ominous dispatches from General Gage in the autumn of 1774. Only the colonial secretary, the earl of Dartmouth, was disposed to make a great effort to conciliate the colonists. The king and the remainder of the cabinet refused to believe that the situation in Massachusetts, indeed in America as a whole, was alarming. They added six hundred marines to the troops available in Boston. Early in 1775, after looking at the papers sent across the Atlantic by the First Continental Congress, they ordered Gage to put his army in motion and arranged to send more troops. They also prepared what they called a Conciliatory Resolution, which they submitted to Parliament. A minority in Parliament protested against the use of force. Speakers for this minority warned that the Americans would fight and fight well, that France and Spain would attack a Britain in distress. The majority scoffed, endorsed resort to the army and navy, and later passed the Conciliatory Resolution. It said that any colony that voted its fair share toward imperial defense was to be excused from parliamentary taxation. The plan was to be presented by governors to private citizens who would introduce it in the American assemblies. Gage received orders to use his army on April 14. He had about 3,500 men available for duty. During the night of April 18 he sent out a detachment of infantry to Concord, about twenty miles from Boston, to destroy military matériel gathered there by the Patriots. The running battle of Lexington and Concord followed the next day. It was hard fought. The British losses were 273, the American, 95. At the end of the day the royal troops were confined to Boston and to Bunker Hill, north of the city.

Immediately after the struggle militia from all parts of New England, about fifteen thousand in number, poured into position on the mainland opposite Boston. There they remained quiet for almost two months. They lacked cannon to attack the British. On the other hand, Gage had neither enough men nor enough equipment to mount a powerful offensive. He concentrated all of his troops in the city. In the meantime, Green Mountain Boys led by Ethan Allen, accompanied by Benedict Arnold, forced the surrender of a small British garrison at Ticonderoga.

Was reconciliation still possible? American legislatures and conventions looked at the Conciliatory Resolution in light of the refusal of Britain to redress existing grievances and the bloodshed of Lexington and Concord. Was it not a device to force American contributions for defense? Did not its framers hope that some colonies would comply with the resolution while others would reject it, that the Americans would divide against each other? Why did Britain ignore the Congress? The scheme found favor in no colony, and it was condemned by the Second Continental Congress.

That body convened as planned on May 10 to consider the situation. Washington set out from Mount Vernon six days earlier in his coach with other members of the Virginia delegation. En route, curious eyes examined the soldier who might soon take the field. At Baltimore he reviewed companies of troops. He and his colleagues were met outside Philadelphia by hundreds of horsemen and escorted into the city, on May 9. That evening he dined at the home of a prominent merchant, Joseph Reed. Among the guests was Judge Samuel Curwen of Salem, Massachusetts, who was not disposed to resist Britain and who afterward became a Loyalist. Curwen perceived that Washington possessed a "fine Figure" and a "most easy and agreeable address."

Washington served in the Congress for only five weeks. The delegates inevitably assumed authority to speak and act for all America, but were otherwise divided upon many questions. Some, including John Dickinson, desired to make another effort to reach an agreement with Britain; a few, like Samuel Adams, were not averse to an assertion of independence. Benjamin Franklin, coming home after serving for more than a decade as an agent for several colonies in London, would not strive to maintain connection with Britain. Upon a time he had dreamed of a noble empire in whch the Americans and the British would be equals. He was prepared to become a citizen of an American republic. The majority continued to hope that it was still possible somehow to secure American rights within the empire, even though they had to face the fact of Lexington and Concord. But what if that goal could not be reached? Accordingly, facing the question of disposal of cannon and other military gear captured at Ticonderoga, the Congress resolved that they should be stored and returned to British custody when the crisis ended, a decision that was reversed after news came of the battle of Bunker Hill. But even before that struggle Congress established a committee for military planning and another to consider specific ways and means to secure and keep control of New York City, the principal strategic place in America because of its location at the mouth of the Hudson River and its splendid harbor. Washington served on both committees. Moreover, the delegates could not but agree that they must assume general direction of the American forces for the sake of the common cause. In consequence, Congress informally "adopted" the New Englanders stationed about Boston and other forces burgeoning in the colonies, undertook to send ten companies of riflemen to assist the Yankees, and framed a Continental army. It then became necessary to choose the officers of higher rank who would serve under the control of Congress. Especially important was the selection of a commander in chief, whose first task was to assume leadership of the Patriots camped outside Boston. He must be loyal to America, obedient to the will of Congress, able, courageous, vigorous, and experienced in warfare.

Congress considered the merits and defects of various persons. Among them was General Artemas Ward of Massachusetts, who was more or less in charge of the Yankees outside Boston. He had not supplied proof of military genius. Besides, it was held against him that he was a New Englander. Among the delegates from the middle and southern colonies there was distrust of the Yankees. Had they not been precipitous in dealing with the British? There was also a suspicion, which would grow, that the New Englanders sought to dominate their fellow Americans. If John Hancock, the president of Congress, desired to be commander in chief, at least to have the refusal of the appointment, as John Adams said long afterward, Hancock was also barred because he was a Yankee. Besides, the good-looking Hancock, wealthy by inheritance from an uncle who had amassed money through British army contracts, had had military experience only as a colonel of showy cadets who marched in Boston in celebration of special events. Israel Putnam, a folk hero of New England because of his exploits in the Seven Years' War, could not be a serious candidate for the high command, and not merely because of his birthplace. He was brave indeed, but there was serious doubt regarding his abilities.

Nor was there an outstanding candidate in the middle colonies for the highest post. There was Philip Schuyler, a wealthy land-owner and member of the Anglo-Dutch Hudson River aristocracy. Schuyler had served in the Seven Years' War, but primarily as a commissary officer. He had not led troops in battle. Richard Mont-gomery, who had been a captain in the British army and who had married into the powerful Livingston clan, was devoted to the cause and attractive, but he was a recent comer to America and had not led a substantial body of men.

There were two other English-born officers who received consid-eration, one of them being Horatio Gates, formerly a major in the British army. Gates had served for many years among the redcoats and had participated in the Braddock campaign, but he had re-signed his royal commission to become a planter in Virginia. He was kindly, amiable, and fond of off-color anecdotes. He had been a desk officer rather than a leader on the battlefield and had given no evidence of superior military talent. There was no serious doubt of his loyalty to the cause. He would prove to be completely faith-ful, devoted to the American republic soon to emerge. He could be useful, but his English background and his record served to deny him serious consideration for the high command. He had made many friends among the New Englanders, including the Adamses, who would later push his claims to lofty preferment.

Much more impressive was his friend Colonel Charles Lee, who had emigrated from England in 1773 and had embraced the cause of the Americans. Traversing the colonies from Massachusetts to Virginia, he had formed acquaintances with many of the American leaders. He had also appeared as a redoubtable propagandist in behalf of American rights. A tall, lean, homely man, he was a hard-bitten veteran of numerous campaigns. The grandson of an English baronet, he had entered the British army as an ensign in the 44th Regiment, then commanded by his father, Colonel John Lee. As an officer in that regiment he had served in the forces that crushed the Scottish rebellion of 1745 in behalf of Bonnie Prince Charlie; had participated in the Braddock campaign and all the succeeding ones that led to the conquest of Canada; and had won laurels in battle in Portugal in 1762. Wandering about Europe after the Seven Years' War, he had been appointed a major general in the Polish army and had seen somewhat of a Russo-Turkish war. Lee possessed a superior intellect and was familiar with the classics and the literature of his time. He had conversed with the great and near great in England and Europe. He would prove to be the ablest strategist in the War of Independence. Of the same age as Washington, he was a vigorous bachelor, altogether a most impressive person. He harbored a personal grudge against George III, who had promised him a promotion and had failed to keep his pledge. An enthusiastic disciple of Jean Jacques Rousseau, he was seeking an ideal society and hoped to find it in America. He had obvious defects. He was slovenly and profane; he was fully aware of his own merits; fond of ribaldry, he was addicted to satire. It was not well known at the time that he suffered seriously from gout and "rheumatism," from maladies that exacerbated fits of high temper. The delegates were otherwise well acquainted with him, for he had hobnobbed with them during the First Continental Congress. He was in Philadelphia and was ready to serve. He was trying to dispose of an estate of eleven thousand pounds in England and to purchase a plantation in western Virginia. He desired a promise from Congress that he would be compensated if his English property were seized. Impressed though many delegates were by Lee, they could not entrust the high command to him, if for no other reasons because he was English-born, because he owned no property as yet in America. Like Gates, he might be able to offer valuable service in the emergency.

Washington was the obvious choice for the supreme command. There could be no question that he was ready to serve in some capacity, for he had a Virginia uniform with him at Philadelphia and wore it at sessions of the Congress. At forty-three he was vigorous. He had given ample proof of abundant courage and of ability to withstand the strains of warfare. He had not commanded a large body of men in the Seven Years' War; nor had he won a great victory. But then, no American had led an army or gained a signal triumph over the French and Indians. There was about him an aura of power, determination, dignity, and probity that impressed everyone. It was as certain as might be that he would neither betray the cause to the British nor seek to establish himself as a monarch or a dictator. Appointment of a Virginian was politically desirable, for it would satisfy all the Americans who wished to keep the Yankees in check. There were men in the Virginia delegation, Edmund Pendleton and Carter Braxton, who were somewhat concerned because they believed that he was too forward in opposing Britain. They were overborne, in part because the New Englanders in Congress gladly supported him. They perceived that he was utterly committed to the American cause. They did not need to see a letter he wrote to George William Fairfax on the last day of May to reach that conclusion. In the letter Washington said that "the once happy and peaceful plains of America are either to be drenched with blood, or inhabited by slaves. Sad alternative! But can a virtuous man hesitate in his choice?" The Massachusetts delegates received a message from two of the Patriot leaders at home, Elbridge Gerry and Dr. Joseph Warren, telling them that the choice of "the beloved colonel Washington" as "generalissimo" would be welcomed as a gesture of respect to Virginia and that it would be acceptable to the officers in the army stationed about Boston.

He was nominated as "General and Commander in chief of the army of the United Colonies" on June 15 and was unanimously elected. John Adams reported to his wife the choice of "the modest and virtuous, the amiable, generous and brave George Washington Esquire." The next day the new general briefly addressed Congress. Accepting the appointment, he declared that he "would exert every power I possess" in behalf of "the glorious cause." He protected himself to a degree against future criticism by asking the delegates to remember that "I this day declare with the utmost sincerity, I do not think myself equal to the command." He also declined to accept any money from Congress except for his expenses, an unnecessary gesture of generosity that many of his fellow officers could not afford. But it is not to be doubted that his modesty was sincere, that his refusal of pay was intended to be altruistic. The responsibility he accepted was enough to weigh heavily upon any thinking man. If there were Patriots who expected an easy triumph over Britain, he knew better; if his leadership ended in military defeat, he was well aware that he might be dismissed in disgrace, that he might die upon a specially high scaffold as an arch-traitor.

During the following week Washington put his private affairs in order as best he could. He sent his "chariot" and horses back to Mount Vernon, drew up his will, and sent the news of his appointment to Martha and family connections in Virginia. He was worried about Martha. Assuring her that he valued one month with her at home more than seven times seven years away from her, he said that "a kind of destiny" had led him to the high command, that "it was utterly out of my power" to refuse it without dishonor. "I shall feel no pain from the toil or the danger of the campaign; my unhappiness will flow from the uneasiness I know you will feel from being left alone." She must bear up as best she could, spend her time as agreeably as possible, and write to him. He urged John Parke Custis, Burwell Bassett, and John Augustine Washington to do everything possible to make Martha comfortable. "I am imbarked on a wide ocean, boundless in its prospect, and from whence, perhaps, no safe harbour is to be found," he wrote to John Augustine. His departure for Massachusetts would be "a cutting stroke" for Martha. He had "many very disagreeable sensations" in consequence, and he hoped that John Augustine and friends would visit Mount Vernon to cheer her. Immediately before leaving Philadelphia, he sent a second letter to Martha. He was going to his new duties "in full confidence of a happy meeting with you some time in the fall." He retained "an unalterable affection for you which neither time or distance can change." He would not see Mount Vernon again for more than six years. His cousin Lund Washington looked after his lands during his absence.

During his last week as a member of Congress, Washington also took part in the selection of other high army officers. He urged appointment of Charles Lee and Horatio Gates. He had probably met both men during the Braddock campaign. He had become well acquainted with Lee during the First Continental Congress and two visits by Lee to Mount Vernon, and he particularly desired the services of that veteran. He also desired the help of Gates, who might be very useful in drilling troops. Washington had his way. Some members of Congress balked at selection of Lee, but the majority gave its consent and agreed to compensate him in the event that his English property was taken from him. In the end the congress chose four major generals, in order of seniority Artemas Ward, Lee, Philip Schuyler, and Israel Putnam, with Gates as adjutant and brigadier general.

On the morning of June 23 Washington, Lee, and Schuyler, accompanied by aides, set out from Philadelphia to assume their duties. They were escorted for some distance by members of Congress, a troop of light horse, and a band. Among the politicians was short and pudgy John Adams, who was jealous of the military men. "Such is the pride and pomp of war," he wrote. "I, poor creature, worn out with scribbling for my bread and liberty, low in spirits and weak in health, must leave others to wear the laurels which I have sown." Adams would be sufficiently rewarded for his labors. Nor was the progress of the generals toward their new duties a continuous glorious parade. They were welcomed at New York City on June 24, but royal Governor William Tryon, who returned to his post there from England on the same day, was also greeted with enthusiasm, a sharp reminder that there were many Americans who would not sacrifice in behalf of the Patriot cause, a warning that many would actively assist Britain in the event that hostilities continued. At New York the party was also supplied with grim evidence that warfare was continuing, that America and Britain were becoming interlocked in a desperate struggle—they learned about the battle of Bunker Hill, which had taken place on the seventeenth. Schuyler undertook the defense of the colony of New York. Washington and Lee rode on through New England toward the American lines outside Boston. They were greeted by students at Yale College in New Haven and by various dignitaries along their path in Connecticut and Massachusetts. They arrived at Cambridge on Sunday, July 2. Attended by several Yankee generals, they went out to inspect the Patriot forces before sunset. The next day Washington formally took command, without fanfare because the army had no powder to waste in welcoming guns. More-or-less Commander in Chief Artemas Ward, not without a feeling of relief, it is to be suspected, consigned his authority to the Virginian.

Washington inherited an army only one-third organized and still recovering from the shock of defeat at Bunker Hill. Or had it won a victory? After Lexington and Concord, General Gage prepared as best he could for a renewal of fighting, at Boston and throughout the colonies. He solidified his fortifications across Boston neck until they became almost impervious to attack. He arranged to send a few troops to Virginia to assist Lord Dunmore, who was gathering a force in the region of Chesapeake Bay. Gage was in grim earnest. He had proposed before the shooting began that Britain augment her small army by hiring European troops for service in America. Now he suggested that it might be necessary to enlist Negro slaves and to call upon the Indians for assistance. He urged the royal Indian superintendents, Guy Johnson and John Stuart, who respectively looked after the northern and southern tribes for the Crown, to see to it that the red men became allies of Britain who might take up the hatchet against the Patriots. Reinforcements trickled into Boston so that his army grew to about six thousand men. With contingents that arrived from Britain late in May came three major generals—in order of seniority, William Howe, Henry Clinton, and John Burgoyne—sent to assist and inspirit him, and new orders from Lord Dartmouth to move energetically against the Patriots.

Gage consulted the three generals regarding the situation of the army in Boston. They had cause for worry, for both the troops and the warships in the harbor could be driven away by cannon fire from hills on Charlestown peninsula north of the city and on Dorchester peninsula south of it. As yet the Patriots did not have artillery, but the generals agreed that it would be prudent to occupy the peninsulas. In any event, as Burgoyne said, the army, cramped in the city, needed "elbow room." Before the British could move, the Patriots, learning of the plan, occupied Bunker Hill on Charlestown peninsula. The generals resolved to drive them off. It would have been possible to cut off the Patriots on Bunker Hill from their army by using the navy and troops to seize the narrow neck that connected the peninsula with the mainland, as Clinton suggested. Instead Howe, who led the attack, landed on the end of the peninsula and undertook to outflank and then to storm fragile Patriot entrenchments erected on the hill. Two charges by the British were bloodily repulsed by the garrison under Colonel William Prescott. It was driven back, after running short of ammunition, by a third desperate attack, and it fled to the mainland. The British had possession of the peninsula, and they kept it, but at very heavy cost. Over 40 percent of Howe's men, 1,054 out of about 2,200 whom he led into battle, were slain or wounded. The losses of the Patriots, suffered chiefly during their retreat, when they were assailed at the neck by warships and a flanking force under Clinton, were above 400 killed, wounded, and captured. The Patriots at first grieved over their defeat, but they came to recognize that the British had won an extraordinarily expensive victory with little military profit. The Patriots had fought well, and the redcoats were still penned against the sea. Such was the situation when Washington assumed command at Cambridge.

XI

———— ✦ ————

The General for Independence

Inheriting the vague semblance of an army out-
side Boston, Washington struggled to create a real one, without too
much success. Even so, his labors were not without reward. At
last, receiving cannon, he forced the British to evacuate the city, a
signal triumph. In the meantime American forces penetrated far
into Canada. After achieving remarkably, they were driven back.
However, the British were compelled to leave all the thirteen colonies before the end of June, 1776. The Patriots simultaneously
moved toward asserting their entire freedom from Britain. Washington and his higher officers were among the first to voice a desire
for separation from the Mother Country. On July 2 the Second
Continental Congress formally severed the last tie between America and Britain. Two days later it endorsed the famous document
that came to be known as the Declaration of Independence. The
task of translating words into reality then fell upon the Patriots,
especially upon Washington. Other Patriots might waver; he would
not turn back.

Inspecting the militia scattered along a line ten miles in length
on the mainland opposite Boston, Washington learned, to his vexation, that the Yankees were not what he had expected them to be.
He had been led to believe that the Patriots facing Gage were all

brave, devoted, virtuous, self-disciplined sons of freedom, determined to make every sacrifice for the great cause, like himself. So they had been described in reports he read and heard in Virginia and Philadelphia. He saw instead men who bore a strong resemblance to those he had led to battle in his youth. There was indeed, as time and trial would prove, a large stock of sturdy and steady Patriots in New England. But at the moment he was disconcerted to see an unorderly, untrained, and heterogeneous collection of contingents from the four colonies east of the Hudson. Most of them, armed with family muskets, were clad in civilian dress. They were casually quartered in huts and tents; their cooking facilities were meager; their latrines were insufficient or entirely lacking. Nor were their officers uniformly superior. Chosen because of local prestige or popularity, perhaps secured by generosity with respect to drinks at the village tavern, they were only too often men who could not demand discipline from independent-minded friends and neighbors. Some of the officers were thieves; others had been guilty of cowardice at Bunker Hill. Profanity and drunkenness were endemic. Although gunpowder was scarce, soldiers discharged muskets skyward for amusement. Disobedience of orders was common, with soldiers defying officers who tried to make them behave. Drilling of the troops was haphazard. If they were to meet redcoats in battle, there was much work to do. With the assistance of Lee, Washington began the slow process of turning balky armed civilians into obedient soldiers.

The labors of the commander in chief were not without a touch of humor. Orders from headquarters on August 22 declared,

> The General does not mean to discourage the practice of bathing whilst the weather is warm enough to continue it, but he expressly forbids, any persons doing it, at or near the bridge in Cambridge, where it has been observed and complained of, that many men, lost to all sense of decency and common modesty, are running about naked upon the bridge, whilst passengers, and even ladies of the first fashion in the neighborhood, are passing over it, as if they meant to glory in their shame. The guards and centries at the bridge are to put a stop to this practice for the future.

But most of Washington's activities were serious enough.

Court-martials became frequent. One William Pattin was found guilty of "threatening and abusing a number of persons, when prisoner in the Quarter Guard." Pattin was sentenced "to ride the wooden horse" for fifteen minutes in the presence of his watching regiment. Daniel Carmiele, for "disobedience of orders, for reinlisting and taking advance money twice over, and for drunkenness" was condemned to be "whipt on the bare back, with 30 lashes, and discharged from the army." A Captain Oliver Parker, for defrauding privates of their pay and embezzling rations, was cashiered. For "deserting his post" at Bunker Hill, Captain Christopher Gardner was similarly punished. The process of establishng order and discipline was tedious and frustrating. Washington was particularly dissatisfied with the Massachusetts troops. He carelessly wrote to Lund that they "would fight very well (if properly officered) although they are an exceeding dirty and nasty people." He informed Richard Henry Lee that there was "an unaccountable kind of stupidity in the lower class of these people which, believe me, prevails but too generally among the officers of the Massachusetts part of the army who are nearly of the same kidney with the privates."

Flatly condemning the Yankee troops in general and those of Massachusetts in particular, in letters to Lund and to Lee that went southward, Washington was indiscreet. Privacy of correspondence was by no means a sacred right among the Americans at that time. Moreover, there was a possibility of interception by the British. Publication of the opinions of Washington would have been most embarrassing both for him and for the American cause. The British did intercept an American courier that summer in Rhode Island and gleefully published a letter written by John Adams in which that crusty politician carelessly described John Dickinson as "a certain piddling genius." Thereafter Dickinson was not fond of Adams. Indeed, supporters of the Crown were so eager to discredit Patriot leaders that they did not balk at forgery. Among the letters that fell into their hands in Rhode Island was a sufficiently official and staid one from Benjamin Harrison to Washington. It was published—with an insertion supplied by someone who did not love Harrison or Washington in which the president of Congress said that he was fitting a laundrywoman's daughter for the embraces of the general.

Washington was fortunate. His remarks concerning the Yankees did not become public. He had another bit of luck that summer. Suddenly he learned that his army was almost without gunpowder

—he had been led to believe that his supply was far larger than it actually was. In near panic he begged the New England colonies to send powder. His supply was replenished before the British could take advantage of the Patriot weakness. His situation actually improved with the passing months, while that of the British deteriorated. Their losses at Bunker Hill were more than replaced by four regiments that appeared from across the ocean, but they continued to lack men, gear, and supplies for a movement out of Boston. "I wish this cursed place was burned," declared General Gage, well aware that his career was ruined, that he would become the scapegoat for the unhappy state of British affairs. Penned against the sea, the British even began to run short of fresh food. Their cruisers prowled along the coasts of New England, seizing cattle and sheep. In exasperation their raiders burned the village of Falmouth (Portland), Maine. Washington added to the difficulties of the beleaguered redcoats by commissioning vessels to intercept their supply ships. The British were reduced to butchering the Boston town bull for steaks and roasts. They and their Tory friends in the city became increasingly dispirited. In the autumn General Gage was recalled. A well-liked officer in the army, he had never given evidence of brilliance. He paid dearly for listening to Howe rather than Clinton before the battle of Bunker Hill. His career came to an end. He was succeeded in command in the thirteen colonies by General Howe, in Canada by General Guy Carleton. The change made no immediate difference, for Britain was unable to make a great military effort before the summer of 1776. When winter came, the Patriots outside the city shivered in their tents and huts, but the British troops within it also suffered from the cold. They cut down trees and tore down buildings in order to secure wood for fuel. They and their Loyalist friends waited impatiently for the help that would come, that must come, from Britain.

Once and again Washington talked with his senior officers about assault against the British lines. The redcoats were well entrenched; the "great guns" of the fleet in the harbor could be used to assist the army; the Patriots had very few cannon. Washington was forced to remain quiet at Boston for many months. He was able to keep more than twenty thousand men in position and to enlist the bulk of them during the winter in Continental service for a period of one year without interference from the British. But he could not move in force against the city until he acquired artillery. He had domestic consolation. Martha came from Virginia in the family coach and stayed with him until spring, a procedure she would follow throughout the war.* She became very friendly with Lucy Knox and Catherine Greene, the wives of Henry Knox and Nathanael Greene, who were to be two of Washington's favorite officers. Martha went home in March, 1776.

In the meantime, the Patriots seized ascendancy elsewhere throughout the Old Thirteen. The British garrison forces in the middle colonies had been withdrawn to Boston, and those colonies came under Patriot sway without a struggle. It was otherwise to the south, where royal forces gathered, but the result was the same. Lord Dunmore took the field for the king. He collected a motley force of Americans loyal to the Crown, Negro slaves, regulars from a garrison at St. Augustine, and marines from British war vessels in Chesapeake Bay. He tried vainly to instigate Indian attacks upon the frontiers of Virginia. Breathing fire, he denounced the Patriots as traitors. Supported by the warships, he challenged the Patriots from the bay. However, early in 1776, he was defeated in the battle of Great Bridge, south of Norfolk. In revenge he set fire to the town before retreating to the shelter of his ships. Eventually, having accomplished nothing except to cause Patriot rage, he sailed away. The story was much the same in North Carolina. There Governor Josiah Martin, expecting help from a British fleet that did not promptly appear, called upon Tories in the colony to take up arms for the king. Some 1,700 men, chiefly Scottish Highlanders, recent emigrants who were feudally faithful to the Crown, responded and moved from the interior toward Wilmington. They were checked and routed in the battle of Moore's Creek Bridge on February 27.

But if the Patriots could rejoice over their victories within the thirteen colonies, they could not be jubilant over their efforts to add a fourteenth one to their number. They were eager to become truly continental, to enlist the province of Quebec in their cause. They desired the help of the French Canadians or at least their neutrality. Accordingly, Patriot agents went to the St. Lawrence Valley even before the battle of Lexington and Concord to appeal to a few new English-speaking residents in Quebec and, more especially, to persuade traditional French-speaking and Roman Catholic enemies of Britain that they ought to join their Yankee brethren in throwing off British rule. For a time after the beginning of hos-

---

* Many soldiers had less formal reunions with camp followers.

tilities the Congress was disposed to take a defensive posture, to avoid sending troops beyond the borders of the Old Thirteen. But the battle of Bunker Hill persuaded the deputies that they had a war to wage, that they should seek help wherever it might be secured. Concentrating his army in Boston, Gage had reduced the redcoats in Quebec to three regiments of infantry and three companies of artillery scattered along the shores of the Great Lakes and in the valley of the St. Lawrence River. Congress gave General Schuyler permission to advance toward Montreal. With help from the French Canadians, might not Quebec be made into a fourteenth colony without great effort? Schuyler and his successor, General Richard Montgomery, moved northward from Ticonderoga late in the summer of 1775. With two thousand men Montgomery finally overcame resistance by the largest body of British troops in Canada, a garrison of seven hundred men at Fort St. John's on the Richelieu River, captured Montreal, and moved down the St. Lawrence toward the city of Quebec.

In the meantime Washington, calculating that the British could not defend both Montreal and Quebec, still the Canadian capital and stronghold, made the redoubtable Benedict Arnold a colonel, gave him more than one thousand troops, and sent him through the woods of Maine against Quebec. Arnold encountered tremendous hardships as he advanced through wilderness; part of his force unheroically turned back; but he reached his destination and joined forces with Montgomery, outside the city—too late to make an easy capture of the strategic place. Lieutenant Colonel Allan McLean and General Guy Carleton, who was governor of Quebec, managed to gather redcoats, marines, sailors, some Scottish Highland settlers, and a few French Canadians in the fortress before the Patriots could strike in force. The invaders received little help from the inhabitants of the province. An attempt by Montgomery and Arnold to storm the fortress on December 31 failed. Montgomery was killed. Wounded, Arnold maintained a siege until heterogeneous reinforcements moved north in the spring of 1776. Renewed efforts by the Patriots to win over the French Canadians achieved little. A British fleet came up the St. Lawrence in May and landed thousands of redcoats. The Patriots fell back helter-skelter, accompanied by dysentery and smallpox, pursued by Carleton. The Americans did not cease to retreat until they reached Ticonderoga. Patriots continued to dream of annexing Canada. Without the help of the French inhabitants, most of whom loved neither the Patriots nor the British regime and who preferred to remain neutral, the Americans could not make Quebec into a fourteenth colony—or state. Indeed, British offensives from the St. Lawrence in 1776 and 1777 were formidable threats to the Patriots.

But the stalemate at Boston was at length resolved in favor of the rebels. The city was vulnerable to cannon attack from the hills on Charlestown peninsula, also from Dorchester Heights to its southward. From those eminences shot and shell could be poured down upon the city and the British fleet. On the other hand, the guns of the royal forces could not reach the top of the hills. After the battle of Bunker Hill the British held Charlestown peninsula, but neither Gage nor Howe thought it necessary to spread their forces to occupy Dorchester Heights, since Washington did not have artillery to open a bombardment. A large store of cannon came into Patriot hands with the capture of Ticonderoga. Washington sent his chief of artillery, Henry Knox, to secure the big guns. Knox, a fat and faithful officer who had been the owner of a bookstore in Boston and who had presumably dipped with profit into tomes containing passages about the use of round shot and shell, was finally able to bring many cannon on sledges over snow and ice into the Patriot camp in the winter of 1775. During the night of March 4, 1776, Washington sent troops to occupy Dorchester Heights and mounted cannon upon them. He prepared for a battle on the next day, the anniversary of the Boston Massacre, when his troops would presumably perform very well. There was no battle. Howe momentarily considered an assault to drive the Patriots from the heights. He thought again. It had been determined in London that the task of suppressing the rebellion required concentration of the bulk of the Royal Army at New York City. An attack upon the Patriot entrenchments might be expensive. Howe chose to leave Boston, to take his army to Halifax, and to remain there until massive reinforcements came from England. Taking with him more than one thousand Loyalists, he sailed away on March 17, St. Patrick's Day, giving the Boston Irish of a later time two reasons to celebrate the anniversary. The time would come when the British consul in the city joined in commemorating the day, but not until several generations had passed. Washington made no effort to interfere with the evacuation—he was delighted to see the British depart.

Washington was committed to independence as the great goal of the Patriots before his triumphant move into Boston. With thou-

sands of other Americans he read the famous diatribe of Tom
Paine, *Common Sense,* which came from the press early in 1776
and which inveighed against kings in general, against British kings
in particular, and especially against George III. The general declared that the arguments of Paine convinced him of the iniquity of
Britain and her monarchy and that there must be a complete separation. Actually, if Washington found the passionate contentions of
Paine to be persuasive, they merely pointed to a conclusion toward
which the Virginian had already been very rapidly and inevitably
moving. The general was not one of the last Patriots to decide that
the last link with Britain must be severed.

It was one thing to clamor for American rights and to employ
economic weapons against Britain; it was another to engage British
forces in battle. In London the Patriots officially became traitors, a
fact formally announced by a royal proclamation of August 23,
1775, which withdrew the protection of the Crown from all the
American rebels. If they yielded to British force, they might face
confiscation of their property; their leaders became subject to execution upon the scaffold. Moreover, it was evident as the year 1775
drew to a close that Britain would make a great effort to crush the
rebellion. The government undertook to expand the small British
army, to hire the services of thousands of Hessians—German
soldiers. Garrison forces in Britain were reduced to a minimum,
and redcoats at Gibraltar were replaced by Hanoverian contingents. It was apparent that Britain would begin to wage war in
grim earnest in the summer of 1776. The Patriots were exasperated
as well as alarmed, for they resented the employment of the foreign
troops, the more so because they feared, with good reason, that
Britain would instigate the Indians to attack them. Because the
lands and the freedom of the red men, even their existence, were
threatened by westward advance of frontier folk, it was to be expected that most of them would favor distant King George. As yet,
servants of the Crown, except for Lord Dunmore, were polishing
chains of friendship between the tribesmen and Britain but were
not urging the warriors to wield the tomahawk. However, the Patriots rightly assumed that the crisis would induce British officials
to seek aid of whatever sort wherever it could be obtained, that
Indians urged on by the British would assail the western fringes of
the colonies. It was one thing to instigate Indians to wrest scalps
from Frenchmen and Spaniards, but quite another for them to take
strips of hair from Americans at the behest of the Crown. The

Patriots, assailed by mercenary troops and red men, were to be treated as if they were Frenchmen or Spaniards as well as traitors? Had not Lord Dunmore even enlisted Negro slaves?

Rising passions drove the Patriots toward a declaration of independence from the Mother Country. Moreover, sober thought among their leaders impelled them toward that measure. Was it even possible to make a stable agreement with Britain that guaranteed American freedom within the empire, that provided absolute protection for those leaders against the halter and the ax? Having laid down their weapons, the Patriots would be at the mercy of the British and the Loyalists, who might or might not live up to guarantees of safety of person and property. There was also the fact that formal announcement of independence was necessary to secure help from Britain's ancient enemies, France and Spain, help that might be militarily indispensable. And might not an America relieved of kings, nobles, and the Anglican church, become republican and prosper in freedom?

The forces that impelled the Patriots toward asserting their freedom from Britain were especially potent among those who confronted the British in battle. The militiaman who engaged the redcoats at Concord and Lexington and the musketman who fired at charging redcoats at Bunker Hill found it a bit difficult to look upon their antagonists as brethren. They and the relatives of slain and wounded Patriots increasingly saw the royal forces as enemies little different from traditional French and Spanish foes. The high officers of the Americans shared the rising hostility of the rank and file toward Britain, the more so because they were peculiarly exposed to punishment and because they understood the need for foreign aid. Less sophisticated Patriots might think such assistance unnecessary. Those who were better informed knew that it would be most valuable, and perhaps indispensable. By the autumn of 1775 several generals serving with Washington outside Boston desired a final separation, among them Charles Lee, who had his personal grudge against George III, and Horatio Gates and Nathanael Greene. Washington was, of course, an arch-traitor. He did not commit himself at that time, but he was ready to accept a declaration of independence by Congress. He was referring in letters to "my country" and even to "my bleeding country." He was obviously prepared to carry on the struggle in behalf of an American republic.

Congress moved unsteadily but rapidly toward complete separation. It took one measure and another to sever ties with Britain. In the meantime royal and proprietary officers were deposed and fled. Patriot conventions and provincial congresses replaced colonial assemblies; Patriot committees seized executive authority. Deputies of North Carolina at Philadelphia were instructed to vote for independence on April 13. Those of Virginia were ordered on May 15 to propose resolutions for that purpose in Congress. On June 7 Richard Henry Lee of Virginia accordingly asked that body to declare independence, to establish an American republic, and to seek foreign alliances. There were men in Congress, especially John Dickinson, who urged delay. They were overborne, on July 2. Congress unanimously—by a vote of twelve delegations, with deputies from New York abstaining for lack of instructions from home—asserted that "these United States are, and of right ought to be, free and independent states." Two days later, by a similar vote, the deputies endorsed the great pronouncement afterward known as the Declaration of Independence, which justified the decision taken two days earlier. The men from New York later gave consent to both measures. Thomas Jefferson earned enduring fame as the principal author of that document, with its melodious phrases; its indictment of George III, his ministers, and a Parliament pretending to exert authority over America; and its immortal proposition that government must have the consent of the governed.

Although it was safer for ardent and conspicuous Patriots to proclaim independence, it was not safe. For it was not at all unlikely that they would encounter defeat in battle, that the British victors and their Loyalist allies, moved by growing bloodlust, would wreak vengeance in proportion to the supposed crimes of the vanquished. It was one thing to assert independence, a very different matter to secure it. Before the shooting began, Lord North told Patriot Josiah Quincy, Jr., that the power of Britain was immense, that every opponent who had rashly challenged her had paid dearly for its impudence. North was trying to frighten a young colonial. Britain was not so mighty as the prime minister claimed.

To be sure, the British population was about four times that of the colonies. Britain was much wealthier than the colonies, possessed ready capital, and could easily produce war matériel. She had the advantage of a long-established system of government. Her navy was far beyond challenge by the Patriots, who were never able to send to sea even one ship of the line, the great war vessel of that time. Indeed, though recently neglected, the British navy was roughly equal to those of France and Spain combined. Its smaller vessels could maintain a blockade of sorts of the entire American coastline. Nor was the royal army to be despised, even though it contained no more than fifty thousand men, many of them needed for garrison duty at home and in scattered possessions beyond the seas. The quality of the infantry—the army had but few cavalrymen—was excellent. Its recruits were often farm boys seduced to enlist by liquor and smooth talk from gay young subalterns. Not a few were young men convicted of crimes and given a choice between severe punishment and service in the army. Others were Scots and Irishmen who preferred the army to civilian poverty. If the men in the ranks were not the crème de la crème of Britain, they were commonly veterans, for, once committed to the army, they remained in it during the pleasure of the Crown. Drilled by sergeants over the years, they maneuvered efficiently. They imbibed the pride of regiments that had crushed the forces of James II in the battle of the Boyne, withstood the armies of Louis XIV in the Low Countries, and overwhelmed the French at Blenheim. The army was their family and home; they were accustomed to discipline; they had that comradeship that leads to ultimate sacrifice for fellow soldiers. They would be assisted by some thirty thousand Hessians, who might not be zealous in the British cause, but who were obedient and useful nevertheless; by Loyalist contingents; and by thousands of Indian allies. It has been urged that the arms wielded by the royal troops were deficient, because they carried muskets with which they could not hit a target beyond close range. But a volley from those guns directed toward a body of opponents could be shattering. Somewhat has been made of the fact that a part of the Patriot forces carried rifles that could be aimed with precision. The riflemen were very valuable, but their fire was much slower than that of the musketmen and their bullets were smaller. Moreover, the musket had a bayonet. The Patriots had not learned how to fasten a bayonet upon a rifle. In formal combat on open ground the riflemen were at a serious disadvantage, for they were exposed to attack after discharging their weapons. In the end, if the rebels were to stand against the forces of the king, they had to oppose musket to musket, bayonet to bayonet.

Britain had serious weaknesses, the greatest one being that the war was unpopular, particularly among the men who in another and appealing cause would have filled the ranks of her regiments

and manned her ships. Few volunteers could be secured either for
land or sea service, and conscription, except for the informal draft
of the press gang used to secure sailors, was as yet unknown in
Britain. The Patriots could put more men under arms than could
be sent across the ocean. Moreover, both transportation and communication were slow and uncertain between Britain and America.
Corruption, especially in the army, was a drawback. Contractors
and commissaries were accustomed to become rich at public expense. One perceives Colonel Lord Rawdon buying horses from
horse-grower Lord Rawdon; one sees army paymasters lending
public money to troops and to the Crown. There was no Pitt to
direct the British war machine. After the autumn of 1775 its levers
were manipulated principally by Lord George Germain, who succeeded Lord Dartmouth in the autumn of 1775. Cashiered from
the army for refusing to obey orders to attack the French at the
battle of Minden in 1759, Germain was brave enough, but was
distrusted, disliked, and undistinguished. Field commanders who
served under him were conventional British officers, brave rather
than brilliant. The British war machine would creak and groan,
but it would run far more smoothly than that of the Patriots.

Could the rebels withstand the assaults of the royal forces, until,
perhaps, they secured European allies? Could they withstand them
even with the help of France and Spain? Washington knew that
they would be sorely tried; he placed trust in Providence. With
thirteen emerging states, with a Congress assuming general direction of the war effort, the Patriots were not politically united. They
clashed among themselves, and they could not make full use of
their resources. Moreover, many white inhabitants of the new republic were neutral or nearly so. Many blacks, if obedient to Patriot owners, were less than ardent for American liberty. Not a
few, to be sure, bore arms for the United States. The Loyalists were
a serious menace to the Patriots, especially in North Carolina and
New York, where they were comparatively numerous. As the
struggle continued, more and more Tories took up arms. The Cherokee, perceiving that their independence and freedom were threatened by the westward advance of the American pioneers, also entered the conflict as allies of the king in the summer of 1776.

The Patriots were assailed in five different areas in that summer.
The Cherokee were driven back by the frontiersmen of Virginia
and the Carolinas. A British expeditionary force that appeared at
Charleston harbor, its fleet being repulsed by the gunfire of Patriot

batteries on Sullivan's Island on June 28, was forced to return to sea. Lord Dunmore was compelled at length to abandon Chesapeake Bay. Much more serious for the Americans was the southward advance of General Carleton from Canada. Heterogeneous and ill-organized troops of New England and New York fell back rapidly before the thrust of Carleton. They suffered terribly from smallpox. Their retreat ceased only at Fort Ticonderoga. Carleton approached that place in the autumn, and he was tempted to attack it and to attempt a junction with the main British army, which began to go ashore on the islands in New York Harbor on July 2, the very day on which Congress resolved that America must be free. As Carleton moved southward, William Howe, with the help of a fleet directed by his older brother, Richard, Viscount Howe, struck heavily at the principal American army under Washington. Correctly anticipating that the British would appear in great force at New York, Washington concentrated there. He arranged to have the Declaration of Independence read to his men. The British appeared in even greater numbers, regulars from Halifax and Britain, redcoats from Charleston, and Dunmore's men. It became apparent to Washington and to his troops that they would be very severely tested.

XII

The General in Flight

*W*hat to do about meeting the British thrust, sure to come, at New York City? Early in 1776 Washington sent Charles Lee there to begin preparations against attack. Lee, aware that Manhattan, as an island, could be flanked by the British navy both from the Hudson River and Long Island Sound, declared that the Patriots could only fight delaying actions before abandoning the city. He began to build fortifications for that purpose before he was sent away by Congress to defend the southern colonies. Taking command at Manhattan, Washington continued the work begun by Lee and collected more than twenty-seven thousand men to face the British. A few weeks after the signing of the Declaration of Independence it seemed to many that the great proclamation was only a literary exercise. Driven from the island, Washington fled with ever dwindling forces to the mainland and eventually across the Delaware River into Pennsylvania.

The British plan for the campaign of 1776 was, perhaps, as judicious as might be. General Howe, with the help of a fleet commanded by his older brother, Richard, Viscount Howe, was to seize New York City, then move northeastward. Guy Carleton was to advance southward from Canada and join General Howe in subjugating New England. It could be believed that reduction of

Yankeeland, the Patriot stronghold, would lead without remarkable delay to the collapse of Patriot morale and resistance elsewhere.

Before resorting to their guns the Howe brothers tried to extend
an olive branch. They were authorized to act as peace commissioners—each of them receiving the handsome sum of five thousand
pounds per annum, in addition to their usual pay, for their efforts
to placate the embattled Patriots. They could accept the submission of rebels, pardon them, and establish the king's peace in areas
where resistance had ceased. Admiral Howe was willing to grant a
generous position in the empire to the colonists, provided that they
recognized the right of Britain to regulate their maritime commerce. He had sought to arrange an accommodation of that sort
with Benjamin Franklin before the clash of arms, and he continued
to seek it. Black Dick, as the admiral was called, was a splendid
fighting man rather than a supple diplomat. The brothers attempted to open a negotiation with Washington. He informed them
that they must deal with Congress.

Then William Howe struck. By mid-August he had about thirty
thousand troops, British and Hessian, available for battle. Another
five thousand men were en route to join him. He considered the
American defenses, consisting chiefly of Fort Washington on the
northwestern side of Manhattan and Fort Lee on the opposite
shore of the Hudson, which were intended to interrupt the passage
of British vessels up the river; batteries on lower Manhattan; and
others on the heights of Brooklyn, erected to guard the East River.
The Americans, Continentals and militia, were strung out from
Fort Lee to Long Island. About one-fourth of them were camped
on Long Island. The Americans were in a perilous position, the
more so because Washington was determined to "use every endeavour" to defend the city, for he believed that possession of it by the
British would enable them to control the Hudson and divide the
Americans into two parts. Before Howe moved, two small British
vessels sailed up the Hudson beyond Forts Washington and Lee
and returned to New York harbor. Batteries that had been built to
prevent their passage did not injure them. It was apparent that
most of the American army was exposed to a flanking attack by
royal troops landed above Fort Washington. Howe had had experience in such operations, notably at Quebec and Havana in the
Seven Years' War, but he chose to move against the Patriots, some
seven thousand men, on Long Island. On August 22 British troops

who were camped on the islands at New York harbor below Manhattan began to land south of Brooklyn. Five days later they went into battle.

The Patriots on Long Island were ill-prepared for the struggle that followed. They were strung out along a ridge from Brooklyn eastward to Jamaica Pass. Their left wing merely ended at the pass. It was exposed, for nothing had been done to ward off a flank attack from the pass—a mistake on the part of the less-than-astute General Israel Putnam, who commanded on the island, and also on the part of Washington, who inspected the arrangements made by Putnam and failed to correct his error.

Brave and experienced, William Howe was by no means a military genius. But he did not fail to take advantage of a splendid opportunity. Before dawn on August 27 he sent Henry Clinton with ten thousand men to the east of the American line. Clinton turned around it without opposition, and rolled it back. Meanwhile Major General James Grant assailed it frontally with seven thousand troops. Grant was held off for some time by a much smaller body of Maryland and Delaware Continentals. They and other American contingents fought very well, but the royal troops gradually drove the entire Patriot army back into a fortified position at Brooklyn. By midday the Americans were penned there with the East River at their back. Howe might then have continued the attack, might have taken all of the Patriots on Long Island. He fancied that he had done enough for the day and stopped to prepare for a final attack. The situation of the Patriots was dangerous. Washington added to the bag of prisoners that the British might take, with General Howe assaulting the entrenchments of the Patriots, with Admiral Howe preventing their retreat across the East River. Unaware that the Patriot position, despite its fortifications, could not be held, that its defenders would likely become rather easy prey to the British, Washington sent reinforcements from Manhattan. Among them, fortunately, were Massachusetts Continentals led by Colonel John Glover of Marblehead, who was accustomed to managing boats. Washington himself assumed command at Brooklyn and awaited a renewal of hostilities with more than nine thousand men. There was skirmishing on the twenty-eighth and twenty-ninth. But it rained, and Howe saw no reason to hurry to seize his prey. In the meantime Washington perceived his danger and began to collect boats to carry his troops to Manhattan and safety. Pretending to be preparing for a struggle, he began to ferry his troops across the East River during the night of the twenty-ninth. Glover and his men performed miracles. Most of the Patriots, together with their weapons and supplies, were quietly put ashore on Manhattan before dawn without arousing the British. Moreover, nearly all of the remainder escaped across the river in the morning under cover of a dense fog. Only three Americans, who had lagged behind for plunder, were captured by the royal forces. Washington had made amends for his mistakes by a masterly—and fortunate—retreat.

But the situation of the Patriots remained perilous. More than a thousand had been captured on Long Island, and hundreds had been killed or wounded. The British rested for more than two weeks before resuming hostilities—they did not bother to bury the slain Americans. But Admiral Howe indicated that he bore them no ill will. Congress had appointed a committee consisting of Benjamin Franklin, John Adams, and Edward Rutledge to meet him and to discover the terms of peace that he had to offer. The four men conferred on Staten Island on September 11. The admiral assured the three rebels that Britain intended to be generous. They were not impressed; they told him that America must become independent. Disappointed, he afterward presented his case to individuals, not without result.

In the meantime Washington and General Howe considered the changed military situation. The Patriots wished to hold Manhattan, but they knew that they could not do it. The majority of the American generals advised Washington to evacuate it without delay. General Nathanael Greene and other officers urged that New York be burned to deprive the British of comfortable winter quarters. Even John Jay, a civilian resident of the city, endorsed that drastic step. But Congress refused to accept a "scorched-earth" policy.* Washington was reluctant to withdraw without a fight. To give up New York without a struggle, he realized, would "dispirit the troops and enfeeble our cause." On the other hand, he recognized that the enemy might "enclose us" by landing in his rear, either from the Hudson or Long Island Sound. He resolved to make a fighting retreat. General Henry Clinton, second in command to Howe, again demonstrated his intellectual superiority to his superior. The British fleet could control the Hudson. He recom-

---

* A Patriot, called "some honest fellow" by Washington, burned down a part of the city after the American evacuation.

mended that Howe put troops ashore from the river on the northern end of Manhattan. Such a maneuver, if successful, would leave
the Patriots only one avenue of retreat, across the Kingsbridge
toward Connecticut. There was very good reason to believe that
the maneuver would succeed. Howe was disposed to ignore any
proposal from Clinton. Instead, he resolved to attack from the
eastern side of Manhattan. On September 15 royal troops in large
numbers put ashore at Kip's Bay.

The result was an easy conquest of the city. British and Hessian
troops brushed aside feeble resistance at Kip's Bay and drove on
westward and northward. The Patriots fled before them. Contingents of Washington's army on the southern tip of the island were
fortunate to escape encirclement. The Patriots went helter-skelter
up the island with Howe's men in contemptuous pursuit. Washington strove in vain to persuade his men to make a stand until they
reached temporary safety on Harlem Heights. However, the next
day he struck a partial and successful blow at the royal forces, and
he was encouraged to believe that further retreat was not immediately necessary. He thought that he could hold Harlem Heights
against the British—if his militiamen would fight. It was most
doubtful that they would. Many thousands of them had already
departed for home in Connecticut and other attractive places. No
more than sixteen thousand men remained with Washington.

Fortunately for the Patriots, Howe spent almost a month occupying Long Island and establishing a base in New York City. But
the situation of the Patriots remained perilous. Some five thousand
British and Hessian troops joined Howe, so that he had as many as
thirty-five thousand men in his command. The Patriots were now
badly outnumbered, and all of them, save for the garrison at Fort
Lee, were exposed to encirclement, either from the Hudson or
from Long Island Sound. Washington perceived the danger but
was reluctant to fall back without offering resistance. Rejoining
Washington after gaining increased repute by directing the successful defense of Charleston, Charles Lee emphatically urged immediate withdrawal from Manhattan. Washington decided to hold on as
long as possible on a line stretching from Fort Lee through Fort
Washington and Harlem Heights to Kingsbridge. Happily for the
Americans, Howe continued to ignore the advice of Henry Clinton. He undertook to outflank the Patriots, not from the north, but
from the east. Fortune continued to favor the Americans. Howe
struck on October 12, moving the bulk of his army with the help of

his brother into Long Island Sound and landing at Throg's Neck.
That peninsula was virtually an island, and small detachments of
Patriots checked the British advance. Howe had lost a chance to
surprise the Patriots. Six days later he began to land his army at
Pell's Point, three miles to the east of Throg's Neck, from which he
could easily penetrate inland. It was too late to encircle the Patriots from the east. Briefly checking the advance of the royal forces,
Washington withdrew to White Plains, where he drew up his army
on high ground and awaited attack. It came, on October 28. The
Patriots were driven back, but formed a new line. The next day the
royal troops again drove forward, forcing a second retreat, but the
Americans fought well and moved away to new positions on hills
at North Castle. They had proved that they were not to be despised.

Howe reconsidered. Winter was not far away, and he knew that
Guy Carleton would not join him in thrusting into New England.
Pushing southward from Canada, Carleton easily drove Patriot
troops opposing him back into New York. But Generals Benedict
Arnold and David Waterbury built a fleet on Lake Champlain.
Carleton had to construct a larger one to clear the lake. He did so,
and his squadron routed that of the Patriots in the battle of
Valcour Island on October 11 and 12. But clearance of the Patriots
from the lake had taken weeks of precious time. A strong garrison
of Americans held Ticonderoga, and winter was approaching in
northern New York. Carleton, prudently, resolved to fall back into
Canada and resume his advance in the following spring. Would it
be profitable for Howe to drive forward alone, pursuing Washington over very rough terrain? He was offered an alternative. Washington had left a garrison of 2,800 men, together with large quantities of military gear, in the fort named after him. Howe "retreated"
westward and moved against that place. There could be no easy
flight from the place under attack, since British ships controlled
the Hudson. Even so, its commandant, Colonel Robert Magaw,
believed that the fort could be held for weeks and that the garrison
could eventually flee to safety. His immediate superior, Nathanael
Greene, who was encamped at Fort Lee, across the river, also
failed to see that Fort Washington was in grave danger. Washington became worried. He went to Fort Lee on November 12 and
proposed to Greene that the garrison and stores be withdrawn, but
left it to Greene, whom he liked and trusted, to decide what to do.
Greene continued to believe that the fort could be defended. In-

creasingly alarmed, Washington went again to Fort Lee two days later. He crossed the Hudson with Greene to examine the situation at Fort Washington. The two generals were in time to see the beginnings of a British assault upon Magaw's men. Returning to Fort Lee, they very unhappily watched redcoats and Hessians swarm up to the Patriot entrenchments, overcome resistance without great difficulty, and force the surrender of all the men and stores collected in the fort, on November 16. The Patriots had encountered disaster—and the responsibility for it rested largely upon the shoulders of Washington, although he tried to ascribe much of the blame for the decision to defend the fort to the wishes of Congress and the bad advice of Greene.

The fall of Fort Washington exposed the Patriots to new attacks. Howe sent Charles, Lord Cornwallis, up the east bank of the Hudson, thence across the river, and down its western side with four thousand men against Fort Lee. Greene fled with the garrison on November 20. Washington, assuming command in New Jersey with three thousand faithful troops, began a harassing retreat, pursued by a reinforced army under Cornwallis. The Patriot general left four thousand men east of the Hudson under Charles Lee to defend New England. The weather remained mild. Henry Clinton, always eager for an independent command in which he could gain glory, came forward with one of his bright ideas, one that was not very bright. He asked that Admiral Howe convey him with a detachment to Chesapeake Bay and up the Delaware River. Clinton would approach Philadelphia from the south while Cornwallis drove toward it from the east—the Patriots would not be able to defend their "capital" against both thrusts. As usual, Howe responded in the negative. The admiral wished to put his fleet in the commodious waters of Newport for the winter, and Clinton was sent to take Newport. He easily accomplished that mission, and Newport remained in British hands for almost four years.

In the meantime Cornwallis pursued Washington across New Jersey. Cornwallis, not yet thirty-eight years of age, was bold and enterprising. Escaping his clutches at Fort Lee, Washington fled southward and westward with only three thousand "much broken and dispirited men." Cornwallis pursued closely as far as New Brunswick, where, happily for the Patriots, he stopped for several days in accordance with orders from Howe, who believed that the pursuit must be orderly rather than swift. Washington went onward to Princeton, to Trenton, and thence across the Delaware

River. He gathered up all the boats along the river for seventy miles north of Philadelphia. He and his men were temporarily safe, but the weather was mild, and he expected the British to drive on, to aim at Philadelphia. The royal troops did begin to advance beyond New Brunswick. Washington thought of challenging them and moved his men to the eastern side of the river, for reinforcements of militia were coming up from Philadelphia, and Charles Lee, urged to bring his four thousand men from the eastern side of the Hudson, was marching slowly westward across northern New Jersey. Lee did not appear, and Washington ferried back to Pennsylvania.

Patriot civilians watching the onward march of the royal army from New Brunswick were in panic. Patriot General John Cadwalader observed "d——d gloomy countenances" among them as he retreated with Washington across New Jersey. The Hessians indulged in plunder and rape. Many in New Jersey concluded that the Patriot cause was about to collapse. Militia remained at home or went home. Hundreds of Jerseymen asked Admiral Howe for pardon and swore an oath of allegiance to Britain. An ardent defender of American rights before the war, John Dickinson advised his brother to exchange paper currency put out by Congress for pounds sterling. It was commonly assumed that the British would capture Philadelphia. Congress became alarmed and removed to Baltimore.

The panic had an effect even at the Patriot headquarters. Joseph Reed, a member of Washington's staff, had lost faith in the leadership of the commander in chief. He wrote to Lee to urge him to join Washington swiftly—the talents of Lee were indispensable on the Delaware. Washington himself, recalling his several defeats in and about New York, had reason to question his military abilities. Lee moved very slowly across northern New Jersey. Aware that the British could not advance with confidence while he and his men hung on the right flank of the royal army, where they could assail the British line of communications, Lee was emboldened by the plea from Reed. Artemas Ward had resigned, and Lee had become the second in rank in the army. He began to act as if he were the equal rather than the subordinate of Washington. Again and again the commander in chief urged but never quite ordered Lee to hasten to his assistance. Lee continued to follow his own strategy—which was, indeed, well conceived.

Then came what seemed to many Patriots a crowning blow. Lee

carelessly spent the night of December 12 in a tavern at Basking Ridge, more than a mile from his troops. He had with him only a few aides. Lord Cornwallis, moving forward toward Trenton, was concerned lest he be attacked on his right flank or rear. Lieutenant Colonel William Harcourt, sent out with almost thirty light cavalrymen by Cornwallis to locate Lee and his army, learned from a Tory and two captured American sentinels that Lee was almost unguarded. Early in the morning of the thirteenth Harcourt and his men surrounded the tavern. He threatened to burn it down and compelled the surrender of Lee before his army could come to his assistance. Harcourt and his party gleefully carried off the discomfited Patriot general to British headquarters. Lee remained a prisoner of the British for many months. Washington wrote to his nephew Lund, "Our cause has also received a severe blow in the captivity of Genl. Lee." Nathanael Greene saw the seizure of Lee as "a great loss to the American states, as he is a most consummate general," and the young Patriot officer John Trumbull wrote to his father that "this is a misfortune that cannot be remedied, as we have no officer in the army of equal experience and merit." The Patriots generally were downcast. John Hancock expressed the sentiments of Congress. The news of the capture of Lee was "alarming," he said. Hancock feared that the loss of Lee "will be severely felt, as he was in a great measure the idol of the officers, and possessed still more the confidence of the soldiery." In England the apprehension of the Patriot general seemed to many to mark the approaching end of the rebellion. Thomas Rodney of Delaware saw a ray of light in the gloom. Might not the departure of Lee enable Washington to make freer use of his own talents? Few Patriots agreed with Rodney. Washington had not hitherto displayed much military ability except for a vital willingness to fight.

XIII

The Hero of the Delaware

It turned out that Philadelphia did not definitely become a British objective until the year 1777 was well under way. William Howe looked about him as the middle of December approached. Not excessively addicted to cerebration, he considered his situation. Lord Cornwallis, keeping an eye on General John Sullivan, who succeeded Lee, was moving toward the Delaware. Henry Clinton had taken Newport. The British army was scattering between Newport and Trenton. Winter was at hand, and it was neither easy nor customary for a northern European army to keep the field in winter. He considered that he had accomplished enough for the year 1776. He decided that he could safely string out troops across New Jersey, with Amboy and New Brunswick serving as bases between Manhattan and the Delaware. He informed Lord George Germain that the "chain" of garrisons he was establishing across New Jersey was "rather too extensive," but that none of his posts, in his opinion, would be seriously exposed to attack. He announced to his army on December 14 that the campaign of 1776 had come to an end. Lord Cornwallis agreed with his superior. He occupied Trenton and Bordentown, placing Hessians in advanced positions to posts of honor because they had led the British advance to the Delaware. He made ready to depart for

England to spend the winter. The two British generals did not know the man who had risen from a sickbed to fight desperately at Braddock's defeat.

Congress had voted to raise a huge army for operations in 1777. Reporting to that body on December 18, Washington said that if the Continental army was not vastly increased, without much delay, "I think that the game is pretty near up." But he did not remain idle, did not wait for overwhelming forces of regiments and battalions voted by Congress to become more than paper, to appear for combat. He now displayed again the utter courage that won for him the enduring trust and admiration of his countrymen. Others might succumb to despair; desperation drove him to action. Safe for the near future behind the Delaware, he determined to strike back. The weather remained mild. Why should the Patriots be as idle as their enemies? As early as December 14 he began to think of taking the offensive. His situation was not so wretched as it appeared to be. Sullivan was joining him with the remains of Lee's army, about 2,700 men. The Philadelphia militia were at hand. About 1,200 troops not needed at Ticonderoga were marching southward. But if anything was to be done, it must be done soon, for the enlistments of his Continentals were to expire by December 31. Learning that Howe was putting his army away for the winter, Washington planned a great counteroffensive. He would attack the two royal garrisons left by Cornwallis at Trenton and Bordentown, then perhaps march against British posts at Princeton and New Brunswick. Meanwhile New York and New England militia should advance toward Manhattan. If Howe left that place to deal with Washington, if he left Manhattan weakly defended, the militia were to attack the main British base. A feeble assault against the outer works of Manhattan by the militia was easily checked by the entrenched British. Two thrusts across the Delaware arranged by Washington also failed. But it was otherwise with a third one that he led in person.

By December 23 Washington was definitely committed to the offensive across the Delaware. That day he wrote, "Necessity, dire necessity, will, nay must, justify my attack." He framed his plan for the seemingly desperate venture on the following day. There were about 1,500 Hessians and Highlanders at Bordentown and about 1,500 Hessians at Trenton, the two villages being about six miles apart. The Hessian Colonel Carl von Donop, stationed at Bordentown, was in general command. Colonel Johann Gottlieb

Rall had been entrusted with the defense of Trenton. Washington planned three separate crossings. He would personally lead 2,400 Continentals in an assault upon Trenton, his principal immediate objective. A second division under Brigadier James Ewing, chiefly Pennsylvania militia, was to go over the river immediately below Trenton and to prevent its garrison from fleeing southward. A third contingent under Lieutenant Colonel John Cadwalader, composed of Continentals and militia, was to pass the river at or near Bristol, to engage Colonel von Donop and prevent him from moving to the assistance of Rall. Washington hoped to surprise his enemies. The Patriots were to cross the river during Christmas night and begin hostilities early the following morning. The attack on Trenton was to take place one hour before dawn. The plan was well framed.

There is a rather famous painting of Washington crossing the Delaware en route to Trenton, done long after the event by a German artist, Emanuel Leutze. In the painting the general is standing up in a small boat surrounded by ice floes. Had the scene been such as Leutze depicted, Washington would almost surely have been pitched into the icy waters of the river. Fortunately the Patriots had boats almost ideally suited for making their way over the rather shallow river. Developed by one Robert Durham, they were from forty to sixty feet in length and eight feet in width. Their draft was only two feet, and they were propelled by poles and oars. The craft were big enough to carry cannon as well as many men. There was no problem of securing sailors to manage the craft, for Washington still had with him the sailors under John Glover who had rescued the army after the defeat on Long Island. Even so, the river was clogged by ice floes. Ewing failed to make the crossing, and Cadwalader did not reach the New Jersey side of the river in time to move against von Donop. Nor did Washington and his men fail to encounter difficulties. But he and his sorely tried and true Continentals did get over the river, with eighteen cannon, at McKonkey's Ferry, nine miles above Trenton, despite a driving snowstorm that turned into sleet and delayed their passage.

About three o'clock they began to march southward toward Trenton. En route, Washington divided his men into two divisions, one approaching the target from the north, the other from the east. Both contingents had artillery, thanks to the efforts and ingenuity of Henry Knox. Dawn came before the Patriots reached the village, but the Hessians, doubtless not at their best after a German celebration of Christmas, were completely surprised. About eight o'clock their sentries fell prey to the oncoming Patriots. Rall, wakened, tried to rally the garrison, in vain. His men were assailed by artillery fire and charging Continentals from two directions. Rall fell, mortally wounded. There was little firing, for both sides were hampered by wet cartridges. The Germans were hemmed in by the swarming Patriots. A third of the Hessians managed to flee toward Bordentown. About thirty of them were slain. The remainder, well above nine hundred men, were compelled to surrender. Washington returned to Pennsylvania the same day with his prisoners. No American was killed in the contest, and only four, including Captain William Washington and Lieutenant James Monroe, were wounded. The general had the pleasure of writing to Congress on December 27 that he had won an important victory.

But Washington was not satisfied. He learned that Colonel von Donop had evacuated Bordentown and had retreated to Princeton, that Cadwalader had finally managed to cross the river into New Jersey, that the militia of southern New Jersey were taking up arms. Elated by his brilliant little triumph, he boldly decided to return to that state, to strike again at the royal forces, to "beat up the rest of their quarters," as he told Cadwalader. On December 30 he crossed the Delaware once more. His troops followed the next day. He was venturesome to the point of rashness, for the enlistments of his Continentals were expiring and it was likely that the British would make a great effort to retrieve their defeat. He had been given sufficient temporary authority by Congress to provide each of his Continentals ten dollars in return for six weeks more of service. He made the offer, and at least half of his veterans agreed to stay with him for that period.

It was not so easy to deal with the royal forces. Lord Cornwallis changed his itinerary. Instead of leaving for England, he hastened across New Jersey, gathering six thousand men, to punish the impudent Patriots. He reached Trenton late in the afternoon of January 2. Cornwallis was eager to retrieve the losses suffered by his men at Trenton. He could be expected to mount an attack that would be difficult to check. Washington, his numbers swelled by militia to about five thousand men, ventured to make a stand on the southern side of Assunpink Creek with his back not far from the Delaware. Retreat would have been very awkward, perhaps even impossible, had Cornwallis attacked successfully. Preliminary efforts by the British to cross the Assunpink were checked by musket fire and cannon shot from the ever efficient artillery of Henry Knox. The approach of dusk induced Cornwallis to rest his men and to defer full battle to the following day, when he would be joined by contingents of his troops then at Princeton. That night Washington considered the situation with his higher officers. They learned that there was a side road to the south and east by which the Patriots might pass around the left flank of the royal army and proceed eastward. It was agreed that the seemingly daring maneuver should be undertaken. Squads of men built fires and made noises during the night to persuade the British that Washington intended to fight. The Patriots began to move along the side road and headed for Princeton. They muffled the wheels of their cannon with cloth and took the guns with them. Cornwallis ruefully discovered at cold dawn that his prey had escaped. Indeed, he heard the roar of battle behind him. He turned about to pursue his puzzling antagonist.

The Patriots were not out of the military woods. There were three regiments of British troops in and near Princeton, the 17th, the 40th, and the 57th, together with three companies of cavalry. Their commander, Lieutenant Colonel Charles Mawhood, leaving the 40th, part of the 57th, and some horsemen behind at Princeton to guard stores, moved forward to join Cornwallis that morning. Outside Princeton on the road to Trenton he was surprised to encounter advancing Patriots. He formed his men in an open field and exchanged fire with the American van, composed of Virginians under Colonel Hugh Mercer. Then the redoubtable Mawhood ordered the 17th to use the fearsome bayonet. The redcoats drove at Mercer and his men with cold steel. Mercer fell, mortally wounded, and his men fled in disorder. A contingent led by John Cadwalader came forward. The British drove it back in confusion and formed a battle line. Were the Patriots to be checked by a few hundred redcoats and even be assailed by the pursuing Cornwallis? Washington entered the scene of action. He much preferred to risk his own life to achieve success rather than to remain safely behind his men and perhaps in consequence to receive reports of defeat. Conspicuous on a white horse, he rode forward within thirty yards of the British line, urging the men of Mercer and Cadwalader to follow him in attack. The smoke of gunfire enveloped him. His men feared that he was slain, but he was unscathed. The Patriots rallied behind him. More Patriot contingents appeared, virtually surrounding Mawhood's force, threatening to overwhelm it by sheer weight of numbers. The remainder of the 55th, coming up to join Mawhood, was driven back and fled. Mawhood, desperate, again resorted to the bayonet, broke through the Patriots, and fled to join Cornwallis. Washington led the pursuit. At last Mawhood's infantry broke down under attack, but the royal cavalry successfully covered its disorganized retreat. In the meantime parts of the 40th and 55th, after their comrades had fled, took post in the Nassau Hall of Princeton College. They were surrounded by overwhelming force. Patriot artillerymen under Colonel Alexander Hamilton fired a cannon shot into the building. Its occupants promptly surrendered. At least 273 royal troops were killed or captured, and Washington was able to resume his march eastward.

Only forty Patriot officers and men were killed or wounded in the battle of Princeton, but the situation of Washington remained perilous, for the disappointed Cornwallis, having turned about from Trenton, was rapidly pursuing his unorthodox enemies. It would seem that Washington had planned, if circumstances were favorable, to "beat up" the British base at New Brunswick. He was headed toward that place. Cornwallis had to be concerned for its safety, especially since its small garrison protected both military stores and seventy thousand pounds in cash assigned to pay the British troops and to buy supplies. If Washington thought about an attack on New Brunswick, he was forced to set it aside. His men were hungry and utterly weary, and the vengeful Cornwallis was much too close for comfort. The Patriot general turned northeastward. Concerned lest Washington and his men should later change course and bear down on New Brunswick, Cornwallis marched directly to that village. Washington was thus free to continue northeastward to Morristown in the high hills of New Jersey. He was able to settle down there on January 6 for the remainder of the winter. He occupied strong ground, and William Howe chose a second time to put an end to the campaign of 1776. Except for minor affrays of outposts the principal armies of the Patriots and George III remained quiet until late in the spring of 1777.

The news of the British victories on Long Island and Manhattan delighted George III and the North ministry. They could believe that the American rebellion was beginning to collapse. They knighted both Howe and Henry Clinton, officially because of their exploits in the battle of Brooklyn. But the triumphs of Washington at Trenton and Princeton discomfited Howe. He abandoned New Jersey except for New Brunswick and Perth Amboy. At the end of the campaign, he held in addition to those posts only New York City, Long Island, and Newport, and he had been deprived of the services of a substantial part of the army that had gathered at New York in 1776. He was able to recoup his losses in large degree by recruiting Loyalists. Even so, he had been given much food for sober thought, and he thought, not very clearly. He was not always sober, for he was fond of alcohol and gambling.

Delighted as he was by his successes in the last two weeks of the campaign, Washington was not altogether happy at Morristown. He solved the problem of housing by putting his men to work constructing cabins and cutting wood. He managed to get enough food for them. But his army dwindled because of expiring enlistments. By the middle of March he had with him perhaps two thousand militiamen and fewer than a thousand Continentals, who were scheduled to depart by the end of the month. He removed one danger, smallpox, a disease that had riddled the American forces retreating from Canada in the preceding summer. He had his men inoculated against the disease. He was himself seriously ill early in March, but recovered in time to welcome the faithful Martha into camp. The wives of other officers also came to camp, and there were festivities. They were innocent enough, for Washington did what he could to discourage gaming and excessive drinking.

As the winter drew toward its end, Washington's military prospects also improved. In September, Congress had authorized the raising of seventy-five thousand men, and later of even more, to serve for three years or the duration of the war, each man to receive a bounty of 20 dollars, 40 shillings per month in pay and one hundred acres of land at the end of his period of enlistment. Some of the states offered even better terms to fill their quotas. So many men could not possibly be raised; nor could Congress, even with the assistance of the states, support so many. Relying largely upon the issuance of paper money backed only by its own promise to make it good, Congress could not hope to maintain a large army. Many Continentals declined to reenlist, but others stoutly adhered to the cause. Gradually, as the news of the victories of Trenton and Princeton spread, new recruits came forward, and a new army began to appear at Morristown in the spring.

Nor was the increasing strength of the army confined to an increase in numbers. The course of the American rebellion was closely watched in France and Spain. Ministers of state in those two countries and their monarchs were eager to take advantage of the distress into which Britain had been plunged. There was an eagerness in Paris and Madrid to assist the rebels, not for their sake, but to injure the detested Britain that had humiliated France and Spain in the Seven Years' War. In Paris, Caron de Beaumarchais, a clever adventurer who afterward became famous as the author of *Figaro* and *The Barber of Seville,* with the support of the French foreign minister, the Comte de Vergennes, secured the consent of King Louis XVI and his advisers for the creation of a fake association of merchants, Rodrigue Hortalez and Company, to send secret aid to the Patriots. Beaumarchais was given a million francs by the French crown and additional money by the Spanish king to begin operations. He commenced to send artillery, muskets, powder, tents, blankets, clothing, and even cash across the ocean. He worked so rapidly that cannon that he obtained from French arsenals still had the royal fleur-de-lis on them when they reached the Patriots. Two ships loaded by Beaumarchais landed at New Hampshire ports in March, and others followed. In consequence of his efforts and those of Patriot civilians, the American forces who took the field in 1777 were much better equipped than they had been in the past. With the matériel sent by Beaumarchais came French army officers, with the blessing of the French government, among them the young Marquis de Lafayette and the Baron de Kalb. The German Baron von Steuben also came across the ocean, and Polish officers as well, eager to serve against the British. Many of them proved to be useful.

There were other great changes. Acquiring new recruits, the Continental army retained a core of trial-tested officers and men. Moreover, it had acquired a leader who had gained confidence in himself. He might, and did, modestly say that his triumphs at Trenton and Princeton proceeded from good fortune, but he knew that fortune had favored the brave and the bold. His plan for attacking the Hessians was, if desperate, well contrived; that part of it that he had executed—with Continentals rather than militia—had been brilliantly carried through to success. If he had been rash in crossing the Delaware when Cornwallis was coming up in superior force, he had retrieved his error by slipping around Cornwallis, forcing his way through the British at Princeton, and marching to safety at Morristown. Some might think that Washington had not done enough, such as the fault-finding civilian and politician John Adams, who claimed to have read more about the history and art of warfare than any Patriot general except Charles Lee. While

Washington and his men, such as were left to him, rested in the hills of New Jersey, Adams wrote, "Are we to go on forever this way, maintaining vast armies in idleness, and losing completely the fairest opportunity that ever was offered of destroying an enemy completely in our power?" Adams was offended by "the superstitious veneration that is sometimes paid to General Washington." He hoped that Congress would undertake to elect all the higher officers of the army annually. They would thus be reminded that they were responsible to Congress. It seems not to have occurred to him that his scheme would introduce confusion into the army. But other informed civilians, with better judgment, realized that Washington had compensated in large part for the mistakes he had made at New York City, that the dauntless general had acquired valuable experience, and that his equal was not to be found among the Patriot commanders. The sentiments of officers and men who had served under Washington, who had gained intimate acquaintance with him, were far more favorable. They had learned to place complete trust in their chief. They saw him calm and dignified in adversity, intrepid on the battlefield. A feeling very much like worship of Washington had developed and was spreading at his headquarters and through the ranks of the troops under his immediate direction.

Had Washington, ever remarkable for learning from experience, also acquired some understanding of strategy? His flight to Morristown could hardly have been entirely accidental. The stationing of his army at that place was ideal for the campaign of 1777. If Howe marched toward the Delaware and Philadelphia, Washington, adopting the thinking of Charles Lee, proposed to move against the British from the north while other Patriot contingents held them off at the river. If Howe moved northward while the British army in Canada came southward, Washington proposed to go to the Hudson to prevent a junction of the two royal forces.

XIV

The Defeated Victor

*B*_{*y the middle*} of May, 1777, Washington had
nearly seven thousand Continentals with him at Morristown, and
more were on the way to join him. A second Patriot army was
gathering at Ticonderoga to oppose the expected advance of the
British army in Canada. A third and much weaker force of Americans was based at Peekskill in the hope that it could retard a
British movement up the Hudson River. Washington had been cog-
itating regarding the British plan for the campaign about to begin.
In mid-April, having received information through a spy that the
British were building flat-bottomed boats at New York—boats that
could be useful to them for a crossing of the Delaware—he was
inclined to believe that the British commander in chief intended to
move against Philadelphia. And yet—the Hudson River "must
also be an object of very great importance" to the royal forces
"whilst they have an army in Canada and are desirous of a junction
with it."

Accordingly, Washington sent troops to join the redoubtable
Benedict Arnold, who had been assigned by Congress to guard the
Delaware, while he himself moved forward to a strong position at
Middlebrook to impede Howe's advance. The Patriot commander
in chief was soon given additional cause to believe that the Patriot

"capital" would be the prime target of Howe, for the British general not only built boats and a floating bridge but also collected a large force at New Brunswick before the middle of June. It turned out that he had indeed decided to move against Philadelphia, but to approach it by sea. During the spring and early summer a great British armada collected in New York Harbor. It would carry Howe and the bulk of his army up Delaware Bay or Chesapeake Bay toward the Quaker city—to the surprise of Washington and many historians.

Planning for the campaign of 1777 before the battles of Trenton and Princeton, Howe proposed to revert to the British scheme for 1776, to send ten thousand men northward to join the army advancing from Canada. It has been frequently urged that the two forces, with the British fleet dominating the lower Hudson, could have secured control of the Lake Champlain—Hudson waterway, cutting off the Yankees from the remainder of the Patriots; even that the combined British forces could have overrun New England; that they could at least have held the line of the river indefinitely, with disastrous consequences for the Americans. Things were not all that simple. It was doubtful, as Washington's astute young aide-de-camp, Alexander Hamilton, pointed out, that the Yankees could so easily be subjugated, doubtful also that the mere separation of the Yankees from their brethren could be long maintained. Were only the line of the river held, the British lacked strength to act vigorously elsewhere. In a war of endurance would Britain inevitably be the victor? In any event, Howe changed his notions after the defeats of his army in western New Jersey. He was informed by Joseph Galloway and other Philadelphia Tories who had come to New York to join him that the Patriots were few in Pennsylvania, that Loyalists were numerous there. Then he could take the American capital and also recruit his forces in Pennsylvania? That possibility was attractive to the general. His informants did not stress the fact that Loyalists in Pennsylvania were in large degree pacifists—Quakers and members of German peace sects. He decided to use the principal part of his army to approach Philadelphia by land, leaving a garrison of four thousand men at New York City and sending a somewhat smaller force northward "to facilitate the approach of the army from Canada."

Then he altered that scheme. Early in April he decided that he and the main body of his army would move against Philadelphia by sea. He executed that plan, leaving a garrison of 4,700 men at

New York City under Sir Henry Clinton, one of 2,700 at Newport under General Robert Pigot, together with a body of 3,000 Tories at Manhattan. His scheme was emphatically condemned to no avail by Clinton, who was assigned the task of holding New York City and maintaining a "d——d starved deffencive." It is obvious that Howe was not seriously concerned for the safety of the army advancing from Canada. He was commander in chief only in the thirteen colony-states. Guy Carleton was commander in chief in Canada, and the troops under him would not come under the direction of Howe until they approached Albany. A feeble effort to "facilitate" their advance was made. General William Tryon with the Tories raided Danbury, Connecticut, on April 25, and defeated Patriots who gathered to oppose him. Howe's final plan was approved by Lord George Germain in London, although Germain did express a hope that Howe would complete his attack on Philadelphia in time to establish linkage with the Canadian army in the autumn. Howe did not know that he was expected to do even that much in its behalf until August 16, when he was at sea in Chesapeake Bay and completely committed to his Philadelphia enterprise.

The final plan of Howe was all the more difficult for Washington to penetrate, because of activities of the British general in New Jersey. Having time on his hands while transports gathered for his voyage, Howe decided that it would be worthwhile to try to entice Washington into battle under circumstances that would ensure a crushing British victory. Such an event might even have opened the way, after all, for movement against Philadelphia by land. Hence the appearance of Howe at New Brunswick with a large force in mid-June. He was foiled. Washington, with New Jersey militia taking the field, had nine thousand fresh troops. He moved to check the royal army, but carefully clung to strong ground. Howe's men fell back to Amboy. They came forward a second time to try to entrap Washington, but he gave them no opportunity, and they retreated to Staten Island after very little fighting. Washington returned to Morristown.

Watching Howe anxiously from Morristown, Washington concluded on July 1 that his antagonist would soon move up the Hudson "to cooperate with the army from Canada," which was then approaching Ticonderoga. On July 10 Washington accordingly began to shift his troops toward the Hudson. He proposed to join a small force of Patriots gathered at Peekskill under General Putnam and to oppose Howe there. Three weeks later he received credible information that the Howe brothers—they had finally completed arrangements for transporting the bulk of the British army—were moving out to sea. Two days later the Patriot commander learned for certain that the brothers had sailed. Accordingly, he began to shift his troops toward the Delaware. But he was so sure that the British army would go northward that he could not "help casting my eyes continually behind me." On July 31 he learned for certain that a huge British fleet had been at the entrance to Delaware Bay on the preceding day. He hastened to move his troops across the Delaware River. Then the British fleet disappeared, and days passed without word concerning its destination. Where was it going? Back to New York City and up the Hudson? Washington began to turn eastward once more. Reconsidering, he concluded on August 20 that the fleet was sailing southward for an attack upon Charleston. The next day, after a council of war, he decided to march toward the Hudson. Then, at last, on August 22, he learned for sure that the fleet was in Chesapeake Bay and moving northward. Relieved, he marched southward through Philadelphia to defend it.

If the decision of Howe to move against that city by sea was ill-considered, its execution was almost bizarre. A huge fleet of more than 250 vessels, including the warcraft of Admiral Howe and transports carrying at least 15,000 troops, perhaps as many as 19,000, with horses and supplies, spent the last week of July careening down the coast of New Jersey. Arriving at the mouth of Delaware Bay, General Howe was told that the Patriots had erected forts along the Delaware River to bar the passage of the expedition. To avoid an early confrontation at the forts, perhaps also in a crude effort to outflank Washington from the south, he resolved to proceed to Chesapeake Bay and march overland from its northern end. He could thus avoid the forts for the time being, although they must be taken sooner or later in order to open the lower Delaware River to British military traffic. Returning to sea, the fleet encountered unfavorable winds and calms. It did not reach the entrance to Chesapeake Bay until August 14, its absence from sight placing Washington on tenterhooks. He was pleased to learn at last the intention of his adversary. The royal troops did not begin to disembark at the northern end of the bay until August 25. They were weary from the voyage in summer heat, and they had lost the services of many of their horses, which had died from confinement and been thrown overboard. Gaining its land legs and foraging successfully for fresh food, the British army moved steadily toward its objective.

The army under Washington was much smaller than the one with which he had opposed the British at New York, but it was much superior in quality. Well clothed and armed, it pleased Patriot onlookers in the City of Brotherly Love as it advanced to confront Howe. Perhaps sixteen thousand men in all, it now contained many officers and not a few private soldiers who were familiar with battle. Washington had faith in it. Learning that the British Canadian army had captured Ticonderoga early in July, he had even sent a detachment of riflemen under General Daniel Morgan to northern New York to help Patriots there. Although the men wielding those fabled guns could not stand against the smashing fire of muskets and bayonet charges delivered by the British regulars on unimpeded ground, they could be, they proved to be, of very great value in the forests north of Albany. Washington had to depend ultimately upon his musketry and his artillery. He was not unwilling to fight from a good position. He could expect reinforcements of militia, and he could if necessary retreat. He could at least retard British occupation of the American capital. After desultory skirmishing the Patriot commander took post across Howe's path to Philadelphia on the northern side of Brandywine Creek, at a place where that stream was rather deep and not easily traversed. There, on September 11, he was attacked by the British.

Washington had chosen good ground. His left wing, downstream from Chad's Ford, was on high ground above the stream. It was reasonably safe from assault, and it was occupied by militia. He stationed General John Sullivan with Continentals on his right wing, well above the ford. The commander in chief took post with Continentals behind the center at the ford. He expected the British to attack at that place. The activities of redcoats and Hessians under the German officer Baron von Knyphausen confirmed his impression. They moved up and formed as if to storm across the water. They exchanged cannon and musket shots with the Patriots during the first half of the morning. Then they remained almost quiet. Washington waited for them to move, but they stayed in their positions. About nine o'clock a report came to Washington that a large body of the royal troops was marching to the westward. More information to the same effect reached him. Howe had divided his forces, and Knyphausen was unsupported? Washington believed that the British general had made a great mistake. Why not take the offensive against the unsupported Knyphausen, assigning other troops the task of preventing those marching royal troops from returning to help that general? Fortunately, Washington abandoned that scheme. Knyphausen had about five thousand men, with the Brandywine in front of him. It was likely that he could repel the Patriots. What was worse, the Patriots were in danger of entrapment. Starting well before dawn, Howe and Lord Cornwallis, with the main body of the royal army, were about to outflank Washington's right wing. They had moved far enough to the left so that they could easily cross the shallow waters of the two branches of the Brandywine, well beyond the American outposts, and they were swinging about to assail that right wing. Washington was told first that they were en route, then that they were not, and then after two o'clock that they were indeed coming down upon his army from the west. Howe and Cornwallis drove back Continentals under Sullivan, threatening to roll upon the entire American line, even to cut off the retreat of the Patriots. Washington hastily sent reinforcements from his center under Nathanael Greene to support Sullivan. Sullivan's men, after giving a good account of themselves, had fallen into disorder and had begun to flee, but Greene came up very rapidly and checked the royal troops long enough to prevent encirclement of the Patriot army. In the meantime Knyphausen broke through the weakened American center. Then the entire Patriot army fled in confusion as night fell. It was saved from close pursuit by darkness and the weariness of the royal troops who had marched and fought under Howe and Cornwallis. Its losses mounted above a thousand; those of the king's forces were about half as large.

It has often been justly commented that Washington ought to have perceived that Howe was attempting to outflank him in time to thwart the British general's stroke. However, it is by no means certain that the Patriot commander could have held the royal army at the Brandywine. Certainly, once he had perceived that his army was endangered, Washington acted quickly and wisely by weakening his center and strengthening his right wing enough so that his army could fall back without suffering immense losses. His men had put up a good fight, and they soon recovered from the panic of retreat. He was able to report to Congress during the night after the battle, "Notwithstanding the misfortune of the day, I am happy to find the troops in good spirits." Howe had little cause to rejoice. The Patriots could afford their losses—indeed reinforcements were en route to join Washington. Recruits for the royal forces were increasingly hard to secure, for the war remained unpopular in England, and Loyalists were not hastening forward to fight for the Crown. Falling back, Washington still barred the path of Howe into Philadelphia.

Resting and recuperating, Howe and his army did not resume their advance until September 16. Washington did not hesitate to challenge the enemy near the White Horse Tavern. But there was no fighting. A deluge of rain wet the cartridges of both armies, and a marsh between the two prevented bayonet charges. Washington then withdrew to secure fresh ammunition and other supplies. One thousand of his men were now without shoes. On September 19 Major General Charles Grey surprised a Patriot force under Brigadier General Anthony Wayne at Paoli, routed it with a bayonet attack, and inflicted many casualties. Washington found it too risky to try both to defend Philadelphia and to preserve his army. When Howe threatened to move to the westward of the Patriot army, Washington had to shift away from the city to meet the threat. Then Howe marched into the city without opposition, on September 26. There was cheering as his troops filed through the streets of the city, but redcoat engineer Captain John Montresor observed that it did not come from adult male spectators.

Triumphant as the British march into the Quaker city might seem, Howe had little reason to rejoice. Congress, hastily packing up its records, judiciously removed into the interior of Pennsylvania, to York. Washington's army was still very much in being, was, indeed, regaining strength. Moreover, the British general did not as yet have a safe supply line. Passage of the Delaware River was barred by American forts. Those obstacles had to be removed. Howe was compelled to assign part of his army to that task and to assist the fleet under his brother, which was moving up the river. The British did reduce the forts, not without paying a price in casualties, and cleared the stream for their traffic. In the meantime, however, their services were not available at Philadelphia. Besides, a part of the royal army was busy for some time in bringing up supplies left behind by Howe as he advanced from the Chesapeake. In consequence, he had, perhaps, no more than nine thousand men in and near the city. He was, to be sure, not much worried for their or his safety. He established a defensive line at Germantown but did not bother to throw up entrenchments.

There was a time when American historians were fond of describing Washington as an American Fabius, comparing him to the Roman general who prudently and lengthily avoided battle with the great Carthaginian commander Hannibal after Hannibal had virtually destroyed a powerful Roman army in the famous battle of Cannae. Actually, Washington retreated when he was compelled to fall back. He was a fighting man. One could contend, with some show of reason, that he was too fond of trial by battle. But it should be remembered that constant retreat without resistance injures morale. Be those considerations as they may, the Patriot general soon returned to the fray. Hovering to the west of Philadelphia and receiving reinforcements, nearly two thousand Continentals together with five hundred militiamen, he saw an opportunity to strike. He laid a plan for a surprise attack upon the British line at Germantown, with two columns of Continentals moving against it and two bodies of militia hitting at its flanks from the side and rear. It was as good a plan as could be contrived. During the night of October 3 the Patriots began their advance from their encampment at Skippack Creek, about sixteen miles from the British line. The militia moved too tardily to execute their assignments—demonstrating the wisdom of Washington in refraining from using them in the vital center of his army. The Continentals attacked in the early morning of October 4 in semidarkness and fog. A division under John Sullivan, accompanied by Washington, struck at the left side of the British line, drove through its outposts, but then halted briefly to deal with British troops entrenched in the Chew house, in front of the main line. The house should have been masked by a detachment while the main body moved on—the Patriot officers committed a tactical error. Then, resuming his advance, Sullivan—he had to restrain Washington from leading the attack—hit at the royal troops. They had been given time to form in battle array by the roar of guns at the Chew house, and they fought back. In the meantime, Greene and his division lost their way in the fog but assailed the British right, forcing it back and threatening to rout it. Then the tide of battle turned against the Americans. In the fog and smoke of gunfire General Adam Stephen, serving under Greene, attacked Sullivan's men. Howe restored order among his troops. Moreover, Lord Cornwallis came up from Philadelphia with reinforcements, strengthened the British line, and then began a counterattack. The

Americans retreated in some confusion, but Cornwallis merely pursued them at a safe distance.

Washington withdrew. He had lost about a thousand men, the British somewhat more than half as many. But the Continentals had again given a good account of themselves. They had been unfortunate. Adam Stephen, found utterly weary and overcome by alcohol in a barn after the battle, was cashiered for drunkenness. The Continentals were exhilarated by their performance rather than by liquor. Washington was able to inform Congress that the result of the battle was "rather unfortunate than injurious." He had the pleasure of assuring his employers that the troops under Sullivan had "behaved with a degree of gallantry that did them the highest honor." He had not seen much of the men under Greene in action. They deserved the same comment. The Continentals had become formidable. He looked forward with a new confidence. "We must endeavor to deserve better of Providence, and I am persuaded, she will smile upon us," he concluded. His confidence was shared by many of his officers and troops—with Washington leading them. Washington-worship was developing, not only among the Americans who served under him but among the European officers who had come across the ocean to join the Patriots.

The campaign in Pennsylvania had not yet ended. The British cleared the forts along the Delaware by the end of November. Howe was then strong enough to take the field again. However, Washington occupied strong ground at Whitemarsh, not far from Germantown. Inspecting the arrangements of Washington on December 4, Howe decided that he had had enough battle for the year 1777. The British commander withdrew within strong lines at Philadelphia to rest for the winter. Washington went into winter quarters at Valley Forge, about twenty-five miles from the city. His troops were weary; many of them were without shoes. He wished to mount another attack upon his enemies, but it was impossible to make one for several months.

Washington had a special reason for desiring to continue fighting. For he was under fire from Patriots who fancied that he had failed to follow up his victories at Trenton and Princeton—he had not driven Howe back to the cover of his brother's ships. On the other hand, critics pointed out, the record of the Patriot army that dealt with the British forces advancing from Canada was glorious. He would have been glad to add a clear-cut victory to his sterling performance in defeat—to confound those critics.

For some weeks in the summer of 1777 things looked bad for the Patriots in the northern theater of war. As everyone had expected, the royal forces in Canada resumed their march southward. Giving his approval to Howe's Philadelphia venture, Lord George Germain saw no compelling reason to worry about that theater. It did not occur to him, until it was too late to change planning, that it was imprudent to send one army through the Lake Champlain–Hudson River passageway toward New York City while another and more powerful one moved away from that place. After the close of the campaign of 1776 General Burgoyne, after service under Guy Carleton, sailed off to England to recuperate and push for preferment. Germain and Carleton detested each other, and Germain decided to entrust the offensive from Canada to Burgoyne, a middle-aged dandy who had not given proof of military genius. Accordingly, Burgoyne returned to Canada with instructions to lead an army southward to Albany. There, at the close of hostilities, he would place himself and his men under the direction of Howe. Burgoyne assumed command at St. John's on June 13 and moved forward at the head of a substantial army containing as many as eight thousand redcoats and Hessians, with several hundred French Canadians and about four hundred Iroquois warriors —most of the Six Nations had decided to help King George put down his disobedient subjects. Burgoyne expected to meet his stiffest opposition at Fort Ticonderoga, and he took with him plenty of cannon to beat down its defenses. He approached that place on July 2. It was garrisoned by only 3,500 Patriots. It fell to him without a struggle, for they had neglected to fortify a hill from which it could be cannonaded. When British guns began to appear on its summit, the garrison fled, on July 5. Rejoicing over his easy triumph, the British general moved on southward during the remainder of that month and in early August through the rough country of northern New York. In the meantime, Colonel Barry St. Leger advanced from Lake Ontario toward the Mohawk Valley with a mixed force of British regulars, Hessians, French Canadians, and Tories, with about one thousand Iroquois braves. St. Leger was to provide a diversion and to move against Albany from the west while Burgoyne came on from the north.

The news of the fall of Ticonderoga created a near panic in Congress. There must be grave fault in the commander of the northern army, General Philip Schuyler, the delegates felt. He was not a vigorous man. But he was doing his best, and the Patriots in his area were beginning to rally. An aristocrat and a New Yorker, he was much disliked by the New Englanders. Their delegates in Congress liked Horatio Gates, and Gates was sent forward to replace Schuyler. Before he could assume command, the tide of battle turned against the British. In August, New England troops routed contingents of 800 and 650 royal troops in the battle of Bennington. Shortly afterward, beaten back at Fort Schuyler by a doughty garrison and threatened with attack by a relieving force led by Benedict Arnold, St. Leger retreated toward Lake Ontario. If Burgoyne needed help to reach Albany, it must come from New York City.

Burgoyne did indeed need help. The army under Gates grew. Morgan's riflemen were a valuable addition, and New England militia took the field in large numbers. Gates threw up entrenchments at Bemis Heights and barred the advance of Burgoyne down the west bank of the Hudson. Gates had with him some seven thousand men, chiefly Continentals. On September 19 Burgoyne tried to turn the left flank of the Patriots in wooded country but was turned back at Freeman's Farm by Morgan's riflemen and other Patriot contingents. The royal losses were heavy. The riflemen were very effective in the forest, and they chose officers as special targets. Burgoyne did not move again for more than two weeks. He hoped that Gates would attack, for he was confident that he could repel American assaults. Gates cautiously and rightly concluded that time was on his side, and remained quiet. The Indian allies of the royal army vanished. Burgoyne hoped that Sir Henry Clinton would come to his assistance. He declined to retreat while he could still save a part of his army. On October 7 he tried again to push back the Patriot left wing but was driven back a second time with very heavy losses. His situation became increasingly desperate. New England militia under General Benjamin Lincoln swarmed to the rear of the British army. It was virtually surrounded by Patriots, who outnumbered it three to one. Clinton did not appear. Receiving reinforcements, he did try to make a diversion to help his fellow general. He moved up the Hudson with three thousand men early in October and broke through feeble Patriot defenses at Peekskill. He sent Major General John Vaughan with two thousand men farther up the river on October 13. Vaughan was stopped, by shallow water, he said, well below Albany, two days later. Burgoyne would receive no help from the south. On October 17 he capitulated to Gates in a convention signed at Saratoga. All of his remaining troops laid down their arms, with the stipulation that the royal troops were to go to England and to take no further part in the war in North America, a provision accepted by Gates to make sure of his triumph. He might have demanded a complete surrender, but he feared that insistence upon it might cause a delay that would give time for Clinton's men to come up from the south.

In the upshot, Burgoyne might just as well have surrendered. He and his army marched toward Boston to take ship. Howe planned to break the agreement. He proposed to claim that he had been cheated in exchanges of prisoners, to let the beaten Germans return to Europe, but to transport the redcoats to New York for further service. Washington and Congress also sought reasons, or excuses, to set aside the stipulation. What would be the gain if Burgoyne's men assumed duties in Britain, thus freeing troops there for duty in North America? Congress managed to discover that Burgoyne had violated the agreement in minor matters and sent his army off to prison camps.

The stunning triumph of Patriot arms signalized by the convention was not the work of a brilliant commander. Many officers had contributed to it. Colonels Peter Gansevoort and Marinus Willett had stoutly defended old Fort Stanwix; General John Stark had performed splendidly in the battle of Bennington; the Polish soldier Thaddeus Kosciuszko had devised the entrenchments at Bemis Heights that checked the advance of Burgoyne; Benedict Arnold had fought very bravely at Freeman's Farm; Daniel Morgan, as usual, had done his full duty; and General Benjamin Lincoln had made good use of the Yankee militia. Even Philip Schuyler had deserved some credit. He had laid groundwork for Burgoyne's defeat. Remaining on the defensive until the British army had exhausted itself, Gates had been no more than properly cautious. Even so, as commander in chief of the American forces in this campaign, he became the victor of Saratoga. He was older than Washington; suffering from diarrhea throughout the war, he was not physically vigorous; he was not intellectually gifted. But his name had acquired luster.

It was inevitable that the defeats of the army under Washington and the victories of the troops under Gates should be compared. The fervent admiration given to Washington by the politicians in Congress who had striven for his appointment as commander in chief had waned. He had been supported by the radicals in that body, the Adamses, other New England delegates, and Richard Henry Lee. Devout republicans, they were uneasy as the campaign of 1777 closed, because he had become the idol of most of his officers and men. Wrote John Adams to his wife Abigail, "Congress will appoint a thanksgiving; and one cause of it ought to be that the glory of turning the tide of arms is not immediately due to the commander-in-chief nor to southern troops. If it had been, idolatry and adulation would have been unbounded, so excessive as to endanger our liberties, for what I know. Now, we can allow a certain citizen to be wise, virtuous, and good, without thinking him a deity or a savior." A suspicion was developing that Washington might be induced to seek power as a dictator. He had offended men in Congress by his constant and only too well justified pleas for men and supplies. Might he be persuaded to turn against his much-tried employers, doing the best they could with limited powers and resources? Other civilians, notoriously Dr. Benjamin Rush, talked and wrote against the Virginian. Rush fancied that the commander in chief should be chosen annually, like Roman consuls, that the Patriots should put their trust in militia rather than a regular army that might become the instrument of a would-be tyrant. It was contended that Washington played favorites, that Henry Knox and Nathanael Greene were his pets—he did indeed rely upon those able generals.

Some army officers added their criticisms of the commander in chief, among them the Baron de Kalb and General Thomas Conway, two of the many French officers who had joined the American forces. They had crossed the ocean with the young Marquis de Lafayette. A brave Irishman by ancestry, Conway ventured in a letter to Gates to assert that Washington was incompetent. Learning of the contents of the letter, Washington became angry and let Conway know that he resented the censure. Informed that Gates had also indulged in the spreading caviling, Washington also sternly challenged Gates to explain and defend his behavior. Gates was embarrassed. Washington was defended by most of his officers. The custom of dueling, hitherto not well established in America, had been strengthened by the war. One of Washington's aides-de-camp, young Colonel John Laurens, eventually came forward as his champion in a duel with Conway. The French officer was gravely wounded and was expected to die, but recovered and returned to France. He was a gentleman. Before he departed, he wrote a letter of apology to Washington, "the great and good man." It has been asserted that there was a "Conway Cabal" to secure the removal of Washington and replace him with Gates. Conway was not the center of a conspiracy against the commander in chief. Indeed, there was no organized effort to set aside Washington. No one in Congress ventured to condemn him publicly. The many prudent members of that body, including its president, Henry Laurens, properly esteemed the sterling performance of the Virginian. They refused to believe that he would turn against the emerging American republic. They saw that he was a man of honor. In any event, there was no one obviously qualified to succeed him. Gates? He might be a good man. He was clearly not a great man.

The censure heaped upon Washington was all the more galling because it continued into the winter—the winter that he spent at Valley Forge trying to keep his army from disappearing. The royal forces, with their supply line open and protected by the fleet under Admiral Howe, spent the winter as comfortably as might be in Philadelphia. They were well housed, and they did not lack food. Many farmers were pleased to sell them firewood, cattle, and grain for good sterling money; other farmers were compelled against their will to deal with the British. It was otherwise with the men at Valley Forge. They quite quickly threw up huts with fireplaces to shelter them against the cold—the Patriots were always efficient in construction. However, they could not manufacture clothing, and they shivered from the cold. Their troubles were compounded by a collapse of the Patriot supply department. Farmers were reluctant to exchange the solid results of their husbandry for paper money issued by Congress that had begun to depreciate rapidly. Transport from distant sources was difficult. Moreover, the region about Valley Forge had been denuded of foodstuffs by foragers of both armies, and the supply department, headed by Thomas Mifflin, failed to compel farmers to give up provisions. Early in the winter Washington's men were briefly almost without food for a few days. In February, 1778, they suffered even more from lack of nourishment, despite the efforts of foraging parties that Washington sent out to commandeer provisions. Desertion by disheartened troops became common. The situation did not improve until Washington arranged for Nathanael Greene to take over the business of securing supplies. The able and industrious Greene executed his tasks with zeal, and the army began to revive.

A reminiscence has it that in the worst part of that winter a troubled Washington was seen upon his knees in snow, praying for divine help. Since the general, as befitted his station, lived in a good stone house, and since he was a gentleman not given to display, it may be concluded that he beseeched the assistance of the Almighty, if he did, in the privacy of his room. It has never been expected of a commander that he should suffer all the woes of his men. There is no evidence that Washington went hungry. Nor did he lack female companionship, for Martha, as usual, came to spend the winter with him. Of course, he welcomed the coming of spring and summer, the more so because the achievements of the two Patriot armies had induced France to enter the war as an ally of America.

XV

The General in a New War

$O_{ccupying\ Philadelphia\ during}$ the winter of
Valley Forge while the Patriots suffered from cold and lack of food,
the British were as gay as they might be. General Howe had his
wine and his mistress, and he gambled freely. His example with
respect to drinking and gaming was followed by several of his
young officers. But the British commander in chief was not happy.
He had not lost a battle, but what had he gained? Possession of a
city that was not vital to the Patriots. The many Loyalists of whom
he had been told by Joseph Galloway turned out to be few, at least
insofar as recruits for his army were concerned. About three hundred Tories enlisted in British service. There was truth in the
bright comment that Benjamin Franklin made in Paris concerning
the capture of Philadelphia. Franklin asserted that Philadelphia
had taken Howe. The army under Washington had not been destroyed. Moreover, the British general knew that he would be
blamed for the downfall of Burgoyne. Lord George Germain
would surely seek to place the burden for the disaster that had
befallen Burgoyne upon that unfortunate officer and Howe. Reporting to London, Howe claimed credit for his victories and asserted that he would have accomplished more had he received sufficient help from England. He would accept no responsibility for

the defeat of Burgoyne. He made it clear that either he or Germain must leave office.

While Howe waited for a decision, the army at Valley Forge revived, just as that of General Robert E. Lee afterward did every spring in the Civil War, until it succumbed to overwhelming force. Continentals on official and semiofficial leave returned to duty as spring approached and joined their comrades who had persevered at the Forge. Supplies of food and clothing and new recruits made their appearance. The American troops, most of them not clad in bright uniforms but in hunting shirts and pants, as they had been almost from the beginning of the war, were not handsomely dressed. But they had been sorely tried, and they had gained both experience and confidence in themselves. They were no longer easy prey to panic. They placed trust in their commander. They had profited somewhat from the efforts of the Baron von Steuben, the German officer who had been unemployed in Europe and had come across the Atlantic in an effort to improve his fortunes. Steuben posed as a former lieutenant general in the army of Frederick the Great of Prussia, a rank far above that which he had actually held. His claim to be a "von," to be of aristocratic birth, was not too well founded; his title of baron had not been conferred by a monarch and was dubious indeed. But Steuben was a good drill-master, and he taught squads of new and old Continentals how to move in German unison. The baron had another virtue for Washington. Unlike several of the European officers who had crossed the ocean to join the Patriots, he was loyal to the commander in chief.

Couriers who entered the camp in the spring brought splendid news that caused rejoicing. The lack of achievement by Howe and the downfall of Burgoyne had stunned Lord North, Lord George Germain, their colleagues, Parliament, and the British public. It became obvious that it would be difficult to put down the rebellion in America. What was worse, it became clear that France, and perhaps Spain, would take advantage of the distress of Britain and would seek revenge for defeat in the Seven Years' War. In consequence, George III and the North ministry asked for and secured the repeal of all the taxes and punitive laws that had stimulated the rebellion. Moreover, they sent across the ocean a commission headed by the Earl of Carlisle with power to offer a complete amnesty to the Patriots and as much freedom within the British empire as was necessary to persuade them to resume their allegiance to the Crown. Congress rejected the overture before the British emissaries appeared in Delaware Bay. Terms that would have been gladly accepted in 1775 were not attractive after three years of war—and was Britain to be trusted to keep her word after the Patriots had laid down their weapons? Besides, might they not suffer at the hands of the Loyalists, abused and eager for revenge?

Washington insisted that America must, if possible, become independent. Any arrangement whereby the Patriots returned to the empire would bring a "peace of war," a condition in which there would be constant quarreling between America and England. "The injuries we have received from the British nation," he wrote, "were so unprovoked, and have been so great and so many, that they can never be forgotten." Moreover, he declared, for the Americans to accept less than an absolute separation, after solemnly proclaiming their absolute independence, was to display weakness and dishonor that would be perceived by the whole world. If America must yield to force, she must, but he did not despair of the outcome of the struggle. A few of the Patriots were disposed to listen to the blandishments of the British commission, but very few dared to say that such was their opinion. One of the British spokesmen, George Johnstone, vainly tried bribery as a method to win the consent of Congress. The delegates were determined to accept nothing less than independence. They refused to negotiate with the Carlisle people without recognition of American freedom or complete withdrawal of the royal forces from the thirteen states. The commissioners could meet neither of those demands, and at length returned unhappily to London. Congress was the more determined to resist British blandishments, however sincere, because the deputies knew that France was about to enter the war as an ally of America.

The reports that caused dismay in London at the beginning of the winter of 1777 were gladly received in Paris. Three American commissioners sent across the ocean by Congress, Benjamin Franklin, Silas Deane, and Arthur Lee, had been trying for many months to stir France to action beyond the secret aid supplied through Beaumarchais. The operations of Beaumarchais under the guise of Rodrigue Hortalez had become sporadic because of British complaints. (Beaumarchais and his heirs afterward petitioned the United States for repayment of sums he had personally forwarded. He was not a rich man, and he could not have lent very much. His heirs received the handsome sum of 800,000 francs from Congress in 1836 to quiet them, but a Madame Beaumarchais was still claiming, two centuries after the Revolution, that the family had not been repaid.) Franklin had performed superbly as a propagandist. He had appealed especially to the numerous French disciples of Jean Jacques Rousseau who believed that man in a state of nature was virtuous and happy. Rousseau had followers even at the court of Versailles. Franklin was pleased to let it be known that the Americans were not far from a state of nature, were undefiled by the wickedness of a sophisticated European civilization. The Patriots became popular in Paris, and not merely because they were striking at detested Britain. But King Louis XVI and his ministers, feeling the weight of public sentiment, had other and more potent reasons for taking part in the struggle. There was a strong argument for remaining neutral. It was advanced by the Baron de Turgot, the minister of finance. The French government was deeply in debt. However, the French navy and army had been renovated after the close of the Seven Years' War, and they were ready for action. So long as it seemed that Britain would almost surely be able to suppress the American rebellion, the king and the majority of his advisers refused to follow the lead of the Comte de Vergennes, who wanted war. Eager as they were to hit at a Britain in distress, they wished to avoid a conflict with their ancient enemy at the very time when the Patriot cause seemed to be collapsing. Then came the news that Washington and his army had performed very well and had survived the attacks of Howe without serious damage. A letter from the Baron de Kalb came, with a prediction that the Patriots would be able to drive the royal troops back into the sea. There followed quickly authentic news that Burgoyne had laid down his arms at Saratoga. Vergennes now had his way. It seemed that an opportunity had come to bring Britain to her knees, to destroy her empire, and to secure much of the maritime trade upon which her power was apparently based. On December 6, 1777, France entered into two treaties with the American commissioners. In one that was to be published France recognized American independence; in a secret document, based upon the certainty that Britain would respond by declaring war upon France, the parties agreed that they would continue the struggle until that independence had been achieved.

The glad tidings for the Patriots were carried across the Atlantic by Simeon Deane, brother of Silas Deane, in a French frigate. He reached York on May 2, and Congress swiftly and unanimously ratified the treaties. Washington heard the news that France had recognized American independence from Simeon Deane on May 1 with "infinite pleasure." Six days later he and his army joyfully celebrated the occasion with a grand review, coupled with music by a band and toasts to victory and the new ally. The troops hurrahed, and the general responded in kind.

Soon after receipt of the glad news Charles Lee returned to active service with the Patriots. He was released early in April on parole by the British while negotiations for his exchange were still in progress. As a prisoner Lee had at first been threatened with death, although he was able to demonstrate that he had resigned his commission in the British army before joining the Patriots. Congress had protected him, against the wishes of Washington, by declaring that execution of Lee would be followed by that of a batch of Hessian officers captured at Trenton. Washington had questioned the wisdom of reprisals, not without reason, but he had not been willing to go to extremes to assure the safety of Lee, who had outshone him in strategy and had exhibited a tendency to act independently of the commander in chief. But if Washington was less than delighted by the release of Lee—he no longer harbored doubt regarding his own competence—he did not display any sign of displeasure. Lee came forth from Philadelphia on April 5. Washington and several of his officers rode out four miles from camp to welcome him. Lee was escorted to headquarters through two lines of troops with military music and entertained by Washington at dinner. He spent the night in a chamber behind that of Mrs. Washington's sitting room. Elias Boudinot, a commissary of prisoners who knew Lee and did not like him, afterward wrote in his journal that Lee brought with him from Philadelphia "a miserable dirty hussy," took her "into his room by a back door," and had the pleasure of her company during the night. In support of the relation by Boudinot is the fact that the bachelor Lee, though often remarkable in behavior, has not, unlike Lord George Germain and the Baron von Steuben, been endowed by gossip with homosexual tendencies.

But had Lee become a traitor during his long captivity? Early in his imprisonment, first at New Brunswick, then at New York, he tried to arrange a negotiation between the Howe brothers and Congress. Also, late in March, 1777, he offered to the British a plan for the approaching campaign that called for sending an expedition to Chesapeake Bay and for an attempt to cut communications between the Patriots in the region of the Susquehanna River. The British distrusted him and his advice, which was secret so far as the world at large was concerned for more than seventy years after his death. If that advice was intended to help the British, he could have offered an excuse for his conduct in the fact that Congress had not yet determined to protect him by threatening reprisal. Apparently he deliberately offered bad military counsel that confirmed the determination of Howe to approach Philadelphia from the south. For, excessively convinced of his own powers and importance, Lee developed a scheme for an Anglo-American accommodation that he presented early in 1778 through British General James Robertson to William Howe. Fancying himself a statesman, he declared that continuation of the war would be financially ruinous to Britain, even if she triumphed. On the other hand, an independent America would suffer from "confusion, anarchy and civil wars." Britain ought to withdraw her forces and offer the Americans complete freedom within the empire except for such channeling of their maritime trade as they were willing to accept. Lee was quite certain that the scheme would not work, but he was willing as a "good man" to risk his own popularity with the Americans by presenting it to Congress. The stipulation that the British withdraw their forces made it impossible for Howe to act upon the plan, but the British general saw a chance to wean Lee away from the Patriots. He conferred amicably with Lee the night before Lee left Philadelphia, and supplied him with wine to smooth his journey to Valley Forge. Lee was not much impressed. He saw Howe as a fine soldier but a lazy and incompetent commander who worshiped "every scepter'd calf, hog, or ass," who "shut his eyes, fought his battles, had his little whore," and then repeated that process. After Lee resumed active service with the Patriots, Sir Henry Clinton, succeeding Howe, tried, again through General Robertson, to win over Lee. But a letter for that purpose from Robertson to Lee apparently failed to reach him. There is some evidence in the papers of Clinton that Philip Schuyler after Saratoga was disposed to seek an accommodation with the British, but none that Schuyler did anything to help them obtain it.

Journeying from Valley Forge to a plantation he had bought in Virginia while negotiations for his final release continued, Lee stopped at York and conferred with Henry Laurens. Unaware that the Patriot army had greatly improved and that France was about to enter the war, he expected that the British army in Philadelphia would soon resume the offensive, toward the Susquehanna. So, en route, he told Henry Laurens and later, Washington. He also expressed the opinion that the Patriots could not withstand the British infantry, an estimate that was sound enough in the autumn of 1776 but that was at least questionable in the spring of 1778. Nor had he learned to set a high value upon Washington. He informed Laurens, "I am well and hope always shall be with General Washington—and to speak again vainly I am perswaded (considering how he is surrounded) that he cannot do without me"—self-praise and disparagement of Nathanael Greene and Henry Knox, frequently and unjustly attacked by critics of the commander in chief as his incompetent pets. Lee wished to undertake reformation of the American army. Returning to York from Virginia, he also asked Congress to promote him to lieutenant general, since many Patriot officers had received higher rank during his imprisonment. Weary from constant appeals for preferment from officers both American and foreign, Congress refused his request. Furthermore, he boldly ventured to hint to Laurens that the Patriots would do well not to insist upon complete separation from Britain.

Washington continued to be gracious to Lee. Receiving a copy of the plan of the Englishman for a new structure of the army, the commander in chief responded facetiously. He hoped that Lee would be more comfortable riding his hobby of army reform than he was when he rode away from Valley Forge on an old nag. At length the negotiations ended, and Lee was officially exchanged for British Major General Richard Prescott, who had been captured by the Patriots in Rhode Island. Sending the news to Lee, Washington wrote to him, "I shall most cordially, and sincerely, congratulate you on your restoration to your country." The commander in chief said that he was "rejoicing" because of the imminent return of his subordinate and urged him to come to Valley Forge as soon as possible.

"To the great joy of the army," Lee rejoined the Continentals on May 21 together with Benedict Arnold, who had recuperated from hardship and injuries. Almost at once Lee recklessly indicated that he was less than utterly devoted to independence. Being required to take an oath of allegiance to the United States, he hesitated briefly, indicating that he might be willing to acknowledge George IV, though not George III, as his prince. So Lafayette, who subscribed to the oath at the same time, afterward recalled. Onlookers were inclined to believe that Lee was merely making a witty remark.

Moreover, Lee was soon criticizing the management of Washington in the campaign of 1777. The commander in chief, acknowledging Lee's proposals for rearranging the army, sent him a mild rebuke. Washington would always be "happy in a free communication of your sentiments upon any important subject relative to the service, and only beg that they may come directly to myself. The custom, which many officers have, of speaking freely of things and reprobating measures, which upon investigation may be found to be unavoidable, is never productive of good, but often of mischievous consequences." Lee would do well not to commit the mistake that Thomas Conway had made. Washington was casting a questioning eye upon his aggressive and self-confident subordinate.

The campaign of 1778 had already opened when Lee joined the army. Washington was eager to please Lafayette, recently made a major general at the ripe age of nineteen. The marquis was brave, zealous, and eager to make a military name for himself. He was important because his family connections in France were influential. He had forthrightly supported the commander in chief against Washington's critics, and he was unhappy that a scheme to send him at the head of an army into Canada had collapsed because of lack of men and means. To placate Lafayette, Washington sent him toward Philadelphia with 2,200 men to gain information regarding the intentions of the British and to deal with their scouting parties, a strange assignment for such a large force. The British, directed by Howe and Henry Clinton, hastily moved out of the city in great force to deal with the impudent Patriots. Almost surrounded at Barren Hill, on May 20, Lafayette barely managed to escape entrapment and return to Valley Forge.

There was no counterthrust on the part of the British. General Howe was going home, for George III and his cabinet preferred to keep the services of Lord George Germain rather than those of Howe. The general, with his brother, was honored by elaborate festivities, including a tournament, the so-called Mischianza, arranged by young British officers who proclaimed that the laurels he had won in America were immortal. He sailed for England on May 21. There he would have difficulty defending his record as a commander in chief. Indeed, he never again held a major field appointment. He took with him one curious relic from the war, an intercepted letter about false teeth from Washington to his dentist that remained in the possession of the Howe family until the twentieth century. Howe ought to have forwarded the letter, ought to have displayed sympathy for Washington's dental distress, since the British general was himself troubled by the absence of incisors, bicuspids, and molars.

Inheriting the powers of Howe, Clinton also received an awkward legacy. He would not march out of Philadelphia in an attempt to crush the army under Washington. Foreseeing that the approaching entrance of France into the war posed a danger that France might send a fleet and troops to assist the Patriots, his superiors had ordered him to evacuate Philadelphia and to concentrate at New York, if necessary to retreat even to Halifax, sending part of his troops southward for a possible thrust against the French islands in the West Indies. Clinton and his troops were indeed in peril, for a powerful French fleet with troops aboard under Admiral d'Estaing sailed to Delaware Bay. Setting forth from the Mediterranean before the outbreak of hostilities between France and Britain, the squadron under d'Estaing, much stronger than that of Admiral Howe, caused alarm in London. Until the French admiral was well beyond Gibraltar, there was fear in London that he might combine with a second French naval force at Brest, even with a Spanish one, to attack the British fleet protecting against an invasion across the Channel. The British army at home, weakened because so much of it had been sent to America, was not prepared to throw back such an invasion. George III and his advisers did not dare send warships across the ocean to support Admiral Howe until d'Estaing was well on his way across the Atlantic. Moreover, when they were sent out, under Admiral Lord Byron, they were delayed by storm. It became possible that the army under Clinton and the fleet under Admiral Howe would be caught between the army of Washington and the fleet of d'Estaing. The trap was not sprung. Lord Howe lacked shipping to carry away the bulk of the British army, but he sailed away from the Delaware with Tories, some Hessians, and military stores a week before d'Estaing made his appearance at the mouth of Delaware Bay. In the meantime, perforce, Clinton, with most of the British army, evacuated Philadelphia, on June 18, and began to march across New Jersey. Howe reached New York without incident; Clinton's march was not unmolested.

Rejoicing over the withdrawal of the British, Washington and his army, revived and strengthened, began to follow Clinton. The Patriot general now had more men, including militia, than Clinton, about thirteen thousand to eleven thousand. The British army, encumbered by baggage, moved slowly. Several hundred Hessians seized the opportunity to desert. A question was posed for Washington. He held a council of war. Should he attack the retreating royalists in great force or strike a partial blow? The majority of his officers advised him to do neither. He called a second council of war, and again, the majority of his officers expressed themselves against opening either a general onslaught or a partial one that might become a full-scale battle. The majority were led by Charles Lee, who contended that it would be unwise to risk an action. He pointed out that the evacuation of Philadelphia was a great triumph for the Patriots, that its rich benefits might be lost by a defeat. He argued that the Continentals were still inferior to the British infantry, that it would be desirable to build a "golden bridge" for the British retreat to New York. General Anthony Wayne, a fighting man, clamored for an all-out attack. Washington was torn between the two views. He, too, was a fighting man. He had not won a victory over a British army. Was there not a chance to strike a decisive blow? In the end, he decided to avoid a general engagement but to make a partial thrust against the British. After choosing Lafayette to make it, he finally instructed Lee to assume leadership of it, because Lee as his senior subordinate was entitled to the honor.

Resting near Monmouth courthouse at Freehold during the night of June 27, the British army started to resume its march the following morning. Lee and his contingent, something like 4,000 men in all, moved forward about eight o'clock and opened an attack upon the royal rear guard of 1,500 to 2,000 infantry. Lee hoped to overwhelm that rear guard, but Clinton soon turned about with some 4,000 troops to deal with the advancing Patriots. The British general was quite willing to engage. Afterward he said that he "fought on velvet" that day. Some of the outnumbered Patriots began to fall back. Concerned lest his force be pinned down against one of three ravines in his rear, Lee at length retreated with most of his men across the gullies and took post on strong ground to await attack by Clinton. There Washington, coming up to support his subordinate, found Lee and peremptorily demanded to know what Lee was doing. The two men exchanged sharp words. Washington assumed command and brought up reinforcements, then instructed Lee to resume duty under his general direction. Again there was an exchange of vigorous language. Then, sending Lee away to deal with some retreating Patriots,

Washington personally took charge of the defense against the on-coming British. Under his leadership the Continentals stiffened and withstood two charges by British infantry and cavalry. Both sides were suffering from the extreme heat. Clinton then fell back, and Washington prepared to take the offensive, but the approach of darkness put an end to the fighting. During the ensuing night Clinton resumed his retreat to New York. It was impossible for Washington to intercept and bring the British into action again before they reached their base at New York.

The action of Monmouth was a drawn battle, both armies suffering about three hundred casualties, caused in part by heat prostration, but its principal benefit went, of course, to the British. However, the Continentals had the satisfaction of holding their ground against the royal troops in the later stages of the struggle. They had won a victory of morale.

Another important result of the battle was the separation of Charles Lee from the American army. Immediately after its close some of the Patriot officers condemned his behavior, probably without full justice—afterward Clinton praised the conduct of Lee in the struggle. The Patriots were disappointed because they had not achieved more; someone must be at fault. Angry and resenting censure by Washington on the battlefield, Lee haughtily demanded an opportunity to justify himself in letters to Washington that were less than polite. Washington undertook to deal sternly with the Englishman. He ordered the arrest of Lee and brought him before a court-martial, charging him with disobedience of orders, committing an unnecessary and disgraceful retreat, and displaying disrespect for the commander in chief. Lee had indeed addressed Washington in less than utterly respectful language. But he had not disobeyed orders, and he was able to assert cogently that his retreat was necessary. He was so confident of acquittal that he did not bother to bring forward as a witness a courier who could prove beyond doubt that Lee had adhered strictly to the instructions of Washington. The court-martial—its members appointed by the commander in chief—softened the charges somewhat, but found Lee guilty on all three counts and ruled that he ought to be deprived of command for a period of one year. Was it suspected that he had been less than wholly devoted to the American cause, that he had been less than zealous in consequence?

The verdict had to be approved by Congress, once more housed in Philadelphia. Lee expected that the delegates would set aside the judgment of the military court. He quipped sarcastically that, regardless of the action taken by Congress, he would "retire to Virginia, and learn to hoe tobacco, which I find is the best school to form a consummate general." The lawmakers hesitated for many weeks. On the record Lee had not seriously misbehaved, a fact indicated by the relatively light penalty imposed by the court-martial. Challenged by Lee, Washington, beset by many troubles, had responded harshly, as he had to criticism by Dinwiddie in his youth, as he had to gossip about him by Conway and Gates. Congress still contained delegates who were concerned lest Washington become too powerful. He had enemies in Philadelphia. It was whispered about in the city that he was guilty of "immorality of life" that was "very secret" and "difficult to detect." But whatever might be said about the planning of Washington before Monmouth, he had given another sterling performance in battle. He had become virtually irreplaceable, and it was necessary to support him against Lee. At length, by a vote of six states to two, Congress confirmed the verdict of the court-martial. After retiring to Virginia, where he campaigned in print against Washington instead of hoeing tobacco, Lee informed Congress that he would not return to service unless the stigma placed upon him was removed. Congress refused to reverse itself and dismissed him from the American army.

There were other troubles for the embittered Englishman. He was challenged to a duel by John Laurens, who again came forward as a champion of the commander in chief. Lee was wounded by a pistol shot. He was also challenged by Anthony Wayne and Steuben but declined to admit that they had reason to shoot at him. He savagely and satirically assailed Washington in newspapers, without much effect. Embittered and restless, he framed a scheme for a utopia of soldiers to be set up in the Mississippi Valley. He consorted with Tories and neutrals as well as Patriots in his last years, and he died obscurely in Philadelphia in 1782. It has often been charitably suggested in behalf of Lee that he became half-mad after Monmouth, even that he was gravely unbalanced before that battle. He was most useful to the Patriots in the early part of the War of Independence. It is certain that he was an arrogant troublemaker and that Washington and the American army were well rid of him. He remained witty to the end. He requested in his will that he should not be buried "in any church, or churchyard, or within a mile of any Presbyterian or Anabaptist meeting-house; for since I have resided in this country, I have kept so much bad company when living, that I do not chuse to continue it when dead."

Were the British safe in their base at New York? Washington, following Clinton, took post at Haverstraw, and Admiral d'Estaing, following Admiral Howe, stationed his fleet off the entrance to New York harbor. Washington saw a splendid opportunity to strike a decisive blow, one that might even assure American independence. The French admiral commanded twelve ships of the line, the big battle wagons of the time, together with four frigates and four thousand troops. Lord Howe had a much smaller fleet. Washington proposed a joint attack upon the British, with d'Estaing forcing his way into the harbor and the American and French troops assailing the royal army from the land. They were outnumbered by well-entrenched redcoats, Hessians, and Loyalist contingents, but Washington could call upon New England militia to help put the finishing touches upon the surrounded British. D'Estaing, a very brave man, an army officer by experience, agreed to the plan. But the royal troops were not put to the test. To deal with the British fleet d'Estaing had to cross a sandbar at the head of New York Bay and to force his way on a rising tide up the Narrows above the sandbar. Lord Howe placed his ships along the shores of the Narrows in such fashion that each of them could fire two broadsides as the French ships came alongside. In effect, he turned his fleet into land batteries, which always had an advantage over moving warships and had a special one over warships carried forward by tide. Howe and Clinton awaited the result with confidence. Howe, a dauntless and skillful admiral, had fought the French successfully before, and he would defeat them again in the wars of the French Revolution. It turned out that the largest French vessel could not get over the sandbar. Without its guns, it would have been risky indeed for d'Estaing to try to force his way through the Narrows. In consequence, Washington and d'Estaing had to abandon their scheme, which would very likely have ended in failure. The French fleet sailed off to the coast of Rhode Island to join Patriot forces there under General John Sullivan in an attempt to force the surrender of the British garrison at Newport.

Capture of Newport, with its garrison of three thousand men under General Robert Pigot, would have been a nice consolation prize. Again the French and the Americans encountered disappointment. Before d'Estaing and Sullivan could mount a powerful

attack, Lord Howe, having at length received reinforcements from
Europe, came to the rescue of Pigot. D'Estaing had to deal with
Howe. Having received reinforcements from England, Howe did
not hesitate to challenge the French, although his fleet was still
inferior. The two admirals jockeyed for position for two days off
Rhode Island and were then separated by a storm. In duels between three smaller British ships and three larger French ones, the
British had a slight advantage. D'Estaing sailed away to Boston to
refit, troops came from New York to join Pigot, and Sullivan was
compelled to retreat.

Washington urged d'Estaing to persevere in joint operations, but
the French admiral had duties that called him away, to the West
Indies. He had not worked well with Sullivan, and a French officer
had been killed in a fracas at Boston. There were recriminations
between the French and the Patriots, who had expected much from
joint operations but had been thrice thwarted. Washington did
what he could to soothe injured feelings. He could do no more. He
could only hover about New York during the remainder of 1778
and hope that another year would bring better fortune. He scattered his army in cantonments outside the city for the approaching
winter and set up headquarters at Middlebrook. Happily that winter was mild, for his army was now confronted by severe inflation
and a much-depreciated currency as well as by cold and by recurrent shortages of food. The economic dislocation caused by the war
was raising prices in sound British, French, and Spanish curren-
cies. Besides, the Continental paper money in which the army was
usually paid, being supported only by faith in Congress and the
American cause, was buying less and less each month. A month's
pay of a private soldier might enable him to buy a bottle of rum,
some tobacco, and another small purchase or two. As yet, the
troops did no more than grumble. They were better off in one way
than they had been, for many of them, though without shoes, were
able to put on uniforms shipped from France.

XVI

Washington in Stalemate

W*ashington seldom left* his army during more than six years. He went to Philadelphia in December, 1778, to confer with Congress. It was now almost universally assumed that he could not be replaced, and he was gladly welcomed. Martha joined him there, and the Washingtons were entertained with dinners and dances amidst general gaiety during the holiday season. Was not all going well for the Patriots, despite the fact that the entrance of France into the war had as yet brought no remarkable benefit to them beyond regaining Philadelphia? Surely, French intervention virtually assured American independence. Washington must have had qualms about those pleasures, for he knew that many more trials lay ahead. There were merchants in the city who were prospering, even becoming rich. Speculators and monopolizers among the Patriots generally were profiting while inflation took a heavy toll among his troops. The general was beginning to wonder whether the ravages of inflation might not be more injurious to the American cause than its armed enemies.

The gaiety of society did not extend to political and military business. Congress voted once more to maintain a large army. To stem the sufferings of the troops and their families from high prices and depreciating currency the delegates offered a new bonus to the troops. It was not large enough to satisfy grumbling private soldiers. Moreover, the delegates actually increased discontent in the army, for they refused a request from officers for more generous half-pay. The officers, less injured by inflation, had been promised half-pay for seven years after the close of the war. They were seeking half-pay for life. Congress considered their request to be excessive and refused their demand.

Nor was it possible for Washington and Congress to devise an offensive for the year 1779 that held promise of putting a successful end to the war. If only New York could be taken—but there was no hope of dislodging the British from that place without the assistance of a French fleet superior to that of the British, and the British navy had regained superiority on the sea. Moreover, Admiral d'Estaing was busy in the West Indies. Something might be achieved if d'Estaing joined the Patriots in a venture less risky than an attack upon New York, but no scheme for one could be worked out at that time. The British were beginning a thrust into Georgia, and it was not likely that they would do much more from New York than continue raids that they had begun to make along the coasts of New England and Chesapeake Bay. It was therefore possible for Washington to spare some troops, without excessive worry, for an operation on land that did not require French help. Accordingly, Washington and Congress decided to strike at the hostile warriors of the Six Nations. (Nathanael Greene, aware of the decision, foresightedly advised his cousin Griffin, with whom he was a partner in business, to establish a store in Albany to deal with the Patriots going to war up the Mohawk River.)

Proud and dominant over their Indian neighbors, the semicivilized Iroquois had remained neutral until 1777, in part because General Guy Carleton did not desire their services, in part because they were divided among themselves. Because of the influence of the Reverend Samuel Kirkland, a missionary from New England, one of the smaller tribes of the confederacy, the Oneidas, favored the Patriots, and another smaller tribe, the Tuscaroras, was disposed to remain neutral. But the other four nations, the Mohawks, Cayugas, Onondagas, and the numerous Senecas, perceiving that their lands and their independence were threatened by the advancing settlements of American pioneers, were inclined to favor King George. Loyalists and British officials, setting aside scruples regarding the use of Indians and the barbarities of war as they waged it, urged them to take up arms against the rebels. Neither Gage nor

William Howe nor Clinton nor Burgoyne nor General Frederick Haldimand, who succeeded Carleton in command in Canada, declined to accept the help of Indian allies. The Iroquois joined Burgoyne and St. Leger in 1777. Incited and supplied by Haldimand, they took the warpath in June, 1778. About five hundred of them, with a large contingent of Tories, staged a bloody raid in the Wyoming Valley in northern Pennsylvania. They slew more than two hundred frontiersmen, laid waste to the valley, and carried off prisoners for later tortures. In the following November the redoubtable chief Joseph Brant, with five hundred warriors and two hundred Tory rangers led by Colonel Walter Butler, appeared in Cherry Valley, west of Albany, and created havoc. In July, 1779, Brant struck again, at the village of Minisink, near the Delaware River in New Jersey. So brutal was the behavior of Tories who accompanied the Iroquois that a British officer who witnessed it expressed the wish that redcoats returning to England in the event of Patriot victory would "scalp every son of a bitch of them."

Indians and Tories ravaging frontiers? Washington detested Loyalists. He endorsed heavy punishments inflicted upon them by the states, including deprivation of citizenship, denial of the right to vote, imposition of special taxes, expropriation of their property, and imprisonment. No one knew better than he the horrors committed by the red men in war, and the barbarities of the Iroquois aroused his anger. He had himself employed Indians, domesticated Stockbridge tribesmen as early as 1775, but in small numbers and under his control. He would not send them against civilians or permit them to torture prisoners or butcher women and children. There was a sure method to bring the Iroquois to heel—the conquest of Canada and cutting off the supplies of guns, ammunition, and clothing they received by way of the St. Lawrence River. Eager to add Quebec to the American union, Congress and Washington had laid a plan for an invasion of Canada in the spring of 1778 and decided to employ Lafayette in the effort. It had been impossible to gather men and stores, and the plan had been set aside, not entirely to Washington's displeasure, for he suspected that France might seek to regain her empire in North America. Looking into the future, he foresaw that British possession of the St. Lawrence Valley would cramp the growth of the American republic, also that Bourbon control of Canada and New Orleans would be seriously injurious to the United States.

Accordingly, it was necessary to strike directly at the Indians and their white allies. Washington arranged for a contingent under Colonel John Brodhead to invade the country of the Iroquois from the southwest, from Pittsburgh, and formed a much larger force to push into it from the south. He offered the command of the principal body of invaders to his senior major general, Gates, who declined to serve on the score of health, and then appointed John Sullivan. While Brodhead created a diversion, Sullivan went forward at the head of some 3,700 troops, chiefly Continentals. Confronted at Newtown on August 29 by about 500 Iroquois under Brant, some hundreds of Tories, and a few British regulars, Sullivan attacked them and drove them into retreat. He then swept through the Iroquois towns, destroying more than forty of them, inflicting a heavy psychological blow from which the Six Nations never fully recovered. They later resumed their raids, but their losses during the war were such that their military power was vastly reduced. (Other Indian allies of Britain, the Shawnee tribe and the Cherokee nation, similarly suffered from invasions by the Patriots and from severe losses in battle.)

What to do with the main body of his army remained a puzzle for Washington during many weeks after his return to camp. Admiral d'Estaing, preparing to return to the North American coast, proposed a joint attack upon Halifax and Newfoundland. Halifax and Newfoundland? Of what military value would possession of those places be to the Patriots? Washington was able to scuttle that project, pointing out that it would not be feasible to supply garrisons for them in the event that they were taken. Did he harbor a small suspicion that d'Estaing was too much interested in areas once claimed by the French crown? Eventually, listening to pleas for help from the Patriots of South Carolina and Georgia, d'Estaing went to their assistance at Savannah, which had been taken by the British before the end of 1778. The Patriots to the far south were in trouble, and Washington was doubtless pleased by the decision of the French admiral.

Moving his headquarters from Middlebrook to New Windsor on the Hudson with a revived and well equipped army of well above ten thousand men, Washington undertook to keep Clinton and the British army in New York in check. The possibility remained that Clinton would try to gain control of the Hudson and to sever the main communication lines between the Yankees and their fellow Americans. In particular, Washington was determined to hold West Point and to bar British war vessels from proceeding up the river. Clinton supplied good cause for worry. At the end of May royal troops supported by war vessels moved up the river against American posts at Verplanck's Point and Stony Point, between which was King's Ferry, much used by the Patriots for transit between New England and the middle states. Both places succumbed quickly to the royal arms. Was Clinton attempting to push far up the river? He was a good fighting man, but he was not so bold as a commander in chief as he had been as a subordinate. He was thinking about an advance up the Hudson, but he chose not to make one. Placing garrisons in the two posts, he withdrew to his base on Manhattan.

Washington determined to strike back. He ordered General Anthony Wayne to make a surprise attack upon Stony Point, on the western side of the river. If Wayne succeeded in his assignment, Verplanck's Point would be a second objective. The result was a stunning small victory for the Patriots. On July 14 Colonel Christian Febiger, who was to serve under Wayne, drew up his will because there was "a probability of my going on a very hazardous expedition in which there is some danger of my taking a place among the deceased heroes of America." Febiger survived. During the night of the fifteenth Wayne led forward 1,200 men against Stony Point, which was garrisoned by more than 500 royal troops. Wayne ordered his men not to fire, to use only the bayonet. They swept up in two columns to the fort early in the following morning, caught the garrison in disarray, and soon forced its surrender. Wayne's losses were fewer than 100. It turned out that it would have been imprudent to try to storm Verplanck's Point, and British reinforcements soon began to appear there. In fact, Stony Point could not be held by the Patriots, since it was open to approach from British vessels in the Hudson. Accordingly, Washington withdrew his troops from that place, and the British reoccupied it. Clinton had succeeded in closing King's Ferry, but the cost of his minor achievement was exorbitant. He could not proceed up the river, for his passage was still barred by American fortifications at West Point and by Washington's army. Clinton later withdrew from the two posts at King's Ferry. Moreover, Wayne had demonstrated that the Continental infantry had become formidable indeed. The Patriots gained enormously in morale.

Mad Anthony persisted in assaulting Stony Point even though he was wounded in the face. Another, younger officer also came to the fore, Major Henry Lee, who became, with Greene, Knox, and

Wayne, a favorite of the commander in chief. Light Horse Harry Lee, a Virginian and later the father of the Confederate general, was brave, devoted, and very aggressive. He was a harsh disciplinarian. Washington had been compelled to reprimand him because he had not only executed a deserter but had had him decapitated. But there was no doubt about the zeal of the major. Accordingly, when Lee asked, in August, to lead an assault on a British post at Powles Hook (modern Jersey City), Washington gave his consent. The attack did not succeed. Lee was finally driven off, but his losses were small and he carried scores of prisoners away with him.

The summer passed, and the deadlock between Washington and Clinton persisted. As autumn approached, Washington began to think once more about an all-out effort to take New York. Was it not possible that d'Estaing, after having assisted the Patriots in the attack upon Savannah, would come north and join in a general assault? Washington planned to call forth many thousands of New England militia for the purpose. "To Count d'Estaing, then, and that good Providence which has so remarkably aided us in all our difficulties, the rest is committed," he wrote. But the French admiral did not give Providence an opportunity to act. In fact, having failed, with the Patriots, to regain Savannah, he left North American waters. There was one bit of good news in October—the British evacuated Newport. But was it good news? Clinton was reducing his commitments in the North for some purpose. It developed that, encouraged by the departure of d'Estaing, he was planning a powerful offensive in the South. Washington went into winter quarters once more at Morristown with the knowledge that all was not going well for the Patriots in Georgia and South Carolina.

There followed the worst suffering for the army under Washington during the war. The winter of 1779–1780 was extraordinarily cold. The temperature at New York fell to sixteen below zero, and its harbor was frozen over. Snow and ice covered the ground for weeks on end. The troops shivered in their cold huts. They lacked clothing, especially shoes, as was so often the case. Again foodstuffs were lacking, until they were vigorously requisitioned from civilians. The Continental currency lost all value by spring, and Congress finally had to ask the states to supply food and clothing for the army. Its condition was pitiful indeed for many weeks. Officers asked for leave because of illness, and private soldiers went off without formality. A committee of Congress, after inspecting the army in May, reported that the patience of the troops was "exhausted. . . . Their starving condition, their want of pay, and the variety of hardships they have been driven to sustain, has soured their tempers and produced a spirit of discontent which begins to display itself under a complexion of the most alarming hue." Late in that month Connecticut troops briefly mutinied. Moreover, reports from the Deep South were discouraging. Washington had earlier sent small detachments to assist the Patriots of South Carolina and Georgia. Now he ordered some of his best troops, Marylanders and Delaware men, to march to the aid of their hard-pressed fellow countrymen. Before they reached their destination, the southern Patriots met disaster. They arrived in time to perform very well in a second serious American defeat.

Sir Henry Clinton was not at all eager to move northward and to encounter both Washington's army and many thousands of hardy New England militia. He had sufficient strength to defend New York and to embark upon a major offensive in the far South. There were many Tories in the Carolinas and Georgia, and the Patriots of those states were far less numerous than those of Yankeeland. In the last days of 1779, leaving Knyphausen in command at New York, he embarked with a fleet and an army of eight thousand men, sailed southward, and undertook to capture Charleston. There he was confronted by Benjamin Lincoln with a much smaller army. Lincoln committed the mistake that Washington did not quite make at New York in 1776. Prudence declared that Lincoln should fall back inland to preserve his army. Instead, listening to pleas of Patriot leaders in the city, he resolved to defend it, without establishing a safe avenue of retreat. Hemmed in by the British army and fleet, subjected to a heavy bombardment, Lincoln was forced to surrender, on May 12, with 5,500 troops and large quantities of supplies. That stunning royal triumph, gained with very little loss, was followed by a collapse of Patriot resistance in South Carolina. Given a choice by Clinton between expropriation of their property and taking a special oath of allegiance to the Crown, hundreds of South Carolinians, including even Henry Middleton, once president of Congress, yielded. Royal troops moved into the interior of the state. Leaving Lord Cornwallis to consolidate the British gains, Clinton returned to New York in glory. Congress sent Gates to replace Lincoln, against the opinion of Washington, who urged appointment of Nathanael Greene. Assuming command in North Carolina, Gates, who had been condemned for caution in the Saratoga campaign, boldly moved for-

ward into South Carolina. He and an army he had hastily
collected, including the Maryland and Delaware Continentals, col-
lided with Lord Cornwallis at Camden on August 16. The result,
despite a sturdy performance by the Continentals, was a complete
defeat of the Patriots, who were routed and lost more than six
hundred men. The remainder fell back into the interior of North
Carolina. Congress then authorized Washington to choose a successor to Gates, and he selected Greene, who assumed command at
Charlotte early in December. By that time the fortunes of the
southern Patriots had improved somewhat. American frontiersmen
had surrounded and destroyed a large contingent of Loyalists,
nearly a thousand men, with a small body of British troops, under
Major Patrick Ferguson at King's Mountain, in October, and Pa-
triot.guerrilla leaders were pestering the British in South Carolina
and Georgia. Even so, Greene faced a formidable task. The British
seemed to be well established in the far South.

The news that reached Washington in the spring and summer of
1780 was not all bad. Lafayette returned from France in April with
word that a French squadron and a French army were soon to sail
to join Washington in an offensive and that a second French fleet
would follow. He learned that Spain—promised Gibraltar by
France as a reward for victory—was entering the war against Britain. In June, Knyphausen moved out of New York in force but
returned to the British base after minor skirmishing. Returning
from Charleston, Clinton kept his troops in New York, except for
punishing raids into New England. But Washington was also unable to take the offensive. The French fleet, under the Chevalier de
Ternay, and the French army of five thousand men, under the
Comte de Rochambeau, made their appearance and took post at
Newport. But Ternay had only eight ships of the line in his squadron, and the British fleet based at New York was far stronger.
Hoping that the second contingent of French warships would soon
appear, Washington prepared for an attack upon New York. But
they were blockaded in France by the British navy and could not
come to assist him, and he was again compelled to abandon his
favorite scheme.

The Patriot cause suffered another blow in the North, seemingly
a heavy one, in September. Since Clinton gave no sign of offensive
action against the Patriots near New York, Washington traveled to
Hartford to meet Ternay and Rochambeau. They conferred amicably at Hartford. General Rochambeau informed Washington that

he had been instructed to obey the orders of the American commander in chief and assured Washington that he would execute his instructions. He kept his word. It was the easier for him to do so because he found Washington to be imposing and admirable. From Hartford, Washington set out for West Point to confer with General Benedict Arnold, the commandant there, and to inspect the defenses of that important post. On September 23 he examined the works, which were in disrepair, for a very good reason. Late in the afternoon he learned that the tree of liberty had borne fruit with a bright sheen but with a rotten core, that Arnold had become a traitor. He had been planning to pave the way for a British seizure of the post. Major John André, then in charge of British intelligence under Clinton, had come to West Point to confer with Arnold. En route to New York, wearing civilian clothing on the advice of Arnold, he had been captured by Patriot militia. Damning papers were found on his person. Learning that André had been apprehended, Arnold had hastily fled to a British ship in the Hudson and to safety in New York. Washington and the Patriots generally were shocked. They soon recovered; no Continental officer, save for Washington himself, was indispensable.

Arnold had rendered valuable service, at Ticonderoga, at Quebec, in the naval struggle for control of Lake Champlain, in the relief of Fort Stanwix, and in the fighting at Freeman's Farm. He had displayed courage, audacity, and fortitude. Had he remained faithful to the Patriot cause, he would have been one of the principal American heroes of the War of Independence. Betraying it, he became the very image of a traitor. There have been those who have attempted to justify, at least to palliate, his conduct. Through no fault of Washington, who had always set a high value upon the services of Arnold, but because of the fact that Congress felt obliged to apportion high-ranking officers among the states, Arnold had not been promoted as rapidly as he deserved. But other men had suffered from the system. They had swallowed their disappointment or had resigned; none of them had gone over to the British. It has been claimed that he went over to the enemy in a moment of frustration and rage. He bargained with them for sixteen months before his flight. Afterward Arnold would say that he wished to prevent France from establishing hegemony over America—English rule was preferable to French domination. There was a streak of meanness in him with regard to money. After the withdrawal of the British from Philadelphia, Washington had given

Arnold an easy appointment as commandant of that city so that he could rest a leg twice wounded in battle. There Arnold had mis-used his authority to make a bit of money and had married a second and young wife, Peggy Shippen, daughter of a Tory family. It is very likely that she had exerted influence upon him in favor of Britain. In any event, he carried on an extensive negotiation with the British and was promised rewards for his services. He received six thousand pounds and a general's commission in the royal army.

There was no reward for the imprudent John André, an intelli-gent and likeable young officer. By putting on civilian clothing within the Patriot lines, he had placed himself in the position of a spy. A court-martial established by Washington unanimously con-demned the unfortunate André to death, and he was hanged. As a final favor he had asked to be shot instead of hanged, but his request had been denied. It will be recalled that Nathan Hale was similarly executed by the British. There is a pathetic monument to the memory of John André in Westminster Abbey. There is none there, or anywhere, to Benedict Arnold.

Far more serious than the defection of Arnold were the contin-ued sufferings of the army under Washington. Unable to accom-plish anything in the autumn of 1780, it went into quarters once more as winter came. Part of it went into huts at Morristown. A larger body settled down at New Windsor, where Washington set up his headquarters. Its officers were rather pleased that winter because Congress at last promised them half-pay during life. It was otherwise with the men in the ranks. The weather was not so harsh as it was in the preceding year, but lack of pay, provisions, and clothing provoked them beyond endurance. On January 1, 1781, Pennsylvania troops mutinied, killed a captain, wounded other of-ficers, and began to march toward Philadelphia to force Congress and the government of Pennsylvania to redress their grievances. Many who had been enlisted for three years or the war and who had served three years insisted upon their release. Their com-mander, Anthony Wayne, and Pennsylvania officials managed to persuade them to halt at Princeton. The situation was grave. Wash-ington was alarmed lest the mutiny spread throughout the army. He begged the governors of New England to send money, food, and clothing. Moreover, it was to be feared that Clinton would take advantage of the situation. Discontent was so rife in the army generally that Washington was forced to consider the placement of New Jersey militia where they could prevent the mutineers from joining the British. Clinton sent out two agents who offered to lead the discontented Pennsylvanians to New York. They had no desire to return to British allegiance. They hanged the agents, and they agreed to return to duty in mid-January, after some of the three-year men were promised their discharge.

The crisis was not ended. No one was as much concerned for the welfare of his men as Washington. He knew only too well the trials the troops had undergone and were undergoing. Over the years he had done everything he could to satisfy their wants. He had again and again begged and importuned Congress, state legislatures, and state officials to act in behalf of the troops, so often and so emphatically that he had incurred the displeasure of the civil officeholders, who were sometimes quite unable to respond to his pleas. On January 20 he expressed hope that the crisis had passed, that the remainder of his army would "continue to struggle under the same difficulties they have hitherto endured, which I cannot help remarking seem to reach the bounds of human patience." But the very next day he learned that some New Jersey troops had begun a second mutiny, at Pompton. Sympathetic as he might be toward the disobedient soldiers, Washington was determined to make no more concessions to men who did not do their duty, onerous as it might be. Discipline must be maintained if the army was to retain strength. He ordered General Robert Howe to move against the mutineers, who numbered about two hundred. With five hundred trustworthy New England men from West Point, Howe was to insist upon their unconditional submission. Moreover, if they yielded, Washington said to Howe, "you will instantly execute a few of the most active and incendiary leaders." Howe's march was delayed by snow, and New Jersey officials made a bargain with the rebellious troops before Howe reached their camp, to Washington's displeasure. But the mutineers then refused to carry out the terms of the agreement, and Howe was free to act. He surrounded them on January 27, ordered them to lay down their arms, and demanded their unconditional surrender. They reluctantly yielded, and two of their leaders were executed after a court-martial. Discipline had been restored in the army, although Wayne found reason afterward to put a third man to death. It once more survived the trials of winter and was able to move again in the spring.

XVII

————◆————

Washington in Triumph

One of the many tasks that confronted the Patriots during the War of Independence was that of creating a constitution for the United States of America. Harassed by many troubles, Congress completed one in 1777, the Articles of Confederation. Submitted to the thirteen state legislatures for approval and amended by Congress, it was not ratified until March 1, 1781, when Maryland gave its endorsement. The new basic document had serious faults, for there were many Patriots, in and out of Congress, who feared that an American central government might become tyrannical. Congress now had a constitutional basis, but it was not given much greater authority than it had been exercising by grants of power from the states to their delegates and by seizure as a revolutionary body. Power to tax and power to enforce its will upon citizens, even within its limited sphere of authority, had been denied it. A long step had been taken toward creating a stable union, but the document did not satisfy Washington. It did not enable Congress to raise more troops or to provide money with which to pay those already in service. The Continental currency had become worthless. The benefits of the new system, such as they were, would come in the future rather than in the continuing military crisis. It was by no means certain that the Articles, along with

the Declaration of Independence, would be more than an exercise
in political science. Receiving the news of ratification without enthusiasm, Washington continued to toil at his arduous tasks.

The military news was not all bad in the early months of 1781.
Nathanael Greene was performing as Washington had anticipated.
Inheriting a small and disorganized army and confronted by the
same problems of money and supplies that plagued Washington,
Greene prudently gathered men as best he could and prepared to
retreat until he was strong enough to take the offensive. The better
to secure supplies, he divided his little army into two parts, placing
one of them under the redoubtable General Daniel Morgan, who
had resigned from the army because of ill health and a quarrel over
rank but had later returned to duty. Greene himself led the second
part of the army. As Greene had expected, Lord Cornwallis took
the offensive. Controlling South Carolina and Georgia, Cornwallis
was eager not only to solidify the British grip upon those states but
to expand British sway. He had invaded North Carolina in 1780,
but had been forced to fall back because of hardships and disease.
Reinforced from New York, he resumed the offensive. The two
American forces retreated. Cornwallis pursued Greene, and Colonel Banastre Tarleton, a bold cavalry officer much feared by the
Patriots, chased Morgan. Tarleton caught up with Morgan at the
Cowpens in South Carolina on January 17, to his own sorrow.
With somewhat more than one thousand men he attacked an equal
number of Patriots. Riflemen under Morgan riddled the ranks of
the royal troops. His Continentals not only withstood their charge,
but counterattacked. The riflemen, having retired in accordance
with Morgan's instructions, returned to the fray, and Tarleton's
men were assailed from three sides. They were routed and fled,
having sustained more than six hundred casualties.

The tide of warfare was beginning to swing in favor of the Patriots in the Carolinas. Greene, joined by Morgan, continued to retreat, with Cornwallis in pursuit, until the Patriots reached Virginia and secured reinforcements. When Cornwallis, his army
reduced by fatigue and casualties, undertook to establish British
authority in central North Carolina, Greene moved southward and
challenged him at Guilford courthouse on March 15. By that time
Cornwallis had no more than 2,000 men. Greene commanded as
many as 4,500, of whom 500 were Continentals. After a hard
struggle the intrepid Cornwallis held the field of battle. But the
profits of the engagement went to the Patriots. Cornwallis could

not maintain his position. He turned eastward to Wilmington, then marched northward into Virginia with the remainder of his army, 1,600 men, leaving the defense of South Carolina and Georgia to subordinates. They performed well, twice defeating Greene in pitched battle, at Hobkirk's Hill and Eutaw Springs. But, with the help of the American guerrillas, the Patriot general captured the royal forts in the interior of South Carolina and Georgia and gradually pushed them back to the coast. When hostilities drew to a close, the royal forces held only Charleston and Savannah in the Deep South. Their grip upon those places was shaky, for they were deprived of reinforcements. Moreover, the Spanish, sending out a fleet and troops from Havana, had overwhelmed British garrisons at Mobile and Pensacola.

Disobeying the spirit, even the letter, of his instructions, Cornwallis turned Virginia into a third important theater of war. To assist Cornwallis, Clinton had sent troops to Virginia to raid, to give the Virginians occupation, and to prevent them from sending help to the Patriots in the Carolinas and Georgia. Cornwallis assumed command of all the British forces in Virginia on May 20. Had Cornwallis had his way, he would have turned Virginia into the principal theater of war. He even ventured to propose evacuation of New York in order to operate massively in the region of the Chesapeake. Clinton vetoed that scheme, but he allowed Cornwallis to retain command of the British forces in the Old Dominion. So it was that Cornwallis and the army under him became a target for the Patriots and their French allies.

Even before the northward march of Cornwallis, Washington had undertaken to deal with the British raiders in Virginia. In December, 1780, Benedict Arnold, now a British general, had sailed from New York to the Chesapeake with 1,600 men. He had done immense damage to the Patriots in the valley of the James River. Unable without a powerful French fleet to move against New York, Washington sought to help the suffering Virginians and to trap the traitor. He sent a contingent of Continentals under Lafayette southward, and he urged the Chevalier Charles Destouches, who had become commander of the French fleet at Newport, to take a squadron and troops to the Chesapeake to cut off Arnold. Destouches sailed toward the bay but was checked at its mouth by a British fleet, on March 16, and forced to turn back to Newport. The trap could not be closed so long as the British retained naval superiority in Chesapeake Bay. The British forces in

Virginia were reinforced before the end of March by 1,500 men
under General William Phillips. Eventually joined by other contingents, Cornwallis was able to collect as many as 8,000 troops in the
Old Dominion.

The raiding begun by Benedict Arnold hurt the Patriots. Ware-
houses went up in flames and smoke, and slaves were carried off. A
British sea captain in the Potomac even threatened to burn down
Mount Vernon unless Lund Washington furnished him with supplies, and Lund bowed to the menace of the captain, much to the
distress of its owner, who preferred that his home be destroyed
rather than give even small assistance to the enemy. Cornwallis
continued the ravaging. Banastre Tarleton penetrated as far as
Charlottesville and forced Governor Thomas Jefferson to make a
hasty flight from his Monticello home. Lafayette, with 1,200 Continentals and Virginia troops, did what he could to give Cornwallis
occupation, but he did not dare to engage in full-scale battle. Once
and again Washington cast an anxious eye toward Virginia. He
meditated about another expedition from Newport, but the Comte
de Barras, who had succeeded Destouches, was unable to move,
because the British commanded the sea. What could be done?
Washington had only six thousand men available for duty. Conferring with General Rochambeau at Wethersfield, Connecticut, after
the middle of May, Washington decided to send Anthony Wayne
and his Pennsylvania troops to the assistance of Lafayette, also to
mount a menace to New York that would induce Clinton to withhold reinforcements from Cornwallis and even recall troops from
Virginia. Rochambeau agreed accordingly to move his army toward the Hudson. Lafayette and Wayne gave Cornwallis occupation for many weeks without risking a general engagement. At
length the British commander undertook to establish a strong base
prior to further adventures. Setting aside a suggestion from Clinton
that he build it at Old Point Comfort, Cornwallis chose an inferior
location at Yorktown near the end of the peninsula between the
James and York rivers. But he was safe enough, so long as the
British navy controlled Chesapeake Bay.

At Wethersfield, Washington and Rochambeau had much more
to discuss than the situation in Virginia. Exciting news had come
from Paris. That powerful French fleet which had not come in
1780 would appear in midsummer. Admiral Comte de Grasse was
to cross the ocean, with transports carrying a small army and with
instructions to go to the West Indies, thence to the coast of North

America to assist the Patriots. Hoping that the French would establish naval superiority in American waters, Washington proposed that Rochambeau, de Grasse, and Barras join him in an all-out attack upon New York. Cornwallis might be a later target. Washington was hopeful. He believed that "the game is yet in our hands; to play it well is all we have to do." He was sure that "it is in our power to bring the war to a happy conclusion." He believed it quite possible to drive "our foes entirely from the continent." Rochambeau did not quite share the optimism of Washington. He sent a message to de Grasse suggesting that Cornwallis was an easier target than Clinton.

Gathering their troops outside New York, Washington and Rochambeau staged the diversion they had planned to give Clinton occupation, in July. A double thrust that they made against the British outposts there was easily repulsed. Clinton was not impressed, for he had more troops than the allies. An effort they made to put fear into him by displaying their power did not alarm him. Moreover, he received a final reinforcement of 2,500 Hessians while his enemies watched outside the city. New York would be a tough nut to crack. Still, if de Grasse came, if Barras joined him, if the French gained control of the waters adjacent—Washington continued to hope to take the city and Clinton's army if these things came to pass. The war could be won at New York. If necessary, the British forces in Virginia and the Deep South could later be forced to abandon the struggle. Should it prove impossible to strike at Clinton, he might be able to persuade de Grasse to join in an attempt to corner Cornwallis. Then came news that de Grasse was not coming to New York, that he was headed toward Chesapeake Bay. De Grasse had accepted the advice of Rochambeau. He let Washington and Rochambeau know that he planned to reach the coast of Virginia in August and that he must depart from North America in mid-October to return to the West Indies, where the French and British were engaged in a struggle for rich sugar islands.

Washington was disappointed, but he quickly grasped the chance of a major victory offered by de Grasse. After all, capture of Cornwallis and his army would be a heavy blow to the British. He perceived "the fairest opportunity to reduce the whole British force in the South and to ruin their boasted expectations in that quarter." He persuaded Barras, who was eager to lead an expedition to Newfoundland, that the Newport squadron should join de Grasse at the Chesapeake, and he ordered Lafayette to do all that he could to prevent Cornwallis from moving southward or northward. He boldly made ready to march to Virginia with 2,500 Continentals and the French army under Rochambeau. Leaving the remainder of his Continentals outside New York under General William Heath, who was to cover Clinton as best he could with the aid of New England militia, Washington feinted as if he were preparing to attack New York in force and began to move southward on August 19. Clinton was soon aware that the allies were headed for Virginia, but he could not quickly follow them. Indeed, it was impractical for him to collect troops and supplies and to go to the assistance of Cornwallis by land. He could proceed to Virginia by sea—if the British navy retained its superiority in American waters.

Washington and the French and American troops under him marched on, reaching Philadelphia on September 2. Gambling upon help from de Grasse, he worried. He knew that the British fleet at New York was on the move. Would de Grasse actually come? Was de Grasse strong enough to deal with the British? Was the squadron under Barras endangered? He wrote to Lafayette that day, urging the marquis to send him any news of de Grasse "on the spur of speed." He resumed his march three days later. Passing beyond Chester that afternoon, he received glad tidings from de Grasse. The French admiral was in Chesapeake Bay. He had reached its entrance on August 26 and had landed three thousand French troops at Jamestown on September 2. There was good reason to believe that his fleet was powerful enough to ward off an attempt by the British to enter the bay. Moreover, it could be hoped that Barras would come to join de Grasse. The allies moved on; they were delayed by bad roads and lack of boats at the head of Chesapeake Bay. The Continentals received a bit of pay, made possible by the exertions of Robert Morris, the superintendent of finance under Congress. Washington rode ahead of his troops and reached Mount Vernon on September 9. His home and lands were not in the best of shape. He remained there until the twelfth, resting and entertaining Rochambeau and other officers, then rode on to Williamsburg, where he was joyously greeted on the fourteenth by Lafayette, French army officers who had accompanied de Grasse, and French and Patriot troops. Washington's army followed him. Cornwallis, cut off at Yorktown by land and sea, was trapped.

But was he? Washington learned that the British fleet stationed at New York had appeared off the mouth of the bay and that de Grasse had sailed out to challenge it. Happily for the allies, the French fleet was easily superior. De Grasse had twenty-four ships of the line and six frigates. One of his vessels carried 110 guns. Admiral Thomas Graves, who commanded the British fleet, had only nineteen ships of the line and seven frigates because the British who had been contesting with de Grasse in the Caribbean had failed to send reinforcements in time to assist Graves. Such odds would not greatly have disturbed Lord Howe, who expected to win when he had three ships to four of the French. But Graves was no Howe. Afterward Admiral Samuel Hood, who was second in command under Graves, said that his superior was "unequal to the conducting of a great squadron." The two fleets engaged on September 5. In a combat that lasted for two and one-half hours the superiority in guns of the French enabled them to inflict heavy damage with little loss to themselves. Minor clashes that followed were without decisive result. Four British ships were badly damaged, one so severely that it was necessary to sink it. Graves lingered near the scene of action with thought of renewing the struggle, then decided to sail off to New York to refit and secure help. In the meantime Barras and his vessels entered the bay and were joined there by the triumphant de Grasse. Cornwallis was at least temporarily cut off by land and sea. Considering that the British fleet would return, de Grasse, concerned lest he be forced to fight in the bay, proposed to leave it and sail toward New York. Washington feared that Graves might appear in the Chesapeake while de Grasse was at sea. De Grasse agreed to stay put.

Washington moved forward to attack, on September 28. He had ample force at his command, about 7,800 French troops and about 8,800 Patriots, of whom almost two-thirds were Continentals, the remainder Maryland and Virginia militia. The allies had plenty of cannon and engineers, largely supplied by de Grasse. To the surprise of the allies they discovered that the British general had abandoned outer fortifications to concentrate. Occupying those positions, French and American batteries opened a heavy bombardment. They did much damage, and British return fire was ineffective. Cornwallis began to lose men in substantial numbers. Allied engineers and sappers pushed forward, building entrenchments from which to assail his works. It became apparent that he could not hold out long. He wrote to Clinton, "If you cannot relieve me very soon, you must be prepared to hear the worst." On

October 15 American infantry led by Colonel Alexander Hamilton stormed one British redoubt while the French burst through a second one. From the hills above the village one hundred cannon began to pour shot and shell down into it. The situation of Cornwallis was indeed desperate. He staged an unsuccessful sortie. There was still a slim chance that he might save part of his army. Gloucester, across the York River, was held by a British detachment that was penned against the river by more than two thousand French and American troops. Might it not be possible to push them aside and march northward? During the night of the sixteenth a large part of his army crossed the river in small boats, but a great storm prevented completion of the movement. Cornwallis brought the troops back to Yorktown the next day. The French and Americans continued their shattering bombardment. On the seventeenth, four years to the day after the capitulation of Burgoyne at Saratoga, a British officer waving a white cloth appeared upon a parapet. A drummer boy beside him beat for a parley. Cornwallis offered to lay down his arms. He proposed that in return his men be allowed to depart upon condition that they refrain from further service in the war against either the French or the Patriots. Washington demanded a complete surrender, and Cornwallis yielded.

On October 19, seven thousand royal troops at Yorktown paraded between lines of French and American soldiers and put down their weapons. The British contingent at Gloucester also stacked their guns. Cornwallis, pleading illness, did not appear at the principal ceremony, at which he would normally present his sword to Washington. It may well be that he was physically as well as psychically disturbed—his situation was most humiliating. He commissioned General Charles O'Hara to act for him. Washington then thoughtfully assigned Benjamin Lincoln, who was of the same rank as O'Hara, to accept the sword, giving Lincoln, humiliated at Charleston, the pleasure of appearing as a victor. A British band performed during the ceremony. It is said that it played the music of "The World Turned Upside Down," a suitable enough tune. There is some reason, however, to believe that there were other words to the tune—"The King'll Come into His Own Again." Cornwallis and his principal officers were released upon parole, and the royal troops were led off to prison camp.

Sir Henry Clinton received the sad news off the coast of New Jersey. With seven thousand men he was aboard the British fleet, with Admiral Graves, sailing from New York. Repairs to the fleet had delayed its departure until it was too late to attempt to rescue Cornwallis. Graves proceeded toward the Chesapeake, but there was now no good reason for risking his fleet or even New York in combat with de Grasse and Barras. The relieving expedition disconsolately turned back to New York. Afterward, there was gossip among British officers to the effect that workmen at New York had staged a slowdown in order to help the Patriots and French. The relieving force would in any event not easily have executed its mission.

Looking back, Rochambeau referred to "the miracle of Yorktown." Washington ascribed the triumph of the Patriots and their allies to Providence. The crestfallen Cornwallis, going off to England, explained that it resulted from shortcomings on the part of Clinton and British naval commanders. Clinton, resigning, went home and ascribed the British defeat to failure on the part of Lord George Germain to give sufficient support, to the incompetence and disobedience of Cornwallis, to defects in the British admirals, and to the strength of the Patriots. Later, French historians said that the French, with aid from the Americans, brought about the downfall of Cornwallis and his army; later, American chroniclers said that Washington and the Patriots, with the assistance of the French, were the victors at Yorktown. In fact there was glory enough for all the allies who took part in the campaign. But would the Americans have achieved their independence without the splendid allied triumph? It is not at all unlikely that a continuing struggle of endurance would have compelled Britain at last to acknowledge American liberty.

The war went on. Skirmishing continued in the Deep South, and the Indian friends of George III fought on into 1782. De Grasse sailed away with the bulk of the French warships to the Caribbean, where ill fortune brought him to defeat at the hands of Admiral Sir George Rodney in the battle of the Saints. Some of Washington's Continentals marched northward toward New York; Anthony Wayne with his Pennsylvanians went southward to assist Nathanael Greene. There was no need for Washington to hasten northward to confront Clinton, since winter was approaching. He lingered briefly in Williamsburg. There was sadness in the very midst of his triumph. Martha had come to join him. Jacky Custis, who had appeared at Washington's headquarters during the siege, had contracted camp fever and died after a brief illness. Washington made arrangements for the funeral and did what he could to comfort Martha. On November 11 he set out for Fredericksburg to visit his mother. She was not at home, and he rode on to Mount Vernon. After a brief visit there he and Martha proceeded to Philadelphia. They were joyously welcomed en route, and he was hailed as a hero. At Philadelphia he received the plaudits of Congress. Admiring crowds gathered wherever he went. He remained in the city until March 23, 1782, making plans with Congress for the next campaign, then traveled onward with Martha to new headquarters at Newburgh, New York. Once more Washington and his army, later joined by Rochambeau and his troops, hovered around the city.

The war continued, but the British at New York remained quiet. Without the help of the French navy Washington could not even consider an attempt to take the city. At Philadelphia he had urged Congress not to relax its efforts in the Patriot cause; neither he nor the delegates knew what the response of Britain would be to the news of Yorktown. The French came forward in the summer with schemes to employ their navy in American waters in another joint venture. Washington and Rochambeau considered an attack upon Charleston. The scheme was impractical without a powerful French fleet, which did not appear. Washington thought of an invasion of Canada. It could not be mounted. However, it became increasingly evident that American independence was assured.

The news of Yorktown had a staggering effect in London. The war against the Patriots had never been popular. It had become impossible to secure recruits for service across the ocean. Without reinforcements the British forces in New York and the Deep South must dwindle and be increasingly exposed to attack. Britain was war-weary, her national debt had doubled, and her merchant marine had suffered at the hands of Patriot and French warships and privateers. Clamor arose in the House of Commons for peace with the Patriots. Germain was forced to resign. George III wished at all costs to continue the struggle, but the Commons resolved on March 4 that "this House will consider as enemies to his Majesty and this country, all those who shall endeavor to frustrate his Majesty's paternal care for the ease and happiness of his people, by advising, or by any means attempting to further prosecution of offensive war on the continent of North America, for the purpose of reducing the revolted colonies to obedience by force." Lord North then resigned, and the king felt forced to accept new ministers who undertook to negotiate with American diplomats at Paris.

Sir Guy Carleton went to New York to replace Clinton, and Admiral Robert Digby assumed command of the fleet there. They officially informed Washington on August 4 that Britain was preparing to acknowledge American independence, provided that the Patriots agreed to deal mercifully with the Tories. Washington suspected that the two British commanders were trying to trick him. Why did they address him rather than Congress? Were they trying to drive a wedge between him and Congress? He sent the notice to that body. A little later Carleton informed Washington that the British would not take the offensive. The British army did indeed remain quiet, and Carleton even withdrew troops from some outposts.

But Washington was quite correct in suspecting that Carleton sought to create, and to take advantage of, dissension among the Patriots. The British general, like the Howe brothers, had power to pardon and to extend the king's protection to repentant rebels. He hoped to make peace with the Americans and doubtless sought to foster division among them toward that end. William Smith, a prominent Loyalist of New York, was a trusted adviser of the British general. Did he tell Carleton that there were Patriots in New York who desired to put Washington upon a throne? In the preceding spring Colonel John Lewis Nicola of New York had written to Washington to urge that he ought to make himself an American king. Nicola claimed that there were other Patriot officers who felt as he did. Washington summarily rejected the notion. He was a devoted republican and a man of honor who would not stoop to conspire in order to gain a throne—he was not a Napoleon. "Let me beseech you, then," he wrote to Nicola, "if you have any regard for your country, concern for yourself or posterity, or respect for me, to banish these thoughts from your mind." Nicola responded that he sought only the public good, but abandoned his scheme. In any event, Carleton was forced to conclude that he could not bargain with the Patriots.

That summer Washington was tested for humanity as well as loyalty. A board of Loyalists in New York had authorized the execution of Joshua Huddy, a captured New Jersey militia captain, held by the Loyalists to be guilty of murdering one of their number, and Huddy was hanged. Washington could not permit Loyalists to exercise such power. He arranged to have a captured British officer, Captain Charles Asgill, chosen by lot for execution in reprisal. Asgill was threatened with death for many weeks, but Washington did not order his execution. The general's menace was enough to give the Loyalists and their British allies pause and to make them behave better in the future. Eventually, Washington was able to use a plea for mercy from Asgill's mother as sufficient reason for abandoning reprisal.

It became ever more likely in the summer and autumn of 1782, so far as anyone in America could tell, that peace was approaching. Rochambeau and his men, no longer needed, came from Virginia and made ready to leave the continent. There was dissatisfaction in Washington's army, now better clothed and fed than it had been for many years because of easier access to supplies. Winter quarters did not bring new harsh trials, but soldiers and officers were worried. What would be done for them when they were disbanded? Would they be repaid, even to a degree, for their deeds and their sufferings? They had leisure in which to meditate about their future, and they began to make much of their grievances.

At last, in March, 1783, reliable news reached America that peace and independence were virtually assured. Benjamin Franklin, John Adams, John Jay, and Henry Laurens, acting for Congress, had signed a preliminary treaty of peace with Britain at Paris. Washington received the glad tidings "with inexpressible satisfaction." It became part of a final treaty on September 5, 1783, after France and Spain had reached a separate agreement with Britain. (Lord North went into St. Margaret's church near Westminster Abbey that day to pray.) The terms, so far as America was concerned, were generous. Britain retained Canada, and Spain acquired East and West Florida, the peninsula and a strip of territory stretching along the northern shore of the Gulf of Mexico to the Mississippi. But the new United States of America, recognized as independent, was given all the lands between the Atlantic, the Mississippi, and the British and Spanish possessions. The French and Spanish had failed to take Gibraltar, and Spain did not get that prize for her efforts. The French gained little for their efforts beyond the satisfaction of humiliating Britain. The American commissioners had performed very well, and much has been written and said about the subtlety and skill they displayed in the game of diplomacy. It should be remembered that they held very high cards. Britain was unable to continue the war in North America, thanks to the achievements of the Patriots at home, to the help they received from Rochambeau and de Grasse, and surely to the devotion and leadership of Washington.

Before the war mercifully came to an end, Washington had to deal with very unhappy officers and mutinous men. In December, 1782, anonymous officers at Newburgh sent an address prepared by Major John Armstrong to Congress asking new provision for their future, for disabled officers and soldiers, and for dependents of those who had been slain. The officers now wanted full pay for a period of years or a single payment in cash. A Congress without means to meet their demands feebly sought to fob them off to the states, which could tax and raise money. Restlessness was not confined to the officers. Men in the ranks were unhappy. In mid-February, Alexander Hamilton urged Washington to use his dissatisfied army in cooperation with "all men of sense" to force endowment of the central American government with power to tax and ability to pay the army. What did Hamilton have in mind? Washington rejected any thought of employing his troops for other than military purposes. On March 10, 1783, anonymous officers at Newburgh, with Armstrong again playing a leading role, called for a general meeting the next day to consider their plight and to take further action. Their language was extreme and rhetorical, containing a threat to move off to the western wilderness unless action were taken toward fulfilling their demands. Washington, alarmed, then called a meeting for the fifteenth in place of that scheduled by the discontented officers and read a paper to the assemblage. He urged them to do nothing to sully their record. They must believe that their sacrifices would be rewarded by their grateful countrymen. He would himself do all that he could to push their claims. His eyesight—he was now above fifty years of age—was not what it had been, and he had begun to use spectacles in order to read effectively. Before he finished the paper, he reached in his pocket and put on his eyeglasses, remarking that he had grown gray in service and that his vision was impaired. Touched, the officers agreed to pursue their claims without unseemly threats.

Then came trouble with the men in the ranks. Washington begged Congress to give them three months pay when they left the service. All that Congress would or could do was to ask the several states to supply the money—six months after the war officially closed. Washington urged the states to act. Before they could stir, in mid-June, five hundred Pennsylvania troops who had done little duty in the war mutinied and marched on Philadelphia, where they were joined by other discontented troops. The mutineers physically bedeviled both the authorities of Pennsylvania and Congress, and the Congress moved off to Princeton. Washington sent five hundred men under General Robert Howe to bring the malcontents back to their duty. It was not necessary to use force against them. They prudently yielded to the authority of their state. The Continentals gradually went home without decent rewards and without serious damage to the cause for which so many soldiers had sacrificed so much. Meditating about these events, Washington declared that the new United States must have a regular army and that it must regularly be paid.

In the summer of 1783 the military situation was so easy that he was able to take a vacation. He made a long tour of New York state, traveling to the shores of Lake Champlain, thence to Fort Schuyler, where he opened a speculation in land, to Albany, and back to his headquarters. The journey enabled him to relax. The lines of worry that had appeared upon his face softened. Perhaps he was also acquiring a little fat. After his return he weighed 209 pounds; Henry Knox tipped the scales at the same time at 280. Called to Princeton to confer again with Congress, Washington spent many weeks at the scene of one of his most brilliant triumphs. He learned that Congress had voted to erect an equestrian statue of him at the permanent capital of the United States—after one had been established. He was wined and dined, thoroughly enjoying himself. He displayed again that sense of humor denied to him by solemn portraits. Informed at a dinner that Robert Morris "had his hands full" with financial business, he expressed a wish that Morris "had his pockets full, too." Informed that the silver goblets used at the dinner had been made by a man who had become a Quaker preacher, Washington commented, "I wish he had been a Quaker preacher before he made the cups." The commander in chief was specially pleased to meet again Nathanael Greene, who had come north after achieving in the far South all that anyone could have accomplished. Washington began to arrange to move his papers and his stock of wine to Mount Vernon. At last, in October, a reliable report reached Princeton that the definitive treaty of peace had been signed at Paris. He sent fulsome "Farewell Orders to the Armies of the United States" and set out to rejoin the remains of his army and to accept the surrender of New York.

The British had already evacuated their forces from the Deep South, carrying off many Tories and blacks. Carleton was making ready to depart. After November 20 Washington and a few Continentals, with militia, moved southward down the Hudson and camped near the British lines. On the twenty-fifth Carleton and his troops withdrew from the city. Carefully letting Governor George Clinton of New York precede him, in order to display respect for civilian authority, Washington rode through the streets with a military entourage. He was tumultuously welcomed. More than seven years had passed since he had been driven from the city by the British under William Howe. On December 4 Carleton, his army, and thousands of Tories set sail. At noon that day Washington said farewell at Fraunces' Tavern to the officers still with him. After they were served wine, Washington said a few words. He was grateful to them for their services, and he wished them prosperity and happiness in the future. Moved to tears, Washington and his officers drank their wine as best they could. He asked them to come forward to shake hands. The ever reliable Henry Knox was the first to approach the commander in chief. Overcome by emotion, Washington embraced Knox, then Generals William McDougall and Steuben, then the rest of his guests.

There remained the matter of his own discharge. The United States must maintain an army, but he was determined not to lead it. He longed for the peace of Mount Vernon, and he was making ready to submit his resignation. He left New York as swiftly as possible, accompanied by Steuben. At Philadelphia he was received again with appropriate ceremony and festivities. Church bells rang, and a Dutch ship captain saluted the United States with thirteen cannon. Washington formally submitted his account for his expenses during the war, about $450,000, to the national treasury. His bill has been likened to the padded one of a twentieth-century business man, precise regarding small items, rather vague concerning large ones. Included was a rather remarkable request for reimbursement of sums spent in consequence of the many visits made to headquarters by Martha. But he had not drawn pay during more than eight years in service, and the bill was doubtless reasonable enough. It was accepted without demur. More important, it would appear that at least eventually he received a balance due to him. As soon as festivities and good manners permitted, he rode to Baltimore, where he was again subjected to celebration. He rode on to Annapolis, where Congress was in session. At that time it contained delegates from only seven states, but that fact did not persuade him to act without due formality. He submitted his resignation in respectful language, ending solemnly, "I consider it an indispensable duty to close this last solemn act of my official life, by commending the interests of our dearest country to the protection of Almighty God, and those who have the superintendence of them, to his holy keeping." Replying for Congress, its president, Thomas Mifflin, responded appropriately, expressing the gratitude of Congress and the United States, not only for his splendid achievements, but also because he had unfailingly obeyed civil authority. There could be no doubt that the retiring commander in chief would come forward again when he could be of service to "our dearest country," to the American republic. Resuming his journey, he pushed on as expeditiously as possible to Mount Vernon, arriving there late on December 24. Martha was there, and they celebrated Christmas together.

XVIII

The Great Man

Freed from military duties, Washington meditated a journey to inspect the boundaries of the United States but abandoned the notion. Urged by Lafayette and other French officers to visit France, he decided not to travel across the ocean. Except for brief visits to the West and Philadelphia he did not go far from home for almost four years. He wished for no public office; he hoped that other men gifted in statecraft would come forward to guide the new republic. He became a farmer again, and he devoted much energy to restoring his home and his fields, both injured by the vicissitudes of war and neglect during his long absence. He sought to profit from his large landholdings beyond the mountains, and he devoted attention to commercial enterprises, for both his own benefit and that of the public. He could not escape from the world. There were Englishmen who wishfully believed that America would not amount to much, and there were ministers of state on the European continent who failed to perceive that a revolution in the affairs of men was in progress across the Atlantic. Wiser observers perceived that a heavy blow had been dealt to the European colonial system, that a vast and beneficial experiment was under way in America. Some well-wishers to the new republic predicted that an ideal society would appear, even maintained that it already existed. To them Washington was a heroic figure, tower-ing among his compatriots. European travelers in America went to Mount Vernon to see him, among them even British officers so recently his enemies in battle. Nor would his fellow Americans permit him to live in quiet retirement. The time came when he was compelled by his sense of duty to devote himself once more to public affairs, when he must take civil office to assure the welfare of the Republic, to reap the rewards of independence.

Not yet fifty-two years of age when he returned home, Washing-ton was still vigorous. He was not fatigued by long rides on horse-back. Whenever the weather and care for guests permitted, he "rid" out to oversee work upon his lands. He had only one bout of illness during several years, an attack of the "ague" in 1786 that left him a legacy of rheumatic pains for some months. Once, dur-ing the war, he had wondered whether he would live long enough to see the end of it. At fifty-four he was well aware that he had passed "the noontide of life," that he was "descending the hill" toward the grave. He hoped that he and Martha would glide "gently down a stream which no human effort can ascend." He remained sexually potent. Considering disposition of his property after his death, he assumed that he would not have progeny. Obvi-ously, Martha, past her climacteric, would have no more offspring. If he survived her, "whilst I retain the reasoning faculties, I shall never marry a girl; and it is not probable that I should have chil-dren by a woman of an age suitable to my own, should I be dis-posed to enter into a second marriage."

There is a temptation to believe that life at Mount Vernon was idyllic. So it was, to a degree, for the Washingtons and their guests, but not for the blacks who waited upon them. Gazing upon the noble house perched high above the Potomac, one also saw rows of humble cabins that supplied shelter of a sort for the many scores of slaves who toiled for Washington. Some of them were indulged as house servants, but the great majority, men and women, worked on the land. His black women wielded the hoe, helped to build fences, and spread manure. His diary records that he had a girl of fourteen or so guide a plow. Lund Washington had sold nine slaves during the War of Independence in order to get money to pay taxes, and eighteen blacks had fled, but the number of slaves controlled by Washington was enlarging again by natural increase.

Announcing devotion to the principle of liberty in the struggle against Britain, no thoughtful and humane Patriot could fail to perceive the iniquity of black servitude. During the war it was proposed to enlist slaves in the Patriot forces, pledging to give them freedom in return for their services. Washington opposed the scheme because it would give the British excuse to raise Negro troops with the same promise—he did not object to the presence of many free blacks in northern regiments. But he did not fail to recognize that it was wrong to hold blacks in subjection. In tranquillity at Mount Vernon he said that slavery ought to be ended. "There is not a living being who wishes it more sincerely than I do," he wrote. He also asserted, however, that there was "only one proper and effectual mode by which it can be accomplished, and that is by legislative authority." He would vote for abolition. He desired that it should come by "slow, sure and imperceptible degrees." Perceiving the sufferings of blacks because of sales, he turned against that "traffic in the human species" and resolved to sell none of his slaves. Even so, as president, later, he opposed steps to put an end to trading in slaves, on the ground that the time was not ripe. Until nearly the end of his life he continued to defend his property rights and those of Martha in human beings. In 1791, when he was serving as president in Philadelphia, he developed a scheme to send some of Martha's blacks and one of his own back to Virginia rather than let them acquire their liberty under the laws of Pennsylvania. He proposed to use "pretext" to deceive both the blacks and the public in order to execute the plan. It turned out that no effort was made to apply state law to the president. Still later he tried, apparently in vain, to secure the return of one of his girl slaves who had fled to New England. At last, perhaps in part because he had found that without selling of blacks slavery was unprofitable, he resolved to free his Negroes when it became possible. But he was never sufficiently concerned about black bondage to mount a campaign against it. Like most of the leaders of the revolutionary generation he consigned the problem of slavery to the future. It may be said in his and their behalf that an attack against it would undoubtedly have prevented the creation of the union and would have destroyed the infant republic.

If life at Mount Vernon was nearly as pleasant as might be for the retired soldier, it was a busy one. The general had much to do with the care of his home and his lands. The house required renovation, and his fields were in disarray. He gradually put things in order, resuming his efforts to improve his lands, crops, and livestock. Corresponding with European agriculturists, he tried to enrich his none-too-fertile soils, and he experimented with novel seeds and plants, without rich result. He sought to breed better stock.

One of his experiments, though it produced little cash, at least supplied him with cause for hilarity. Long interested in breeding mules, he had come to believe that "this mongrel race" might replace horses, not only for heavy work, but for show. He intended "to drive no other in my carriage," he asserted. The local mules were poor specimens. In 1784 he informed Richard Harrison, the American consul at Cadiz, that he wanted "a good jack ass, to breed from," for Spanish asses were of the very best quality. The jack must be "at least fifteen hands high; well formed; in his prime; and one whose abilities for getting colts can be ensured." His Most Catholic Majesty, King Charles III, informed of Washington's wish, arranged to have two jacks sent across the ocean. One of them died en route, but the other, which acquired the name Royal Gift, arrived safely at Mount Vernon. Learning of Washington's desire for a jack, Lafayette also sent one, which came to be known as The Knight of Malta because he came from that Mediterranean island, along with two jennets. The Knight of Malta was smaller, younger, and more energetic than Royal Gift, a large and impressive creature. After Royal Gift had recovered from his long journey, Washington advertised in newspapers that the jack was available for fathering mules at a suitable price. However, the big jack for some time displayed little interest in the mares who were brought to his attention, supplying inspiration for much joking by Washington in letters to Lafayette and other friends. The ass, reported Washington, was "too full of royalty, to have anything to do with a plebeian race." King Charles, though "past his grand climacteric, cannot be less moved by female allurements than he is; or when prompted, can proceed with more deliberation and majestic solemnity to the work of procreation." Washington hoped that when Royal Gift "becomes a little better acquainted with republican enjoyments, he will amend his manners and fall into our custom of doing business." Eventually, apparently with the cooperation of one of the jennets supplied by Lafayette, Royal Gift produced a Son of Royal Gift, then fathered other jacks. The Spanish animal also at length was the sire of mules. "He never fails," Washington wrote in the autumn of 1787. Son of Royal Gift was also at first disinclined to do his duty with respect to mules; however, to the amusement of his owner, he begat mules when he was enticed simultaneously by the charms of a jennet and a mare. Washington sent Royal Gift as far as Charleston to breed. He acquired a substantial body of asses and mules, but the venture was not very profitable.

The correspondence of Washington was not confined to that concerning the breeding of mules. Letters poured into Mount Vernon from both America and Europe. He could not manage to write all the necessary replies or to supervise all his plantations. He needed help. His nephew John Augustine, succeeding Lund, joined the household to assist in operating the lands. John Augustine married Fanny Bassett, a niece of Martha's who had come to stay with her aunt and uncle, and the young people provided good company. Eventually Washington also acquired the services as secretary of Tobias Lear, a young Harvard graduate who had studied abroad and who knew French. Lear was highly intelligent, industrious, and reliable, a fine young man. He was a treasure, and he remained in the service of Washington until after his employer became president of the United States.

Tobias Lear could lift part of the burden of correspondence off the shoulders of Washington, but he could not relieve the general of his duties as a host. In the style of Virginia planters Washington had generously entertained all visitors before the war, and he resumed that practice. Relatives and friends from Virginia and Maryland were welcomed. Artists came to take his likeness, and politicians to secure his opinions. Travelers from north to south and from south to north stopped in at Mount Vernon. Visitors came from all parts of America and from Europe, with and without invitation, with and without letters of introduction, to renew or to make acquaintance with the famous man. The house seldom lacked guests. All were politely received, even British army officers, for Washington did not harbor a grudge against individuals. Politeness was not enough for all of the visitors—one European stranger, a self-styled "gentleman," wrote to Washington after his departure to complain that he had not been treated in accordance with his lofty station. The general tried to be gracious to everyone but was doubtless too tired or bored on occasion to devote all his attention to a guest. Moreover, he avoided expressions of opinion to strangers that they might spread to his embarrassment. He was solicitous for the welfare of those who were congenial. One traveler, Elkanah Watson, racked during the night by a cold, was surprised to see his host enter his room with a comforting dish of tea.

In 1784 Washington welcomed Lafayette, whom he had come to like very well, back to America. When Lafayette set out to return to France, the general accompanied him beyond Annapolis. He feared that he would not see his French friend again, and such proved to be the case. Noah Webster, the dictionary Webster, who sought to frame a superior American version of the English language, sojourned at Mount Vernon, along with John Fitch, the steamboat inventor, and Mrs. Catherine Macaulay Graham, the distinguished English historian who was a republican by principle and a friend of America. He was undoubtedly pleasant to Mrs. Graham and her husband, a man young enough to be her son, but he preferred to entertain good friends and relatives with whom, warmed by wine, he could be informal and merry. He also rather enjoyed association with the artists. At first reluctant to submit to their directions, he learned to be an obedient model. Somehow, perhaps because they fancied that they must emphasize the majesty of their subject, they invariably endowed him with stiffness, if not solemnity.

Washington now had time to devote to his speculations in land beyond the mountains and to other economic projects, for his own benefit and also for the benefit of Virginia and the nation. He became interested in a scheme to drain a part of the Great Dismal Swamp, hoping to develop it into a rich farming area. In 1784 he made a journey over the Appalachians to see his property in the Ohio Valley. He hoped that it could be thoroughly developed, that commerce could be opened between Chesapeake Bay and the valley of the Mississippi, which was in the process of occupation by American pioneers. Seeking means whereby Virginia would play a principal role in that commerce, he tried when in the West to find a good road by which people and goods could pass from the headwaters of the Potomac or the James River to the Ohio. Toward that end, he also became interested in schemes for locks and canals by which boats could pass beyond the falls of the Potomac. But he was no longer solicitous only for his own profit and the welfare of Virginians in rivalry with Pennsylvanians, as he had been before the war. Now he wished that Pennsylvanians would also gain from opening the West, indeed, that the entire American nation would benefit from forming economic links between the Atlantic seaboard and the Mississippi Valley. He had become an American. Management of his lands beyond the mountains proved to be vexatious rather than profitable—he had trouble with squatters, and his schemes for opening up the West could not be immediately executed.

He met with other difficulties, and sorrows as well. Living generously, assisting relatives and friends, contributing to good causes, he could hardly make ends meet. His Mount Vernon plantations were not profitable. With most Americans he suffered from an economic depression that followed the war. He doubtless lost rather than gained money from his agricultural experiments. He was averse to economizing. Even though he was under financial stress when Nathanael Greene died, he offered to pay for the education of George Washington Greene, the son of his good friend. He received at last the money due him from the estate of Patsy Custis. It must have been a great help to him. There was nothing he could do but to accept some blows. His brother Samuel died, leaving an embarrassed estate; then John Augustine, his "beloved brother," died from "a fit of gout in the head." Religion gave him less consolation for those sad events than it would have provided before the war.

For Washington was no longer a faithful Episcopalian. Soon after his return home from the war he resigned from the vestry of the nearby Truro church. Thereafter he continued now and then to attend religious services, but then or somewhat later ceased to take communion. Precisely why his attitude toward religion had altered, one cannot say. It has been suggested that he had learned as a Mason to believe in a ruling Providence rather than an orthodox Christian deity. Certainly during the war he expressed faith many times in that Providence. It would seem that, like Thomas Jefferson, John Adams, and many another Patriot leader, he was affected by waves of Unitarianism and deism that accompanied the Revolution. He did not become an enemy of organized religion. He did not support his good friends Jefferson and James Madison in their long struggle to divorce church and state in Virginia. He agreed with them that the Episcopal church, established by law in the Old Dominion and supported by public money, ought to be deprived of its special advantages over other sects. However, he could see no good reason why members of all churches should not be forced to pay taxes to support the one they preferred. Like Patrick Henry, he liked a scheme of "general assessment" by the Virginia assembly, the proceeds being apportioned among the various Christian sects and the Jewish and Mohammedan churches. Nonbelievers could assign their contributions to charity. It did not trouble him that "general assessment" would tend to enforce the status quo in religion. His view was not illiberal, but it cannot be claimed that he was a thoroughgoing champion of religious freedom. Let it be remembered that Jefferson would hardly have been able to have himself described upon his tombstone as the framer of the Virginia Statute of Religious Liberty had Virginia remained in the British empire.

If Washington did not go quite so far as Jefferson and Madison in the direction of religious freedom, he matched them in opposition to the creation of a special aristocracy. At the end of the war Baron von Steuben and other officers undertook to form the Society of the Cincinnati, membership in it to be confined to officers who had served in the war and eldest sons of their progeny. Chapters of it were formed in each of the states and also in Europe. Their appearance caused a furor in America. Why should membership be confined to officers? And why should it be extended to eldest sons to eldest sons to eldest sons who had not fought in the war? Was not the society a scheme to form a martial aristocracy, "a race of hereditary patricians"? Inevitably, Washington was elected its national president. He was inclined to believe that there was no good reason for the existence of the Cincinnati. He asked Jefferson and Madison for their opinions, and they condemned its hereditary membership. Accordingly, at a general assembly of the society at Philadelphia in 1784 Washington secured the abolition of its hereditary feature, so far as its national body was concerned. State chapters continued to elect eldest sons, but the society languished, although it continued into the twentieth century. Washington came to believe that the society was a nuisance. There was a squabble over it even in France. General Conway, technically not eligible because he had not served long enough, was nominated for an honorary membership. Lafayette opposed the nomination but was overruled by higher French officers, among them, no doubt, Rochambeau. When Lafayette reported about the affair to Washington, the general said that the French officers must settle their disputes among themselves.

Whether he would or not, Washington could not indefinitely remain absent from the great world of affairs. Not well read, he was not, and he did not pretend to be, a profound political and social philosopher. During the war it was not possible for him to take a considerable part in a great remolding of American institutions that began in consequence of the separation from Britain.

Nor was he active in that "internal revolution" after the end of the war. Many wholesome changes came in the several states in that reformation, including written constitutions, bills of rights, expansion of the suffrage, abolition of hereditary rights and privileges, greater religious freedom, steps toward abolition of slavery above the Mason-Dixon Line, and provision, at least on paper, for education at public expense. Washington was not hostile to healthy changes. He urged, for example, that America found a national university, so that her young men would not need to go to Europe for advanced education—they were corrupted in Europe. He continued to push for such a university after he became president. There were men, conservatives, who were reluctant to make alterations far beyond those necessary because of the separation from Britain, men who wished power to reside in the good hands of the planters, merchants, and lawyers who had formerly shared it with the British. There were democrats who desired universal suffrage for males and the sharing of power among all of them. Washington was a liberal conservative.

Nor was Washington active in national politics. Of course, he spent the war years striving to secure American independence rather than in helping to construct a central government. But he did condemn the Articles of Confederation even before they were adopted, and he continued to express dissatisfaction with them after the war. The regime that that constitution established lacked a strong executive and had a very limited judiciary. Under it Congress, voting by states, was unable to tax, being forced to requisition money from the states in proportion to their populations and landed wealth. Congress could neither compel the states to meet their obligations nor force citizens to obey its will. It could not regulate commerce between states or commerce with foreign countries. To be sure, Congress was given power to manage foreign affairs and to make treaties, and it acquired authority over the territories of the United States beyond the Appalachians, authority that it eventually used to frame the famous Northwest Ordinance and to arrange for the creation of many new states equal to the original thirteen. For Washington, as he pointed out in 1780, the new constitution had a grave defect in that Congress was not given means to maintain a regular army and a navy. He desired a stronger central government that would supply stability at home and provide for an adequate defense.

Washington had become an American devoted above all to his

country. He had fought for America, not for Virginia, not for the South that nurtured him, not for a collection of squabbling states. Indeed, his fame must be greatly diminished if the republic did not endure and prosper mightily; but he was concerned for its welfare rather than for his own repute. There were Virginians who continued to render their first loyalty to Virginia; there were men in all of the states whose primary political affection was local rather than national. There were men who lived in the smaller states who were jealous of the larger ones. There were conservatives and democrats who were more determined to have their way, to check each other, than they were to achieve the common good. Southerners had appeared, in Maryland, Virginia, the Carolinas, and Georgia, who believed that they had special, even vital, interests opposed to those of the northerners, particularly the New Englanders. Many Yankees viewed the southerners with distrust. Those jealousies had appeared with the beginning of the war, and they continued to flourish. Southerners in Congress were eager to open commerce through the lower Mississippi; northerners wished to enhance trade from the Atlantic seaboard. The lawmakers engaged in a long sectional dispute over the location of the national capital. In the mid-1780s some observers believed that the nation would divide into two parts, northern and southern, or three divisions, northern, middle, and southern. Washington harbored no southern jealousy. He remained fond of Virginia, but only as his home and as a part of the new nation. He would not even classify Virginia as a southern state. To him it was a middle American state.

In June, 1783, preparing to return to private life, Washington emphatically called for a stronger union. Aware that he might be condemned for meddling in civil matters, he nevertheless sent a circular letter to all the states in which he asserted that if the Americans were not completely free and happy, "the fault will be intirely their own." They were "the sole lords and proprietors of a vast tract of continent . . . abounding with all the necessaries and conveniences of life." To assure a glorious future it was only necessary to create "an indissoluble Union of the states under one federal head," maintain a regular army, and set aside "local prejudices and policies." America could become "a blessing to millions yet unborn." But the Articles of Confederation were "a rope of sand."

Discontent with the Confederation grew after the war, especially among conservatives who were elbowed aside in several of the states and whose power was threatened in others. The internal revolution had gone too far for them. They were alarmed lest they be submerged in the mass of citizens, lest they be compelled to submit to "mob rule." They feared for the safety of their property. Among them were many former Tories, the bulk of whom had chosen to remain in the United States rather than emigrate. The conservatives saw that they might be able to hold or regain their power by securing and dominating a stronger central government. But there were good reasons for dissatisfaction with the system. Congress was compelled to abandon the small navy built during the war and to reduce the army to a skeleton. It could not deal forcefully with hostile Indians in the Northwest Territory, since they were being supplied with guns, ammunition, and tomahawks by the British from Canada. The British clung to posts south of the boundary with Canada and declined to move from them. Congress was unable to protect American ships and sailors against the attacks of North African pirates, to compel Britain to refrain from imposing restraints upon shipping that injured American trade, even to prevent the states from interfering with the flow of commerce. It could do nothing to reduce the ravages of the depression that followed the war. American pride was injured. Britain declined even to send a minister across the ocean to negotiate with the new nation. John Adams, appointed minister to the Court of St. James's, was politely received by George III, then treated very coldly by the advisers of the king. The troubles of Congress were created or exacerbated by lack of money. The states responded tardily to requisitions for money if they responded at all. There was an obvious remedy, imposition of duties upon imports, but Congress was unable to resort to it. The Articles could not be altered without the consent of all the states, and changes in them to give Congress the power to levy such duties could not obtain the approval of all the states. Little Rhode Island alone was able to make impossible the adoption of one such amendment.

The failure to pass that amendment and another that would have endowed Congress with authority to impose restrictions upon British trade with America supplied Washington with new evidence that something must be done to change the new nation's system of government. He wrote that "the Confederation appears to me to be little more than a shadow without the substance." The Americans must set aside the jealousies that had prevented the formation of a stronger central government, for if "we are afraid to trust one another under qualified powers, there is an end of the

Union. . . . We are either a united people, or we are not," he declared. "If the former, let us in all matters of general concern act as a nation." At that time he hardly dared to hope that more than a salutary change or two could be made in the Articles. In the spring of 1786 he despairingly expressed fear that the system could not be improved "without another convulsion." By that time, however, many other men had begun to make an effort to call a national convention to correct the defects in it, and he hoped that one could be held. "That it is necessary to revise and amend the Articles of Confederation," he wrote, "I entertain *no* doubt; but what may be the consequences of such an attempt is doubtful. Yet something must be done, or the fabric must fall, for it certainly is tottering. . . . I do not conceive," he asserted, "we can exist long as a nation without having lodged somewhere a power which will pervade the whole Union in as energetic a manner as the authority of the state governments extends over the several states."

There was indeed a growing body of men who were determined to arrange for a general convention. In September, at the invitation of Governor Patrick Henry of Virginia, fourteen delegates from five states met at Annapolis, officially in order to propose ways of removing barriers to commerce among the states. Since eight states, including all those of New England, were not represented, the delegates could do nothing regarding the business for which they were ostensibly assembled. However, led by Alexander Hamilton and James Madison, men as eager for reform of the union as Washington himself aggressively undertook to call for a general convention to meet at Philadelphia the following May to devise provisions "to render the constitution of the federal government adequate to the exigencies of the Union; and to report such an act for that purpose" to Congress and the state legislatures for approval. The call was not ignored. The conservatives rallied to support it, and they were joined by many men who were moderate in politics but who perceived that a change was necessary for the welfare of the Americans as a whole.

The call was the more welcome because it was accompanied by news of Shays's Rebellion in western Massachusetts. Rebelling against high taxes, the farmers and villagers of that area defied the authorities of that state. Led by Captain Daniel Shays, a revolutionary veteran, they took up arms and closed the courts in the region. Reports spread that the Shaysites proposed to redistribute property in Massachusetts and to seize weapons stored in a national arsenal at Springfield. In other states debtors were urging emission of unsupported—and depreciating—paper money in order to escape from their obligations. Washington shared in the widespread alarm. "Good God," he wrote, "who besides a Tory could have foreseen or a Briton predicted" that independence would lead to such attacks on property and public order. Eventually, in January, 1787, militia mustered by Governor James Bowdoin defended the arsenal against 1,200 Shaysites and slew 4 of them. The remainder were gradually dispersed. Later the grievances of the Shaysites were redressed to a degree, but not before a worried Congress had undertaken to raise troops to deal with the emergency—troops that did not move. Washington was not happy with the outcome. It ought to have been possible to put down the uprising quickly and efficiently.

But he was not at all eager to participate personally in revising the union. On February 21 Congress endorsed the call from Annapolis, declaring that it was "expedient" to hold the general convention at Philadelphia "for the sole and express purpose of revising the Articles of Confederation." State legislatures began to choose delegates to the meeting. Inevitably Washington was urged to accept appointment as one of those to be sent from Virginia. Despite his zeal for reform of the union, he was reluctant to serve. He had all sorts of excuses for declining appointment. He was not versed in statecraft; he was suffering from rheumatism; his property needed his attention; and he was pledged to attend a meeting of the Cincinnati in Philadelphia at the very time when the convention was to begin its work. He feared that it would accomplish nothing, that his efforts would be wasted. Heavy pressure was brought upon him, by Madison and Governor Edmund Randolph. His presence, his very name, would give strength to the assemblage. He was the first of seven Virginians chosen to represent their state. At last, after much backing and filling, he agreed, on March 28, to serve, provided that his health permitted him to act. Late in April he was called to Fredericksburg because of the illness of his mother and his sister, but he was able to depart for Philadelphia on May 9. Martha preferred to remain at home. With greatest reluctance departing from Mount Vernon, Washington rode northward in his coach and arrived at the Quaker city on the thirteenth. He was greeted there, as he usually was when he entered a city or town after the war, by welcoming horsemen and cannon fire. Church bells also rang to announce the coming of the hero. He did not return home until four months had passed.

XIX

———————✖———————

The President Under the Constitution

W*ashington was one* of the first delegates to reach Philadelphia and one of the last to leave. By May 25 representatives from seven states were present, and it was possible to open the convention. Robert Morris, with whom Washington lodged, moved that the general be chosen as president. No other person, except for Benjamin Franklin, could bring as much dignity to the appointment. Franklin was now in his eighties and not strong enough to serve. Washington was accordingly elected unanimously. Too modest regarding his political genius, as he had once been concerning his military abilities, Washington diffidently accepted the post. His fine manners, together with his refusal to try to inflict his ideas upon the delegates, enabled him to perform superbly. He did not serve upon committees, and he seldom spoke to issues. He maintained good order; others had to solve the many thorny questions that arose.

More and more of the fifty-five chosen delegates appeared, until all of the states except Rhode Island were represented. There was an ample supply of able men among them, despite the absence of Thomas Jefferson, who was serving as American minister in Paris, and John Adams, then envoy to Great Britain. Two other notables of the revolutionary generation, Samuel Adams and Patrick

Henry, who saw no pressing need for constitutional revision, were not present. They were not missed, since they were not remarkable as constructive statesmen. Alexander Hamilton, a delegate from New York, attended only a few sessions. Expressing the view that constitutional monarchy was the ideal form of government, he set himself apart from the other delegates. Besides, the two other members from New York, who could outvote him, were opposed to basic reform. He went home, and they later did likewise. The assemblage contained former revolutionary officers, governors, legislators, lawyers, merchants, and southern planters. Many were college graduates. Outstanding in their contributions were Madison, small, shy, and astute, afterward dubbed Father of the Constitution; lawyer James Wilson of Pennsylvania; John Rutledge and Charles Cotesworth Pinckney of South Carolina, who magnanimously refused to place the interests of their state above those of the nation; and Roger Sherman and Oliver Ellsworth of Connecticut, moderate and sensible men who were most useful in settling quarrels between men from the large and the small states and between northern and southern delegates. There was even a skillful penman in the body who could put the result of its deliberations in decent English, the one-legged Gouverneur Morris, otherwise famed for haughtiness and amorous exploits.

Toiling in secret in order to avoid appeals to spectators and the public, in order to give men opportunity quietly to change their minds and present an appearance of substantial unity regarding the result of their labors, the delegates persevered throughout the heat and humidity of the Philadelphia summer. There were times when it seemed that they would fail to accomplish anything. On July 10 Washington wrote to the absent Hamilton that he could "find but little ground on which the hope of a good establishment can be formed. . . . I almost despair," he said, "of seeing a favorable issue to the proceedings of our Convention, and do therefore repent having had any agency in the business." Presiding for five, six, and even seven hours a day, he must often have been weary and bored as well as discouraged. To be sure, there were pleasures as well as toil that summer. He was entertained at tea and dinner; he attended a convivial meeting of the Sons of St. Patrick; he inspected the garden of botanist William Bartram; he went fishing; and he visited the encampments of the army at Whitemarsh and Valley Forge.

Having decided that they would prepare *the* Constitution rather than try to patch up the Articles of Confederation, the delegates gradually overcame all difficulties and completed the document. They managed to find a compromise between the conflicting notions of champions of the large states and those of the small ones. They succeeded in forging another between southerners and northerners quarreling over the extent of the power of the central government over the oceanic traffic in slaves. There was no debate regarding destruction of the institution of slavery. However much delegates had committed themselves in speech or in print to American liberty, even to liberty in general, they knew that action against black bondage would make acceptance of their handiwork impossible in the South. They agreed upon description of a new central government and its relations to the states and to the people. Only forty-two men were present on September 17 when the Constitution was finally approved by the convention, and three members declined to affix their names. Two Virginians, Edmund Randolph and George Mason, refused to sign. Randolph wished for a second convention to weigh amendments that might be submitted by the states; Mason believed that southern interests had not received sufficient protection. Elbridge Gerry of Massachusetts found many faults in the document. Officially the signers represented only eleven states—Hamilton, returning to the convention, put down his name for New York, but was not authorized to act singly for his state. Nevertheless, as Washington remarked, their achievement was momentous. Dining together at the City Tavern to celebrate the occasion, the signers, aware that they had not devised a perfect document, nonetheless knew that they had performed very well. They were able to return home with the knowledge that they had produced a new system that merited adoption.

The Constitution was far superior to the Articles of Confederation. It provided for a central government endowed with sufficient authority and resting, like those of the states, upon the people. The central government could enforce its will, within limits, upon the people. Its powers were listed, and specific prohibitions were placed on it. Thus, it could not impose export taxes or create a titled nobility. But it could levy import duties and internal taxes; maintain an army and navy; regulate interstate and foreign commerce; emit currency; make treaties; govern the territories of the United States; create new states equal in status to the existing ones; and abolish the abominable oceanic slave trade after the year 1807. The document also contained valuable restrictions upon the states.

They were forbidden to grant hereditary titles or to put forth currency. The central government was to have three branches. There was to be a Congress consisting of a House of Representatives elected by the people in proportion to population and a senate containing two members from each state chosen by its lawmakers. Provision was made for an independent and potentially powerful federal judiciary with judges appointed for life, with a Supreme Court as its capstone. There was to be a president chosen by a majority of electors authorized to vote by the several states. If they failed to make a choice, Congress would have that power. The president would dominate an executive branch. He was to have a veto over acts of Congress. It could be set aside by a two-thirds majority in both houses—Washington, eager for a strong executive, favored a three-quarters requirement. The president was to play a prime role in foreign affairs, to direct the army and navy, and to make federal appointments subject to the approval of Congress. Checks and balances were inserted, so that the three branches might serve to prevent any one of them from usurping the authority of another. Arrangements were included for future amendments. The Constitution has been lavishly praised, and not without reason. Formally amended, elaborated by judicial decisions, further defined by acts of Congress and by custom, it has endured for two centuries. It had defects, including lack of a Bill of Rights, omitted chiefly, no doubt, because the framers of the document thought one unnecessary, since the powers of the central government were specifically enumerated.

The framers of the Constitution made another important contribution. Foreseeing that their work would hardly receive the endorsement of all the state legislatures, as amendments to the Articles of Confederation required, they prescribed a different method for gaining the necessary approval—ratification by state conventions. Moreover, they stipulated that the new system was to go into effect as soon as nine states gave their consent. (Washington, eager to set the new system in motion as soon as possible, favored seven states as the minimum requirement.) It has been contended that the convention exceeded its authority both by making a new basic law and by altering the manner in which it was to be adopted. It should be observed that requirement of unanimous ratification, technically desirable, would very likely prove to be impractical. Certainly the method of adoption proposed by the framers was more democratic than that prescribed by the Articles of Confederation, for the members of the state conventions who had the task of considering the Constitution were to be elected specially for that purpose by the voters in each state. The existing Congress, meeting in New York, declined to stand upon punctilio. It referred the Constitution to the states for action.

Arriving at Mount Vernon on September 22, Washington resumed his routines as a farmer. He was short of cash and had trouble accumulating it to pay his taxes and other debts. But he also spent much time and energy in behalf of the Constitution. He could not decently come forward for it in public and could not vote in support of it as a member of the Virginia assembly or convention, because it was generally assumed that he would become the first president under the new system—if it was established. He knew, of course, that he would be nominated for the office and that he would in all likelihood be chosen. He could urge his friends to strive for adoption, and he did so, encouraging Madison, Hamilton, Light Horse Harry Lee, and Henry Knox to exert themselves. He also vainly tried to soften its opponents, among them the redoubtable Patrick Henry, at that time the most influential Virginia politician. He wrote to Henry that he wished the Constitution "had been made more perfect; but I sincerely believe it is the best that could be obtained at this time; and, as a constitutional door is opened for amendment hereafter, the adoption of it under the present circumstances of the Union is in my opinion desirable." Indeed, he declared, "anarchy" was the alternative. Actually, he did not believe that the Constitution was seriously defective. It was prudent in asserting its merits not to claim perfection for the document. He wrote to his good friend, the Marquis de Chastellux, in May, 1788, that he expected endorsement of it and that "America will lift up her head again and in a few years become respectable among the nations. It is a flattering and consolatory reflection that our rising republics have the good wishes of all the philosophers, patriots and virtuous men in all nations, and that they look upon them as a kind of asylum for mankind. God grant that we may not disappoint their honest expectations by our folly or perverseness." He wrote to Lafayette, "A few short weeks will determine the political fate of America for the present generation and probably produce no small influence on the happiness of society through a long succession of ages to come." He believed that he could see the fingers of Providence at work.

There were many men, Anti-Federalists, who refused to concede that the divine had anything to do with the Constitution. Some even contended that the Articles of Confederation were adequate. Others argued that the Articles needed only small changes to be quite suitable, while still others urged that the Constitution be submitted to a second national convention for revision. Vehement opponents found all sorts of defects in the proposed new system. Was it not an act of usurpation for its makers to set aside the Articles of Confederation, to declare that it would become operative with the consent of only nine states? The states would be reduced to unimportance. The document contained no Bill of Rights, no protection for the individual against an overweening oligarchy. The methods of choosing senators and the president would serve the purposes of the few rather than permit assertion of the wishes of the many. The federal courts would also be of benefit to a class rather than to the mass, some said. The Constitution was framed for the purpose of establishing a national tyranny. It was favored, was it not, by planters, merchants, and lawyers, by the wealthy and the well born, who intended to dominate plain folk? In the South it was hotly contended that the national government under the Constitution would be under the control of northerners, especially New Englanders, who would use their power to further the interests of merchants and to injure those of the planters and farmers of the South. The merits and faults of the document became subjects of hot controversy.

There were potent arguments for the Constitution, aside from its contents, and its Federalist champions made much use of them. Had it not the approval, they asked rhetorically, of the great Franklin, the American sage? And of Washington, the hero who had always been faithful to the trust placed in him? And was it not certain that Washington would become the first president in the new union? He had never sought to become a tyrant, and he never would. It could be contended, and it was, that the proposed new central government, endowed with sufficient powers, would enable America to defend her citizens on land and sea, to prosper, to acquire respect among the nations, to expand her settlements to the Mississippi, even eventually to the Pacific Ocean. Adoption of the Constitution would solidify the gains achieved in consequence of the struggle for independence. Such arguments appealed to many plain folk, tradesmen, farmers, teachers, physicians, and others. Conceding that the Constitution pleased wealthy planters, lawyers, and merchants, they perceived that they also would benefit from its adoption.

The debate over the virtues and faults of the Constitution went on for months in coffeehouses, tearooms, taverns, and the newspapers, of which every city and town had at least one. Sentinels, Brutuses, Catos, and other writers using classical names as pseudonyms filled the newspapers with their essays. At that time it was customary for such a contributor to withhold his own name and for a newspaper to deny its columns to persons who opposed the views of its owner. Accordingly, newspapers were partisan and commonly abusive. It is not likely that they exerted decisive influence. The famous *Federalist* essays put forth by Hamilton, Madison, and Jay in defense of the Constitution, being abstruse, probably convinced only the already persuaded, although the notions about government put forth by the three authors continue to supply grist for students of history and political science. The debate continued, of course, in the state legislatures, where Anti-Federalists often strove to prevent the meeting of the ratifying conventions; in the elections of members of the conventions; and in the conventions themselves.

The outcome was long in doubt. Delaware, Pennsylvania, and New Jersey quickly voted for the Constitution, then Connecticut, Georgia, Massachusetts, Maryland, and South Carolina. It became apparent that New Hampshire would supply the ninth ratification. But the issue remained unsettled until the summer of 1788. It was clear by that time that Rhode Island would vote in the negative, that New York hung in the balance, and that North Carolina would follow the example of Virginia. If the new union was to get under way, it must have the support of Virginia. Given the endorsement of Washington's home state, the remaining holdouts could be persuaded or coerced into joining.

Accordingly, the decisive struggle over ratification took place in the Virginia convention, in June. The Anti-Federalists were numerous in the state, and they were led by Patrick Henry, who had lost none of his oratorical gifts. He had the support of Arthur Lee, Benjamin Harrison, George Mason, and Richard Henry Lee, the latter of whom had once powerfully exerted influence to secure the appointment of Washington as commander in chief. They were dominated by fear that the proposed new government would be tyrannical and would favor the interests of commercial northerners against those of agricultural Virginia. Washington had encouraged the Federalists from Mount Vernon. They had a small majority when the convention began its deliberations, and he expected that they would triumph. They had won over Edmund Randolph. But many of the Anti-Federalists were bitterly opposed to the proposed union, and Henry vehemently appealed to prejudices and local interests. He stood forth for liberty—the Constitution did not contain a Bill of Rights. He foresaw not only a national tyranny, but a Congress under northern domination using exigencies of a future war to destroy slavery. He pointed out that the federal courts under the Constitution would have power to force Virginians to pay their debts to British creditors—many planters had neglected to meet obligations incurred before the War of Independence and had managed to hold off those creditors. Madison, a short man and a diffident one, led the Federalists. He had the help of Light Horse Harry Lee, who rudely pointed out that he had fought for liberty while Henry talked about it. But it was Madison who quietly demolished or reduced the force of Henry's principal arguments. Promising that the Federalists would work to add a Bill of Rights to the Constitution to protect citizens and Virginia, after the new government was under way, he held his followers together and secured ratification by a vote of 89 to 79, on June 25.

The new union was then assured. New Hampshire endorsed it while the Virginians were debating it. The promise of the Federalists to help pass a Bill of Rights was soon effective in New York, where Hamilton spoke brilliantly for the Constitution, and later, in 1789, in North Carolina. Rhode Island did not accede until 1790, after the new union was in operation. North Carolina and Rhode Island had little choice, since the new system could proceed without them, since they could not prosperously proceed as independent republics, and since their people felt compelled to join their lot to those of their fellow Americans.

Much has been said about the achievements of the Founding Fathers—the makers of the Constitution and the leaders who secured its adoption. Even more remarkable was the behavior of the American people as a whole. The contest over the Constitution was marked by strong language regarding issues and occasionally by pungent remarks concerning the intellectual power and integrity of participants. There was minor mob action at Albany and Harrisburg. One debater in North Carolina received a black eye from an opponent who was trying to make him see the light. There was a residue of rancor from the struggle. Both Patrick Henry and

George Mason had been insulted by Federalists who pointedly referred to the fact that neither of them had performed military service in the War of Independence. Henry saw to it that Madison was denied a seat in the new Senate. Moreover, Anti-Federalists, including Henry and Governor George Clinton of New York, tried vainly to call a second national constitutional convention. But most of them accepted the outcome with good grace and learned to be satisfied with the new system. Even Henry eventually discovered that it deserved his support. Long afterward scholars asserted that the Constitution would not have obtained approval had it been subjected to a plebiscite in each state. They were undoubtedly correct in that conclusion. Would it have been set aside had it been considered by a plebiscite among the Americans as a whole? We cannot know the answer to that question. We do know that they accepted the verdict and that they executed a basic reform in their governmental system in a truly republican contest, without convulsion, even without loss of a single life.

The new machinery began to move. The old Congress of the Confederation, before it adjourned forever, did what was necessary to set the new national government in motion, arranging for meetings of the presidential electors at the state capitals and for convening the new Congress at New York on March 4, 1789. In the choice of members of the two houses the Federalists were easily victorious, although Virginia, under the influence of Henry, elected as senators the Anti-Federalists Richard Henry Lee and William Grayson. Happily, Madison secured election to the House of Representatives. There could be no doubt that Washington would be chosen as president. The prospect did not delight him. He found all sorts of reasons why he should not serve. Had he not done enough for his country? He was not so strong as he had been. The duties of the office would be arduous, and he would be forced to abandon the peace and quiet of his beloved home for the vexing world of politics. His property required his attention. If he accepted the office, would he not be assailed as a selfish seeker of power and place? In October, 1788, he wrote that "if I should receive the appointment and if I should be prevailed upon to accept it, the acceptance would be attended with more diffidence and reluctance than I ever experienced before in my life." But his friends, Hamilton, Light Horse Harry Lee, Benjamin Lincoln, and others, urged him to yield to the popular will, and newspaper editors throughout the country clamored for his election. In the end, he was flattered as well as disconcerted by the prospect. Foreseeing agonies in the presidency, he also knew that he could add greatly to the contribution he had already made to America.

Bowing to the inevitable, Washington resolved to do his civic duty. He entrusted care of Mount Vernon to George Augustine Washington, and he prepared to leave for New York. His feelings continued to be "not unlike those of a culprit who is going to the place of his execution," but he began to phrase a paper indicating his acceptance. He had no need for it until mid-April, 1789. The new Congress assembled slowly, in part because of winter weather. As soon as sufficient members of the two houses had appeared, they met under the chairmanship of Senator John Langdon and counted the ballots cast by the electors. According to the Constitution each of them was to cast two votes. The person having the largest number, if a majority among the electors, was to be president; the person having the next largest number of votes was to be vice-president. To the surprise of no one, all of the electors had voted for Washington. John Adams, popular in his native New England, was named on sufficient ballots to receive the vice-presidency. Washington was prepared to act as soon as he received official notice of his election. It came on April 14, carried by Charles Thomson, the perennial secretary of Congress, in the form of a letter from Senator Langdon. Washington read to Thomson a paper prepared for the occasion. He wished that "there may not be reason for regretting the choice," and he informed Thomson that he would be ready to depart for New York, which was to be the temporary American capital, within two days. He sent off a letter of acceptance to Langdon. Leaving Martha behind, to follow at her convenience, he began the journey on the sixteenth in his coach. He was accompanied by his good friend Colonel David Humphreys and by Thomson. He wrote in his diary for that day, "I bade adieu to Mount Vernon, to private life, and to domestic felicity, and with a mind oppressed with more anxious and painful sensations than I have words to express, set out for New York."

There followed a triumphal procession along roads now as familiar to him as those that he had earlier followed to Williamsburg and Winchester. Everywhere he was welcomed by cheering crowds, escorted by horsemen, and banqueted by almost adoring citizens. Officers and men who had served under him in the War of Independence came forward to greet him. He was honored with a farewell dinner at Alexandria. Cannon saluted him when he entered Baltimore, again when he left that place. Delaware men entertained him at Wilmington and rode with him as far as the boundary of Pennsylvania, where Pennsylvanians appeared to escort him into Philadelphia. They brought with them a splendid white horse, and he rode it into the city. His arrival there was celebrated beyond any other event in the history of the city. People, perhaps twenty thousand in number, lined "every fence, field and avenue" to see him. He was the guest at a great dinner at which fourteen toasts with accompanying wine were drunk. He went on as rapidly as his none-too-sober admirers would permit. At Trenton, the scene of his most brilliant victory, he was specially greeted by lines of women and girls, and he read on a welcoming arch, THE DEFENDER OF THE MOTHERS WILL ALSO DEFEND THE DAUGHTERS. Flowers were strewn in his path. On he went, through Princeton, New Brunswick, and Woodbridge, to Elizabethtown. There he was met by a committee of senators and representatives sent to escort him to New York. After more festivities the party boarded a barge for the last leg of his journey. As the barge approached Manhattan, on April 23, larger and smaller vessels followed it. Then a second barge, owned by Henry Knox, appeared, to carry the president to a landing at the end of Wall Street. Aboard it were Knox and John Jay, who had been in charge respectively of affairs of war and foreign relations in the Confederation. British, Spanish, and American ships fired cannon in Washington's honor. He rode in parade upon his white horse amidst wildly cheering throngs and at last found a little peace and quiet in lodgings prepared for him.

During the next few days, while the president settled into his new quarters, received numerous visitors, and made duty calls upon officials and friends, arrangements were made for his inauguration. A trivial, yet important question arose. How should the president and vice-president be addressed? Vain John Adams, presiding over the Senate, accustomed to European formalities, desired a sufficiently high-sounding title for himself and an even loftier one for Washington. He proposed that the president be known as "His Highness, the President of the United States of America and Protector of their Liberties." Congress declined to accept the notions of Adams. He was given no special epithet, to his distress. Washington was pleased to accept "President of the United States of America" as his official designation. So it was that the head of the American republic came to be addressed as "Mr. President," a simple title that would acquire republican dignity. On April 29 Washington was inaugurated with proper ceremony at Federal Hall. He rode part way to it, then walked to the hall along with other citizens. There, before a throng of onlookers he took his oath of office. "Do you solemnly swear," he was asked by Chancellor Robert R. Livingston, "that you will faithfully execute the office of President of the United States and will, to the best of your ability, preserve, protect, and defend the Constitution of the United States?" Washington repeated the oath, adding solemnly, "So help me God." There was no doubt that he would keep his pledge. It was observed that the passing years and their cares had lined his face. Hurrahs came from the crowd. He spoke, not at great length. The new system must work. He indicated his approval of addition of a Bill of Rights to the Constitution and said that he opposed any change that would weaken the authority of the new government. His very presence at its head gave it strength. He towered above the kings and emperors of his time.

XX

---※---

The President of a Nation

The new president lived well, as formally and majestically as republican principles permitted. He was supplied with a good house on Cherry Street—this without any reference to the legend that as a boy he had refused to lie concerning his improper use of a hatchet. He later rented a house on Broadway. Congress set his salary at twenty-five thousand dollars per annum, a sum that he considered to be money for expenses rather than pay. It seemed sufficiently liberal. However, it proved to be no more than adequate, and he frequently drew it in advance. He was accustomed to the good things of life at Mount Vernon, and he insisted upon having them—upon having more of them—than he had enjoyed in Virginia. He had fourteen white servants and seven slaves in his house on Broadway, and he rode about in a coach drawn by six horses. After Martha came on from Virginia, the Washingtons entertained lavishly at dinners, offering bounteous food and free-flowing wine. The president and his wife also held a reception every Friday evening, a gathering so dignified that it bore resemblance to the levee of a European monarch. Ice cream and lemonade were served. Everyone who was anyone attended. After 1790 his birthday was celebrated, like that of an English king. Citizens who were fond of pomp began to refer to "Lady Washington."

Martha remained modest and sweet-tempered, gaining universal respect and much affection. It is to be suspected that the constant adulation to which her husband was subjected, so long continued, threatened to make him self-important.

But Washington was chastened by private troubles, and public vexations mounted, although the new nation flourished. His mother died in August, 1789. He had known that he would not see her again when he said good-bye to her before leaving Virginia for his inauguration. Her death was expected, for she was old and had suffered from cancer of the breast. He had never been close to her. Still, he was reminded of the transitoriness of life. He was sharply reminded of his own mortality in 1789 and again in the following year. In June, 1789, he became feverish and was sorely troubled by a growth upon his left thigh. It proved to be a carbuncle rather than a malignant tumor, and it was cut out by his physician. He suffered acutely both before and after the operation. Then, on May 6, 1790, he came down with a bad cold, which soon proved to be influenza. His condition worsened, with fever and pneumonia developing. Doubt grew that he would survive. On the fifteenth his life was "despaired of." But that strong constitution that had carried him through so many difficulties saved him once more. That afternoon he began to sweat, and the fever subsided. He was soon himself again, but he knew that another such illness might end his life.

The time would come when the agonies of office seemed almost worse than those of the body, but those ailments were minor for many months. The First Congress under the Constitution was a very productive one. Washington wrought well as the chief magistrate, bringing talented and worthy men into office, and the United States government acquired respect at home and abroad. Britain at last sent a minister, George Hammond. Congress easily found a source of substantial revenue, import duties, the proceeds of which both nourished the federal machinery and went far toward establishing the credit of the nation. Congress also prepared the Bill of Rights, which secured the consent of the states by 1791. It will not surprise students of politics that Anti-Federalists who had thundered against the lack of it during the debates over the Constitution were not remarkably eager to enact it—not a few of them had used its absence merely as a debating point. Other achievements of the lawmakers included the founding of the Departments of State, Treasury, War, and Justice, all of them small in size, that of Justice only in embryo. A postmaster general made a modest and inexpensive appearance. The federal judiciary was developed, consisting of district courts, higher circuit courts to hear appeals, and, at its apex, the Supreme Court. The cabinet, not provided for in the Constitution, came into being by 1793, when Washington began to hold meetings with the heads of the departments as a group, a practice that endured.

The offices had to be filled, primarily by the president, who suffered in consequence, as did all of his successors. He was plagued with applications from men who were willing to sacrifice themselves at a suitable salary for the good of the country. Even his nephew Bushrod Washington, a young lawyer, asked for the post of federal district attorney for Virginia, a request that his uncle denied; for Washington, unlike Benjamin Franklin and John Adams, was not addicted to nepotism. Arthur Lee, mentioning that he had been accepted at the bar in England, sought a place on the Supreme Court. He had opposed ratification of the Constitution, and moreover, he was a troublemaker. Washington refused to put him on the bench. Washington appointed the best and most experienced men he could find, rewarding especially officers who had served under him in the War of Independence, men who deserved well of their country. Thus Benjamin Lincoln, who needed a job, became customs collector in the port of Boston; thus Henry Knox became secretary of war. He also chose for high office individuals who had not performed military service but had contributed to the republic as civilians, including John Jay and Thomas Jefferson. Jay became chief justice of the Supreme Court, but there was little judicial business for several years and his duties were very light. The key appointments made by Washington were those of Jefferson as secretary of state and Alexander Hamilton as secretary of the treasury. They were the dominant figures in his cabinet. Knox had much less influence, and Attorney General Edmund Randolph also played only a minor role. Jefferson and Hamilton clashed almost as soon as they came into close contact.

It is no secret that Jefferson was a most remarkable man. He was a graduate of the College of William and Mary, a lawyer, a scholar, a philosopher, a skillful writer, a diplomat, an architect, an inventor, a gifted politician, almost everything but a soldier. Inheriting a large Virginia estate in youth, he had added to it, like Washington, by a happy marriage of convenience. In youth he owned more land than Washington ever had. Born in 1743, he lived handsomely in his commodious Monticello mansion when not in office. Tall, lanky, freckled, sandy-haired, he was in life less handsome than he is in marble commemorating him, but he was sufficiently imposing in physique. He differed from Washington, and much more from Hamilton, in his political views. Minister to France when the Constitution was drawn up and adopted, he had found it satisfactory rather than altogether splendid. One defect that he saw in it was the power of the House of Representatives with respect to taxation, for he feared that it would be abused. Indeed, for the same reason he disliked all central authority in domestic affairs except when it rested in his own true hands. Accordingly, he desired that state power should be preferred to national except in foreign relations. More important, he wished that the individual should be as free as possible from all governmental interference. He did not have in mind just any individual. He hoped that the typical American would be, into the distant future, a landowning and economically independent farmer. He detested orders of nobility and aristocracy in general, and had it seemed possible entirely to abolish slavery, he would have urged that it be done. He believed that the spread of education, in considerable part at public expense, would improve the plain citizen. The citizen should choose able and virtuous officeholders who would use their own judgment when wielding their limited authority in his behalf. He was an optimist, looking forward to an American utopia. Somewhat has been made, by his admirers, of the fact that he walked to his inauguration as president in 1801. He did so only because his coach was not available—Washington may have walked just as far toward Federal Hall. Jefferson's tastes were not simple; he was a sophisticated man. In France, where he served as American minister for five years, after the death of his wife, he engaged in a torrid love affair with the artist Maria Cosway, a married Englishwoman. It has been asserted, without sound proof, that he fathered at least one child in a liaison with one of his mulatto slaves. He did not lack flesh or blood. He would become the principal founder of the first Republican party and eventually an idol of the Democratic one.

Washington was well acquainted with Jefferson, liked him, and trusted him. Selecting him as secretary of state, the president took into account the fact that his fellow Virginian as minister to France had acquired knowledge of European affairs in general and especially of the great revolution that was under way in France. When Jefferson returned home from Paris on leave of absence early in

1790, he found in his mail a letter from Washington asking him to serve as secretary of state. He accepted the post and made his way to New York, taking over from John Jay, who had temporarily looked after foreign business. Jefferson found Hamilton well established at the Treasury. The two men would become inveterate enemies.

Hamilton had an exotic background. Born on the island of Nevis in the West Indies in 1755 or 1757, he was a product of the union of a Scottish merchant and the wife of another merchant who had refused to give her a divorce. Long afterward John Adams nastily referred to Hamilton as a "bastard son of a Scottish pedlar," but the unofficial union of his parents was not brief or sordid. Compelled to make his own way in the world, Hamilton moved to New York, where he studied briefly at King's College, then entered the Patriot forces as an artillery officer. Good-looking, modest in stature, he had already given evidence of great intellectual power. He became an aide to Washington and resigned that appointment after a tiff with the general, but returned to service for the Yorktown campaign. He was brave, honest about money, industrious, and charming. Becoming a lawyer, he married Betsy, the eldest daughter of Philip Schuyler, and so became allied to New York aristocrats. He was less than faithful to his wife, but he was devoted to aristocracy. Acquiring experience in public affairs, he had campaigned effectively for a stronger central government and had brilliantly debated in behalf of the Constitution in the New York ratifying convention. Washington was well acquainted with his merits, and he was recommended for the Treasury by various men. He was in several ways, despite his youth, an excellent choice. But Hamilton had struggled in behalf of the new system only because it was superior to the Confederation. He believed that government ought to be in the hands of an able few, that the mass of people formed a "great beast." Hence he conceived that the British system, with its dominating monarch and aristocrats, was nearly ideal. Announcing his admiration of it in the Constitutional Convention at Philadelphia, he never abandoned the notion that a similar structure would be ideal for America. He would toy with the idea that it might be necessary to create an American dictatorship. He would become, along with John Adams, a principal founder of the Federalist party.

Adams was also a person of importance in the new regime. He had little to do with the making of policy, but he was the heir apparent to Washington, either through the death of the president or by election after Washington left office. He was not happy as vice-president. His salary was only five thousand dollars per annum, he was compelled to live simply, and his powers as presiding officer of the Senate were minor. He felt slighted, as if his contributions to the republic had not been suitably rewarded. In his middle fifties when he took his oath of office, he suffered from palsy and had lost all his teeth—apparently outdoing Washington in that respect. But his speech and his pen retained bite, for he had the New England habit, not unknown elsewhere in America, of giving all and sundry a piece of his mind. Unlike many who cannot afford to donate part of their cranial equipment, Adams was intellectually gifted, though less astute in politics than he believed himself to be. His notions of government were in several ways similar to those of Jefferson, who was his very good friend until the two men became rivals for the presidency. Like the Virginian, he was a Unitarian, but he was also a pessimist. He doubted that the Americans would possess enough virtue into the far future to maintain the republic. But it must be given ample opportunity to demonstrate its worth. He believed that the voting citizens should vest authority in a natural aristocracy of worthy, talented, and liberally educated men, especially lawyers, men like himself. Inevitably, since families of means would be able to provide educational opportunity for their young, part of that aristocracy would consist of persons of means who would devote much of their energy to defense of their property and other special interests. Such selfishness would be checked by a division of power among citizen voters, legislators, and a strong executive. Time would reveal that he did not see eye to eye with his cofounder of the Federalist party.

The struggles among those politicians were still in the future in September, 1789, when Congress recessed in an atmosphere of good feeling. The postwar depression had begun to lift as early as 1787. A rather general prosperity had made its appearance, and many of the states had managed to put their finances in order. Washington took advantage of a lull in public business to make a tour of New England—except for Rhode Island, which had not yet ratified the Constitution. He traveled as far as Maine in his coach, spending the night in taverns along the way and mounting on horseback when necessary for the social functions of welcome that had now become a routine for him. Having long since developed great respect for the military qualities of the New Englanders, he now admired their way of life, their prosperous farms, their attractive villages and towns, the fewness of the very rich and the very poor among them. Only one incident marred his progress. In Boston, Governor John Hancock, claiming to be ill, attempted to arrange matters so that Washington would make the first call upon him. Washington let Hancock know that the governor must come to greet the traveler if he expected to receive any act of politeness from the president of the United States, and Hancock quickly recovered sufficiently from his illness to pay his respects. There were a few places in New England where Washington did not sleep.

After the return of Washington and the Congress to New York a serious controversy arose. It developed from a remarkable scheme devised by Hamilton, with the approval of the president, to establish the credit of the new nation. Congress had issued about twenty-two million dollars in certificates of indebtedness to persons supplying goods or services during the War of Independence. The states had also contracted large debts in the common cause. Hamilton proposed that the nation undertake to pay all of the debts. Money necessary to meet the resulting expense was to be secured by raising customs duties and imposing excise taxes. The scheme would surely indicate to the world that the United States was determined to meet its financial obligations. But it was open to very serious criticisms. Many of the certificates of indebtedness had passed from the hands of their original holders and had been cheaply purchased by speculators. Hamilton proposed to pay the present holders of the papers—stimulating a rush on the part of unscrupulous members of Congress to acquire certificates before their owners learned about the measure. Madison, trying to obtain an arrangement whereby the original lenders would share in the payments, was overborne. The assumption of the state debts was even more dubious. It was hardly necessary in order to demonstrate the financial reliability of the nation. Hamilton seems to have had it in mind that the creditors of the states, becoming creditors of the nation, would accordingly give their allegiance to the central government. Assumption had another defect. Some of the states, Virginia in particular, had paid off much of their debt, taxing their citizens for the purpose; other states, especially in the North, had not.

The Virginians angrily opposed assumption. There were not enough votes in Congress to secure its adoption. Hamilton found a way to obtain it. The question of the permanent location of the capital, a source of dispute between North and South during the days of the Confederation, was also arousing antagonism. Men from the South favored a site on the Potomac; men from the North were for New York or Philadelphia. Hamilton hinted to Jefferson, recently arrived from Virginia, that enough northern votes to move the capital to the Potomac would appear if assumption was adopted. The implied bargain was executed. Hamilton's proposals were endorsed in their entirety by Congress, except for excise taxes, and it was agreed that the capital should be moved to Philadelphia for ten years, thence, after arangements had been made, to a site near Georgetown. Thus it was that the new city of Washington, with its sultry summers, became the permanent center of the national government. Commissioners appointed to oversee its development almost inevitably named it after the national hero. The credit of the United States was also firmly established. The national debt increased while Hamilton was at the Treasury, but it became evident that the prospering United States could and would pay its debts.

In June, 1790, after Congress had gone home, Washington went on a holiday to Long Island with Jefferson and others. He did a bit of fishing. In August he visited Rhode Island, which had at last joined the new union, with Jefferson and George Clinton, then removed to the new seat of government at Philadelphia. After acquiring the handsome house of Robert Morris for his home—with a hairdresser as a next-door neighbor—Washington traveled on to Mount Vernon for a holiday. All went as smoothly and happily as might be until he reached home. As always he enjoyed a quieter life there. "I had rather be at Mount Vernon with a friend or two about me," he wrote, "than to be attended by the officers of state and the representatives of every power in Europe." But he had been informed before he left Philadelphia that the Hamilton measures were very unpopular in Virginia. He now received complaints from men who had stood forth for the Constitution as well as from former Anti-Federalists. They contended that the new national government was dominated by northern lawyers, bankers, merchants, speculators, and thieves who were hostile to southern interests. They especially profited from redemption of the certificates of indebtedness and from assumption. The new tariffs raised the prices of goods imported from England, and would benefit Yankee shipowners, who were prospering. Since he had given his consent to the measures, it was implied that he had made a serious mistake.

But he refused to admit that their grievances were enormous. He had made it a matter of personal policy to buy from Americans or Europeans other than the English. Britain was doing all that it could to injure American commerce. Did the dissatisfied Virginians prefer to give business to foreign enemies rather than to their fellow countrymen, he asked. The Virginians had a remedy, he said. Let them defend their interests in the chambers of Congress. They did not cease to complain; nor were they soon able to check Hamilton and his allies in Congress.

At the beginning of December, 1790, after the return of Washington and Congress to Philadelphia, all seemed reasonably well with the nation. An expedition led by General Josiah Harmar against hostile Indians in the Northwest Territory had encountered defeat. It was not irretrievable. Vermont and Kentucky were about to become states, and the country was prosperous. But Hamilton soon supplied additional cause for discontent to Virginians and many other Americans. He proposed and secured the passage of an excise tax on whiskey, which would offend its imbibers in general and, much more seriously, would offend frontier folk who both drank the liquid and used it in lieu of currency, folk who were not in any event fond of law or taxes. Indeed, seeking to create a commercial and industrial America, Hamilton was preparing various measures for that purpose, including protective tariffs. Copying the British, he hoped to create a sinking fund, a device without signal merit. His goal pleased enterprising and speculative merchants and bankers. It was anathema to Jefferson and a host of men who believed that America should remain agrarian and, presumably, more virtuous.

Toward developing his system, much of which he was unable to secure, the ingenious Hamilton brought forward his scheme to charter the Bank of the United States, modeled upon the Bank of England, although in an attempt to stifle criticism on that score he said that it was basically copied from the Bank of Amsterdam. His bank, to function for twenty years, was to be both public and private, the nation to hold 20 percent of its stock, investors the remainder. It was to have power to establish branches and exclusive right to emit a paper currency. It could be contended that the bank would both supply a sound currency and useful loans to the federal government, as it did. The scheme was defended by New Englanders and other northerners; it was opposed, chiefly by southerners, on the grounds that it favored northern speculators and also that it violated the Constitution, which contained no specific authority for the founding of the bank. The measure was endorsed by Congress early in 1791.

Constantly seeking to promote prosperity and strengthen the national government, Washington perceived the merits of the scheme. But was it constitutional? Should he sign the bill or veto it? He asked the advice of Jefferson, Randolph, and Madison. All three contended that creation of the bank, since it was not specifically authorized by the Constitution, would violate the basic document. They contended that the phrase in the Constitution that gave Congress authority to enact measures "necessary" to execute its specific powers should be strictly construed, that *necessary* meant essential, not merely convenient or suitable. Washington also sought the opinion of Knox and Hamilton. The secretary of the treasury, with the approval of Knox, pointed out that Congress possessed authority to tax, to issue currency, and to borrow money. It was, then, reasonable to infer that "all the means requisite and fairly applicable" to exercising its financial powers were constitutional so long as they were not specifically forbidden by the Constitution, immoral, or "contrary to the essential ends of political society." For him *necessary* meant convenient, suitable, or well adapted. Hamilton laid down the doctrine of implied powers, which was afterward to be so frequently employed to expand national authority. Washington accepted the argument advanced by the secretary of the treasury and signed the bill into law. Jefferson submitted gracefully to the decision of the president, and the bank proved to be useful. Northern speculators who bought shares in the bank did not profit remarkably. But a constitutional issue was now added to the economic clashes between North and South. Rivalry between Jefferson and Hamilton became increasingly intense.

Soon after the bank was enshrined in law, the First Congress went home. Considering its accomplishments and his own, Washington wrote, "Our public credit is restored, our resources are increasing, and the general appearance of things at least equals the most sanguine expectation that was formed of the effects of the present government." Jefferson was not so well pleased. He perceived a growing "sect" led by Hamilton and permeated by aristocratic and even monarchical notions. The *Gazette of the United States,* a newspaper edited by John Fenno, was consistently supporting Hamiltonian ideas and projects. Jefferson encouraged Philip Freneau to establish a newspaper to challenge Fenno, and

Freneau founded the *National Gazette*. The lines were beginning to form between a Federalist party led by Hamilton and John Adams and a Republican party led by Jefferson. Washington continued to think of himself as a man above faction, but he became increasingly Federalist in action, without admiration for things British, with continuing respect and affection for Jefferson and other emergent Republicans.

But Washington did indeed have reason to be satisfied with the progress of the republic. Leaving Philadelphia, he stopped off at the site of the "Federal City," then went on a tour of the southern states, visiting Richmond; Halifax, New Bern, and Wilmington in North Carolina; Georgetown and Charleston in South Carolina; and Savannah and Augusta in Georgia. Turning back northward, he passed through Columbia and Camden in South Carolina to Charlotte, Salisbury, Salem, and Guilford in North Carolina, thence to Fredericksburg and to Mount Vernon. He visited battlefields of the War of Independence and was warmly welcomed wherever he went. He noted that the widespread prosperity he had seen in New England was lacking in the South. Still, all was well there. He enjoyed the plaudits of his numerous hosts, and he contentedly rested at home before setting out again for Philadelphia. There were a few places in the South where he did not eat.

Although Washington had good reason to be pleased with the achievements of his first two years in office and with the wealthy economy of the nation, he faced troubles during the following year beyond those of growing political strife, especially difficulties in the West supplied by Spain, Britain, and Indians. During and after the War of Independence, American frontier folk flooded into the Old Southwest, especially into Kentucky and Tennessee. After the war they also began to push westward through Georgia. The confederacy of the Creeks, warlike and numerous, inhabiting what is now northern Georgia and northern Alabama, perceived that its independence was threatened and became increasingly uneasy. Spain claimed territory north of the southern boundary line of the United States as it was described in the treaty of peace in 1783, maintaining a post in that territory at Natchez on the Mississippi. Spain also fomented feeling among the Creeks and other southern Indian tribes against the new republic and used its possession of both shores of the lower Mississippi to bar American use of the river, much desired by Kentuckians, Tennesseeans, and other frontiersmen as an avenue for sending their produce to market. Britain was cramping the commerce of the Americans on the Atlantic and in the Caribbean by applying the Navigation Acts to them as foreigners, an action that the Patriots had not fully foreseen when they struck for independence. Moreover, contending that America had failed to execute all the provisions of the treaty of peace, Britain continued to hold a series of posts on American soil adjacent to the boundary with Canada—Point au Fer, Oswegatchie, Oswego, Niagara, Miami, Detroit, and Michilimackinac. The forts also served as bases for disseminating propaganda against the United States among the Indians of the Northwest Territory and for supplying them with muskets, ammunition, and tomahawks, in theory for use in hunting down deer and buffalo rather than American frontiersmen.

What to do? It was obviously imprudent to challenge Britain or Spain militarily. Washington perceived that it was necessary to negotiate with those powers, that the growth of population and wealth would enable America to assert her rights and claims more and more emphatically with the passage of time. He bargained with them as best he could, without much result for several years. It was all the more important to avoid armed clash with Britain or Spain, because even more serious troubles were beginning to loom in consequence of the mighty revolution that began in France in 1789. It was apparent before the end of 1791 that a great European war was about to erupt.

The awkward situation in the Old Southwest worsened before it improved. The Kentuckians became restless, not only because they could not freely use the Mississippi, but because they were unhappy citizens of a Virginia that gave little heed to their interests and desires. A separatist sentiment developed among them, some Kentuckians even turning toward establishing some sort of connection with Spain by which they would be able to carry goods to and from the Gulf of Mexico. Creation of the Commonwealth of Kentucky as the fifteenth state in 1792—Vermont had been admitted to the union as the fourteenth in 1791—greatly reduced separatist feeling, although it did not entirely vanish. It was also possible to avoid war with the Creeks. Washington hospitably received their chief, King Alexander McGillivray, in New York in 1790, and agents of the president soothed the successors of McGillivray and the Creek warriors with smooth talk and presents. The Creeks remained quiet, and Washington even managed to secure from them a cession of land in Georgia. A war that broke out between them and their western neighbors, the Chickasaws, in 1793, providing the Creeks with military occupation, also served to moderate their behavior toward the Great White Father in Philadelphia.

Matters went from bad to worse in the Old Northwest. Pouring across the Appalachians south of the Ohio during and immediately after the War of Independence, pioneers effectively occupied Tennessee and flooded into Kentucky, not without bloody warfare with the Indians. The lust of the backwoodsmen for fresh lands was not satisfied. They began to move into the Old Northwest, founding Marietta, Ohio, in 1788, and establishing themselves in the region of Cincinnati. The Indians of the Old Northwest insisted that the settlers evacuate their new homes. They had been in the habit of raiding into West Virginia and Kentucky; now they gave their unwanted attentions to the new settlements north of the Ohio. The result was an armed conflict that became ever more distressing for Washington in the early years of his presidency, one that he could not prevent.

In the spring of 1792 Washington considered his personal situation. He was sixty years of age, and he was tired at times. The second presidential election was approaching. He rather thought that the condition of the United States was good, that he was no longer needed at the head of the nation. He was weary of political squabbling. Lacking the thick skin of a veteran politician, he wondered whether frequent Republican newspaper attacks upon governmental policies were indirectly aimed at him. He indicated to members of his cabinet and to Madison that he was thinking of retirement to Mount Vernon. Ought he not to announce his purpose, so that he would not be considered for a second term? All of his advisers urged him to continue in office. Early in May he conferred with Madison regarding his wish to leave office and a suitable farewell address. There was no doubt that he would be chosen president again unless he let it be known that he was determined to retire. Madison pleaded with the president to continue. The rise of party spirit, said Madison, supplied an argument against, not for, retirement; the Republicans were in no way hostile to Washington. If he retained the presidency through a second term, the national government would acquire added prestige and stability. Washington was not convinced. He sought the opinion of Jefferson. The secretary of state, coming forth as an ardent party man, emphatically advised the president to continue for at least one or two years. "Your being at the helm," said Jefferson, "will be more than an answer to every argument which can be used to alarm and lead the people in any quarter into violence or secession. . . . North and South will hang together if they have you to hang on." During that time "monarchists" could be put down; "an honest majority" of Republicans could appear in Congress. Jefferson soon afterward added to his advice a thoroughgoing denunciation of the Hamiltonian measures and of their framer and his allies.

The president withheld his decision. Asked by Washington to respond to the charges made by Jefferson, Hamilton asserted that they were utterly unwarranted, that the republic was menaced only by the Republicans, by those who excited jealousies and apprehensions among the people that would lead to civil commotion and anarchy and thus toward monarchy. Late in the summer Washington, urging that "the fairest prospect of happiness and prosperity that ever was presented to man will be lost, perhaps forever," if internal dissension could not be checked, requested the two men to make "liberal allowances" for each other, to exercise "mutual forbearances." He now learned, from their replies, that both of them had taken an active part in the newspaper war between the Federalists and Republicans, that they were personal as well as political enemies. Both halfheartedly said that they were willing to try to work together, but they expressed so much animosity that an accommodation was obviously impossible. Indeed, Jefferson announced that he would in any event resign from the cabinet when Washington left office, and asserted, "I will not suffer my retirement to be clouded by the slanders of a man whose history, from the moment at which history can stoop to notice him, is a tissue of machinations against the liberty of the country which had not only received and given him bread, but heaped honors on his head."*

Deferring his declaration, Washington continued to try to make peace between his two aggressive advisers, in vain. The clash between the Republicans and the Federalists became even sharper as the year 1792 drew toward its close. It was increasingly evident to Washington that he could moderate party passions by remaining in office. Although he had not contracted the eight-year itch that commonly afflicts occupants of the presidency, its agonies were as yet inferior to its ecstasies. There was no one who could oppose him, and he was assured of the support of both the Federalists and the Republicans. At the beginning of October in a friendly confer-

---

* Jefferson fantastically accused Hamilton of cowardice.

ence at Mount Vernon, Jefferson again assured him that the Republicans might disagree with the president regarding Hamilton and his policies but that they desired him to remain at the helm. Accordingly, Washington refrained from announcing a wish to retire, making it clear that he would accept reelection. Again the electors voted unanimously for him. The Republicans confined themselves to campaigning for seats in Congress and against Vice-President Adams. They put forward against Adams the leading Republican in the North, Governor George Clinton of New York. Adams was chosen a second time, by an electoral vote of 77 to 50.

Although the Republicans voted for Washington, party warfare was increasing rather than lessening. The contest between Adams and Clinton was warmly fought. The newspapers—there were scores of them—took part, each of them glorifying its favorite and denying its columns to his opponent, as was then the custom. John Fenno and other Federalist editors had long been in the habit of heaping fulsome praise upon Hamilton and Adams and abusing Jefferson. They condemned the Republicans as irresponsible enemies of good order. Freneau and other Republican editors had denounced Hamilton and Adams. Attacking the Federalists as would-be monarchists and would-be aristocrats, Freneau had even suggested that another American revolution might be necessary. In the fall of 1792 an essay in his newspaper referred to Adams' "breadth of belly" and Hamilton's "length of nose." Washington had hitherto escaped newspaper abuse. Now Freneau made much of the "monarchical" tone of the weekly levee held by the Washingtons and the annual celebration of Washington's birthday. Ought the president to behave as if he were a king? Ought his birthday to be honored as was that of George III of Britain? Much more severe censure would eventually come from some Republicans. Partisan feeling was running higher and higher.

In December, 1792, one James Reynolds accused Hamilton of improper speculation in federal securities. Hamilton was able to establish his financial integrity only by offering proof that he had engaged in a passionate love affair with Reynolds' wife and that the couple had blackmailed him. A committee of Congress exonerated the secretary of the treasury, and the sordid affair was kept secret until after Hamilton returned to private life. In the following January, William Branch Giles of Virginia, with the approval of Jefferson, opened another attack upon Hamilton. Giles sought, vainly, to secure a vote of censure upon the secretary of the treasury. He could offer no evidence of misconduct on the part of Hamilton. As Washington took his second oath of office, he must have found a measure of relief in the thought that Congress would not meet again until December.

XXI

The President and the West

Washington set two American armies in motion in the year 1794, one against aboriginal Americans who lived between the Great Lakes and the Ohio; the other against recalcitrant whites who were also contemptuous of his authority, frontier settlers of the western parts of the thirteen states who engaged in the Whiskey Rebellion.

The situation in the Old Northwest galled Washington. He did not think of Indians as a people who possessed inalienable rights to the lands they occupied, who must be allowed to live in their own way, who must be protected absolutely and permanently against whites who sought to seize and occupy their lands. It was prudent when possible to preserve peace with the aborigines by making treaties with them that limited expansion of white settlements. He did not wish benevolent-minded men to think of him or his fellow white Americans as cruel despoilers of the red men, and he did not perceive that all treaties protecting their thinly occupied lands would be revised or set aside when they were coveted by the numerous whites. Had he sought to stop the advance of the pioneers into the Old Northwest, he could not have prevented it and could not long have retarded it. He favored it because of the presence of the British garrisons south of the boundary with Canada. It was important for the republic to push forward, to do everything possible to prevent permanent occupation of territory south of the Great Lakes by the British and their Indian allies.

The Indians of the Old Northwest proved to be formidable. The Shawnees and Miamis, whose homes were especially threatened by the advance of the whites, had been reduced in number in consequence of border warfare during the War of Independence and were not able to check the whites. But they were determined to defend their freedom and their way of life, and they fought on after the British made peace in 1783. They were joined by Delawares, Wyandots, Ottawas, Pottowatomis, Chippewas, and other tribesmen who perceived that they too were threatened by the oncoming tide of whites. The Indians insisted that all pioneers who had put down north of the Ohio return to its southern bank. Making frequent raids against the new white settlements on its northern side, they committed their customary atrocities. In 1790 General Josiah Harmar, a Continental officer who had remained in the small American army after the War of Independence, was entrusted with the task of reducing the Shawnees and Miamis to reason. He was not a military genius, and he did not have overwhelming force to execute his mission, for the United States army had been small and half-starved throughout the period of the Confederation. He moved forward from Fort Washington (modern Cincinnati) with four hundred ill-trained regulars and one thousand militiamen into what is now northern Indiana. The Indians, carrying arms supplied by Canadian traders and led by Chief Little Turtle, made a surprise attack. They caught Harmar's army when it was divided in two parts, one led by Colonel John Hardin, the other by Harmar himself. They drove back Hardin and his men, then routed the force under Harmar. Losing more than two hundred men, Harmar retreated back to the Ohio.

Raids led by Major John Francis Hamtramck and General Charles Scott angered rather than injured the hostile tribesmen, and Washington replaced Harmar with General Arthur St. Clair, who had begun his military career in the British army, had served creditably in the War of Independence, and had become governor of the Northwest Territory. The president urged St. Clair to guard against surprise attack, a warning that ought not have been necessary. But St. Clair also encountered disaster. He advanced into the valley of the Miami River in the autumn of 1791 with 1,650 regulars and 350 militia. He was sick and did not manage well. Like

Braddock and Harmar, he was assailed by the Indians, under Chief Little Turtle, at a time when part of the army was too far in the rear to be of service. Colonel Richard Butler, leading the van, was killed at the opening of the battle. His men fell back in confusion. The result was almost a repetition of the Braddock disaster. The army was half-surrounded, finally fled in disorder, and suffered more than 900 casualties.

The victories of the Indians over Harmar and St. Clair created shock and anger in Philadelphia. The president and Congress resolved to seek revenge and to bring the red men to heel. The new government had money, and Congress voted substantial sums to raise and equip a good new army, a Legion of the United States, of more than four thousand men. Washington had the task of selecting its commander in chief and other officers. There must not be a third setback in the Old Northwest. Who should lead the Legion? The president reviewed the merits and faults of officers who had served under him in the War of Independence and had left the army at the close of hostilities. Nathanael Greene was dead. In the end, the choice lay between Light Horse Harry Lee and Anthony Wayne. The two were much alike, bold, vain, haughty, utterly brave, devoted to discipline, and Federalist in politics. Lee was younger, and he had not commanded a large body of troops. Wayne had acquired some experience in Indian fighting, for he had fought against Creek allies of the British in Georgia toward the end of the War of Independence. Accordingly, in April, 1792, the appointment went to Mad Anthony, who had failed to develop a plantation given to him by Georgia at the end of the War of Independence and failed to win a seat in the House of Representatives. He was at loose ends, and he was pleased to have more exciting occupation. He was an almost ideal choice.

Proceeding promptly to Pittsburgh, Wayne established headquarters there. Henry Knox saw to it that men and supplies went to Pittsburgh. Wayne drilled his men assiduously and established rigid discipline, executing three deserters. He trained his troops for battle, teaching his men to fire their muskets while charging and then to drive forward with the bayonet. He staged mock engagements in which some of his men played roles as shrieking Indian warriors. He taught his troops to fear him as much as the enemies they would meet, and he also won the respect and admiration of his men. Taking plenty of time to prepare for his task, he began to move his army down the Ohio toward Fort Washington in November, 1792. He was ready in the following summer to move forward from that place into the Indian country, but he was restrained by orders from Henry Knox.

Informed that many of the hostile tribesmen were disposed to negotiate, Washington resolved to try diplomacy before resorting once more to the sword. Wayne was instructed to remain quiet until it became clear that an agreement could not be reached with the Indians. The "great mass of the citizens of the United States are adverse in the extreme to an Indian war," Knox explained to Wayne—referring to residents on the Atlantic seaboard rather than to those who lived near the red men. Washington was swayed by "fair and humane motives," wrote Knox. "If the war continues, the extirpation and destruction of the Indian tribes are inevitable." The president was concerned lest that "extirpation and destruction" injure "the honor and reputation" of the republic. Washington feared that "if our modes of population and war destroy the tribes the disinterested part of mankind and posterity" would class the conduct of the Americans with that of the Spanish in Mexico and Peru. He sent out Benjamin Lincoln, Beverly Randolph, and Timothy Pickering to try to bargain. The commissioners traveled westward to the Detroit River in the summer of 1793 and conferred there uselessly with the dissatisfied Indians. Most of them would accept nothing less than withdrawal by the whites to the south bank of the Ohio, and the minority refused to desert their recalcitrant brethren.

Wayne chafed at the leash, especially because the negotiations compelled him to defer his attack upon the Indians. But he was given time in which to prepare with the greatest care for the task confronting him. He collected a body of mounted Kentucky riflemen to accompany his regulars—he would have preferred to have more regulars. He taught the Kentuckians to believe in their rifles, his infantry "in heavy buck shot & the bayonet," his dragoons in the sword, and all of his men in the Legion. He moved northward from Fort Washington in the autumn of 1793 into the Miami River Valley, putting his troops in armed camps as he advanced. By winter he was established at Greenville, Ohio. He did not permit a successful attack upon one of his convoys to disturb him.

By that time Little Turtle was not eager to resume fighting, and again there was discussion about peace. But most of the Indians were disposed to fight, and they were encouraged by a message they received in February, 1794, from Guy Carleton, who had become Lord Dorchester and governor-general of Canada. Dorchester was hoping to establish a neutral zone occupied by Indians between the United States and Canada, and he indicated to the tribesmen that they could expect to have British allies in a coming war between America and Britain. His message was accompanied by the erection of a new British post, Fort Miami, near the mouth of the Maumee River. On June 30, two thousand braves attacked one of Wayne's convoys near Fort Recovery, an advanced post the American commander had established at the site of St. Clair's defeat. They drove the convoy back into the fort but were pushed away by its garrison the following morning. Wayne was at last free and ready to strike. He had been compelled to use many of his regulars to guard his line of communications. But he was able to move northward on August 1 with some three thousand men, half of them the Kentuckians.

Pushing forward slowly and using advanced guards and flankers to prevent an ambuscade, Wayne was confronted at the Fallen Timbers, near Fort Miami, early in the morning of August 20 by a heterogeneous army of Delaware, Wyandot, Shawnee, Ottawa, Miami, Pottowatomi, and Chippewa warriors, about two thousand in all, accompanied by Canadian whites. The Indians were stretched out in three long lines behind the fallen trees—the debris of a tornado—that supplied the name of the battle that followed. They opened fire upon the first of two lines of the advancing troops. Wayne promptly put his men in motion, sending his infantry against the Indian center, his dragoons against their left flank, and the Kentuckians against their right wing. The flanking movements proved to be unnecessary. The infantry quickly broke through the Indian lines. Assailed on three sides, the braves gave up the struggle within a half hour and fled for safety. Their losses in the brief battle were double those of Wayne. Many of the red men sought safety at the British fort but were turned away by its garrison. Destroying Indian villages while the garrison helplessly looked on, Wayne was pleased to learn that more Indians were about to take the field. But it turned out that the warriors, disgusted by the failure of the British to come to their assistance, had had enough of war for some time. A year later the Indians of the Old Northwest signed a treaty with Wayne at Greenville that opened eastern and southern Ohio and a small part of Indiana to white settlement. Only eight years later Ohio was sufficiently occupied by the whites to be granted statehood.

Had it been within his authority, Wayne would have stormed Fort Miami. After the battle of Fallen Timbers he requested its commandant to withdraw from American territory. The demand was refused. The British would fight rather than yield. Wayne managed to control his desire to storm the post. He would later have the great satisfaction of receiving the surrender of Fort Miami and of Detroit as well.

Almost the whole world has learned, through books, motion pictures, radio, and television, that government had to deal with rebellious frontier folk as well as hostile red men in the great West beyond the Mississippi in the nineteenth century. Buffalo hunters, trappers, miners, cowboys, and gamblers had to be reduced to more or less peaceable citizens. The process was often painful. It is not so well known that backwoods people of the eighteenth century did not greet the coming of law and order with joy, that they engaged in three uprisings in the second half of that century. In the 1760s Regulators in the interior of the Carolinas revolted, claiming that they were charged excessive legal fees that must be reduced— hence their name. At length Governor William Tryon of North Carolina found it necessary to procure cannon and raise a body of militia to put down the Regulators in 1771. He defeated them in the battle of the Alamance and executed six of their leaders. It will be recalled that the farmers of western Massachusetts took up arms under the leadership of Daniel Shays in 1786 and that it was again necessary to call out militia to restore order. Only eight years later Washington was faced by the Whiskey Rebellion in western Pennsylvania.

One may believe that alcohol had somewhat to do with the upheavals in North Carolina and Massachusetts—that men emboldened by imbibing spirituous liquor dared to defy government. There was certainly a relationship between the uprisings in North Carolina and Pennsylvania. The rebels in both cases were chiefly Scotch-Irish, men of Ulster Presbyterian background, a willful lot from whom sprang such stubborn men as Andrew Jackson and Woodrow Wilson. Moreover, the rebels were men who had lived on or near the frontier for decades and who were unaccustomed to the exactions of a settled society. Even the most obedient citizen is vexed by excise taxes, levies upon the things that he enjoys, that seem essential to him. Politicians take advantage of his desires and wants; in the fourth quarter of the twentieth century every American state and also the federal government demand special and heavy tribute from individuals who seek solace from tobacco and liquor. Those who impose such levies even venture to assert that they reduce addiction to vicious habits, that they help to create a more wholesome society. Actually, most imbibers of alcohol and tobacco smoke, grumble, pay the taxes upon those comforting luxuries, and cling to their beverages and their nicotine. The backwoodsmen of Pennsylvania and of the states to the southward were made of different stuff. They fought rather than yield meekly to tax gatherers who sought to execute the excise duties imposed upon whiskey by the revenue acts of 1791 and 1792.

The laws were the brainchildren of Hamilton and were sufficiently noble in purpose, for their proceeds were to be used to help liquidate the foreign debts of the United States. The act of 1791 established federal collection districts and stipulated that distillers of whiskey must pay either an annual sum in accordance with the capacity of his still or nine to eleven cents per gallon upon his production. The rates were slightly modified in May, 1792, but there was no major change in the system. Even before the passage of the first law there were broad hints of resistance. Declared Scotch-Irishman James Jackson in the House of Representatives, "The time will come when a shirt shall not be washed without an excise." Committees of correspondence modeled upon those that had served as engines to combat British tyranny began to spring up in the backwoods in the summer of 1791. As Jackson indicated, any excise duty was detested by many people. What was worse, Hamilton's levies hit especially hard at the backwoodsmen. Gentlemen might drink wines taxed as imports, and common folk along the seaboard might imbibe dutied rum. Moreover, common folk in the northeastern part of the nation could turn to untaxed beer and hard cider. The backwoodsmen of the Southwest, who lacked breweries and orchards, could not evade the new levies. Their tipple, to which they made frequent resort, was whiskey made from rye—bourbon whiskey was then in its birthpangs. There were thousands of stills in the backwoods, so many of them operated by the Scotch-Irish that their product was erroneously often called "Irish." As Presbyterians, eager to obey scriptural commands, they could find endorsement of their habits in the biblical admonition, "Give strong drink unto him that is ready to perish." Even Presbyterian clergymen must have been irked by the duties. They were accustomed to drinking whiskey, as Episcopalian rectors were accustomed to sipping wine, as Congregational preachers were accustomed to imbibe rum. Was it right for government to make expensive a practice enjoined by Holy Writ? The new duties were all the more galling because distillers could make three gallons of liquor from a bushel of rye and send it profitably to eastern markets—there were economic reasons as well as local thirsts that encouraged resistance against the novel levies. Money was scarce in the interior, and whiskey was even used as a medium of exchange.

Accordingly, the new duties had been condemned in Congress by sober and thoughtful men, including Madison and Albert Gallatin, a young politician of Swiss birth then rising to power among the Republicans. It was to be assumed that distillers would protest and would seek to evade payment of the duties. But they reacted much more vigorously than might be expected. Many of them conceived the notion that the taxes were the equivalent of the detested British Stamp Act levies and that they were unconstitutional. The committees of correspondence labored toward forming a common front for resistance. Unhappy distillers began to bedevil revenue collectors as they and their forebears had earlier assailed the stamp distributors. In Lexington, Kentucky, a mob dragged a dummy of Colonel Thomas Marshall, a collector, through the streets of the town and hanged it. Deputies who served under Marshall were insulted and assaulted, their papers were destroyed, and injury was done to their horses and saddles. Opposition was particularly forceful in four counties of western Pennsylvania, Fayette, Allegheny, Westmoreland, and Washington. The "revenooers" suffered more in that region than elsewhere. In September, 1791, one Robert Johnson, collector for Washington and Allegheny counties, was waylaid by a mob of males disguised in women's clothing. They cut off all his hair, clad him in tar and feathers, and seized his horse, so that he was compelled to walk home in his wretched new garb. When a process server sought to hand warrants to the perpetrators of the attack on Johnson, he was beaten, robbed, tarred, and left tied to a tree in the forest. In August of the following year William Faulkner, threatened with both scalping and a coat of tar and feathers unless he withdrew an offer to let a deputy collector use his house as an office, prudently complied with the wishes of a mob. There were numerous similar incidents, and the mails were plundered and burned. The rioters refused to listen to Gallatin, Hugh Henry Brackenridge, and other citizens who urged that opposition to the detested duties should be peaceable, that their repeal should be the goal of the protesters.

Paying the duty upon his own activities as a distiller, Washington became disturbed by the uproar in western Pennsylvania. Although the duties were the brainchild of Hamilton rather than of the president, Washington did approve of them. Informed by Hamilton of the activities of the enemies of the duties who appealed to force, the president took a firm stand, in September, 1792. He said that the proceeds of the taxes were to be used for the benefit of all Americans, especially the very persons who were refusing to pay— just how they would gain more than other Americans, he did not explain. But if his logic with reference to the money collected from the duties was faulty, his thinking was otherwise clear and decisive. The behavior of the recalcitrants was "unaccountable, and the spirit of it much to be regretted." Hamilton should encourage law-abiding residents of the troubled region to restrain their tumultuous neighbors. Hamilton should also use the federal courts to enforce obedience to law. But if opposition to it continued, Washington would, however reluctantly, "exert all the legal powers with which the executive is invested, to check so daring and unwarrantable a spirit." Government must not "remain a passive spectator of the contempt with which it is treated." There could be no doubt that Washington would, if necessary, use whatever force was necessary to compel the rebellious backwoodsmen to yield.

The rioters continued to balk. They found a special grievance in the fact that violators of the excise law had to go to distant Philadelphia for trial in a federal court there. They were not appeased by an arrangement that permitted trial in a nearer state court. In April, 1793, a mob gathered around the house of Benjamin Wells, the collector in Fayette County. He was absent, but his family was threatened and terrified. In the following November another mob surrounded his home and forced him to give up his tax records and his commission. In June, 1794, rioters burned down the house and barn of John Wells, the collector in Westmoreland County. In the following month General John Neville, who had been given the responsibility of collecting the duties in the area of disaffection, was shot at by "Whiskey Boys" who attacked him in his handsome mansion. In the affray that followed, one of the Whiskey Boys was killed, four wounded. The next day, a dozen soldiers from Pittsburgh came to defend the house, and rioters led by Major James McFarlane, a revolutionary veteran, resumed the conflict. McFarlane was killed in the onslaught, but the soldiers were forced out of the house. The mob then burned down the mansion and all its outbuildings, destroyed crops, and drank up Neville's liquor supply. Neville, luckily for him, was absent at the time. At the funeral of McFarlane, David Bradford, the prosecuting attorney of Washington County, a hotheaded man who was disposed to declare the independence of western Pennsylvania rather than pay the duties, orated to a large crowd about "the murder of McFarlane." An epitaph placed over the grave of the fallen Whiskey Boy proclaimed that he had been slain by "an unprincipled villain in the support of what he supposed to be the rights of his country." At the beginning of August, Bradford occupied Pittsburgh with several thousand men. Acclaimed major general of the impromptu army, he paraded about as a conquering hero. He and his followers arranged for a congress that debated whether or not to declare independence.

At last Washington lost patience with the rebels. Hamilton urged him to employ force to reduce them to obedience. Washington needed no urging. He was the more determined to act, because he believed that the rebels were Republicans dominated by French revolutionary madness—Edmond Charles Genêt, the French minister to the United States, had been aggressively stirring up enthusiasm in behalf of his terrorizing government. The president sent commissioners to talk to the malcontents. He promised them amnesty in return for a pledge to obey the law. The state of Pennsylvania made a similar offer. Gallatin, Brackenridge, William Findley, and other responsible citizens urged the rebels to yield. In the meantime, Washington, unable to use the Legion, occupied by the Indian war in the Old Northwest, called upon the governors of Pennsylvania, New Jersey, Maryland, and Virginia to raise militia. Some of the Whiskey Boys, aware that they might see large bodies of militia descending upon them, declared that they would behave themselves peaceably in the future, but others were obdurate. Thousands of militia then began to move toward the disaffected area. They were to gather at Bedford. Washington resolved to command them in person, at least until it became certain that resistance would collapse. On September 30, 1794, he left Philadelphia with Hamilton, who had an excuse for taking part in that he was temporarily serving as secretary of war in the absence of Henry Knox, who was in New England at the time.

The militia moved forward cheerfully. Those of New Jersey were adjured poetically to do their duty.

> To arms once more our hero cries,
> Sedition lives and order dies;
> To peace and ease then bid adieu
> And dash to the mountains, Jersey Blue.
> Dash to the mountains, Jersey Blue,
> Jersey Blue, Jersey Blue
> And dash to the mountains, Jersey Blue.
> Since proud ambition rears its head,
> And murders rage, and discords spread,
> To save from spoil the virtuous few,
> Dash over the mountains, Jersey Blue.

The hastily gathered army advanced steadily in two columns. Five nephews of Washington were among the champions of order. At Norristown, on the day after he began his westward journey, Washington received joyful news, a report from Wayne of the victory of Fallen Timbers. He traveled onward steadily, amidst the plaudits of civilians. Commissioners from western Pennsylvania came to see him; they said that it was unnecessary to employ so much force. They could not give evidence that the troops were not needed. He rode on to Fort Cumberland, that place so important to him in his youth, thence to Bedford. There more than twelve thousand militia gathered by October 20. It was then clear enough that the insurrection would collapse before overwhelming force. The president was needed in Philadelphia. Congress would soon convene, and it was expected that the text of an extremely important treaty with Britain would reach the capital in the near future. He turned eastward, placing the command of the expedition in the hands of Light Horse Harry Lee, who had become governor of Virginia and who led the troops of that state.

The army moved on toward Pittsburgh. It was accompanied by Hamilton; his presence lent a bit of color to a Republican charge that he had concocted the levy upon whiskey in part to foment the uprising and demonstrate the power of the federal government. There was little fighting. Two Whiskey Boys were slain. Twenty of them were made prisoner and taken to Philadelphia for trial. Several hundred rebels, concluding that the sun would shine bright upon new Kentucky homes, fled down the Ohio River. David

Bradford, who had been made an exception in Washington's offer of amnesty, found safety in Spanish Louisiana. Eighteen of the prisoners were kept without trial in Philadelphia for many months. Two, one of them Hermon Husband, who had taken part in the uprising of the Regulators in North Carolina as well as the Whiskey Rebellion, were tried for treason, found guilty, and sentenced to death. The Whiskey Boys, and any other citizens who might be tempted to challenge the authority of the United States, had been taught a sufficient lesson. Washington sensibly pardoned Husband and his ally.

XXII

Washington and the French Revolution

Soon after taking his oath of office for the second time, Washington and the American nation were confronted by a dangerous situation in foreign affairs. Toward the close of the 1780s the absolute Bourbon monarchy in France began to totter. Despite the rich natural resources of France, many of her people, exploited alike by the monarchy, nobility, and Roman Catholic church, were poverty-stricken. Long wars waged by Kings Louis XIV and Louis XV for territory in Europe and elsewhere had led to heavy taxes, a huge national debt, and near bankruptcy. Reformers—middle-class folk, some altruistic nobles, and priests—took advantage of the distress of the Crown and began to remodel the French government and society. Infected by the teachings of Jean Jacques Rousseau, Voltaire, Montesquieu, and many other critics of the ancient Bourbon regime, encouraged by the birth of the American republic, perceiving the British constitutional monarchy and the American republic as models for change, the reformers secured from Louis XVI a National Assembly in 1789. On July 14 of that year a Parisian mob invaded and destroyed the Bastille, an old and feebly garrisoned fortress in which the French kings were accustomed to incarcerate troublesome individuals without trial. The tremendous French Revolution was then under way. The king yielded to the reformers, and France became a constitutional monarchy. Privileges of the Crown, the nobility, and the church were abolished. But the Revolution went on and on, amidst disorder and tumult, and the condition of the country approached anarchy. The king tried to flee to Germany in June, 1791, but was stopped at Varennes and brought back to Paris. Thereafter he was virtually a prisoner.

The other absolute monarchs on the European continent became concerned. There was an inclination among them to take advantage of the troubles of France for their own aggrandizement. But they came to fear that the Revolution would spread to their own domains. In August, 1791, the king of Prussia and the Austrian Habsburg emperor announced that they were ready to join a coalition of all the European rulers to restore Louis as an absolute monarch. In the following February they agreed to put their armies in motion, and France declared war upon both rulers in the spring of 1792. It seemed that the Revolution would quickly be stifled. The Austrians advanced into France from the north and the Prussians from the east. The crisis exacerbated political passions in France, and republicans came to the fore. Lafayette, leading a French army on the Belgian frontier, vainly tried to use it to strengthen the monarchy, was forced to flee to the Austrians, and became their prisoner. The republicans seized power in Paris in August amidst much shedding of blood. It seemed that they would soon be overthrown by an army of Prussians and Austrians under the duke of Brunswick advancing steadily from the Rhine. But a smaller defending French army took post parallel to the line of march of the allies at Valmy and withstood furious and long-continued cannonading on September 20. Other French contingents were gathering to bar the path of Brunswick. It was apparent that they would fight. He did not dare proceed with French forces on his flank and rear, and he began a slow retreat toward the Rhine. The Revolution continued.

The French republicans survived not only the attacks of the Austrians and Prussians but monarchist uprisings at home. Under the leadership of an elected Convention they dealt sternly and bloodily with internal enemies, sending to the guillotine Louis XVI, Queen Marie Antoinette, and others who sided with the invaders; they also slaughtered nobles, priests, generals who failed to win battles, and politicians who happened to be in a minority in the Convention. The revolutionaries resorted to conscription and raised large armies, well equipped by Lazare Carnot, "the Organizer of Victory," a great war minister. They took the offensive, calling upon republicans in adjacent countries to overthrow their masters. A successful French invasion of Belgium brought Britain into the war in February, 1793—a cabinet under the leadership of William Pitt the Younger could not bear to have mad republicans control the shores of Europe adjacent to the British Isles. Spain and the Netherlands entered the conflict against the republicans. The French, assisted by their republican allies in Europe, more than held their own, and Prussia and Spain withdrew from the struggle in 1795. At that time the French dominated Belgium and the Netherlands, and were confronted militarily only by Britain and the Austrian Habsburgs.

In its early stages most Americans favored the French revolutionists. Washington received with pleasure the key to the Bastille as a present from Lafayette. Even Hamilton approved of the upheaval so long as the goal of the uprising seemed to be the creation of a constitutional monarchy in Paris in accordance with the English style. But he along with many Federalists turned against the French republicans when they began to massacre their real and suspected enemies and when they attacked organized Christianity as they strove to reach their goals of liberty, equality, and fraternity. The attack upon Christianity was especially offensive to New England Federalists, devoted to their Congregational churches. Federalists began to fear that the Revolution would spread across the Atlantic. It was otherwise with the American Republicans. They rejoiced over the triumphs of French arms; they were delighted by the overthrow of the Bourbon monarchy; they were less than horrified by the executions of real and suspected enemies of the French republic. Were not those killings necessary for the safety of the republic, justified, at least in part, by the long-continued tyrannies of king, nobles, and bishops? Some of the Republicans fancied that the American Revolution had not gone far enough, that America ought to be transformed into a democracy. No Federalist is known to have hastened across the ocean to fight the wicked and atheistic French, and the names of only three Americans, including Colonel John Skey Eustace and Colonel Eleazer Oswald, formerly aides of General Charles Lee, are known to have served with the French. Even so, feeling regarding the war ran high among both Federalists and Republicans and supplied new reasons for party rancor.

There were many Americans, of course, who sought to be neutral in mind as well as deed, among them Washington. He could not give his blessing to the monarchs of Europe, including Britain; he could not endorse an extremist republic that sent his former comrade Admiral d'Estaing to the guillotine, that imprisoned his old friends Rochambeau and the Comte de Saint-Simon, that forced his disciple Lafayette and other French officers who had served with him to flee from France for their lives. America could not tip the scales of war one way or another. Either Britain or France might use the existence of the war to injure the United States. It was his duty and desire above all to make America stable and prosperous, to stimulate the growth and power of his country. He was firmly determined to do everything possible to avoid entanglement in the struggle between the French and the European monarchs. Avoiding war, America would become respectable, and her citizens would be "among the happiest people on this globe." America must do nothing that would embroil her in the war. "I ardently wish," he wrote, "we may not be forced into it by the conduct of other nations."

The great European war could not be ignored by the Americans, if only because of their extensive shipping on the Atlantic, certain to be interrupted by a Britain using naval power to limit oceanic traffic with France. There were other difficulties. According to the Franco-American treaty of alliance of 1778 America was pledged to help defend the French islands in the West Indies against British attack. Moreover, it was not unlikely that France, at war with Spain, would seek to regain New Orleans and Louisiana, where the creoles were restive under Spanish rule. It was bad enough that Spain—weak as she was—was able to close the lower Mississippi to American commerce. It might not be a formidable task to force Spain to open the river, even to secure possession of New Orleans. To compel the powerful French to abandon New Orleans, even to permit passage of American shipping to and from the Gulf of Mexico, might be difficult indeed.

The French republicans soon put America to the test. Early in April, 1793, Edmond Charles Genêt, a young man who had acquired a little experience in European diplomacy, appeared in Charleston, South Carolina, in the guise of a new minister from France to the United States. It soon became apparent that both he and his employers in Paris looked upon the American republic as a client state of France, a nation that owed its existence to the achievements of the French army and navy in the War of Independence. They assumed that it would gladly help its more powerful sister republic in a struggle against tyranny, not only in Europe but in Spanish America. Genêt immediately began to authorize Americans to engage in privateering. They soon were seizing British merchantmen on the Atlantic. Moreover, as he gradually moved northward to present his credentials in Philadelphia, he commenced to enlist volunteers for an attack upon Spanish Florida. He planned another expedition, against New Orleans, and he appointed as its leader George Rogers Clark, a disgruntled hero of the War of Independence who believed that his exploits had not been sufficiently rewarded. Genêt gave Clark a commission as a brigadier general. Later, Genêt offered a commission in the French army to Light Horse Harry Lee, which Lee, on the advice of Washington, declined to accept. Genêt also undertook to raise an army of Americans to invade and liberate Canada from Britain. The French minister displayed both ignorance and arrogance. He was encouraged in his bizarre behavior by Americans who did indeed think of the French republic as a champion of universal liberty. Dozens of Democratic and Republican clubs sprang up that enthusiastically rallied to the cause of France. Their members, numerous southwest of the Hudson River, were followers of Jefferson, Madison, and George Clinton.

Washington was at the Potomac laying plans for the permanent capital when reliable news reached him that Britain and Spain were indeed entering the European war. He promptly returned to Philadelphia. Congress was not to meet until December. He held several cabinet meetings to consider the situation. His advisers were divided in sympathy, Hamilton and Knox favoring Britain, Jefferson and Randolph, France. But all of them agreed with the president that America should remain neutral. Hamilton urged the president to refuse to recognize the Convention as the government of France, whereas Jefferson insisted that the Convention ruled France and must be treated as such. There was also that troubling treaty with France of February 6, 1778. Was it still valid, since the government of France had altered so remarkably? If it were, was America required to help the French defend their islands in the Caribbean against British attack, certain to come? Hamilton contended that the treaty applied only to the French monarchy, that it had been nullified by the overthrow of King Louis XVI, hence that the obligation had vanished. Jefferson correctly pointed out that the treaty had been made with the French nation, accordingly that it remained valid. However, the secretary of state found other reasons for denying military assistance to the French. It could be argued that the French had not lived up to the treaty. They had guaranteed the territory of the United States as defined in the Peace of Paris, but they had done nothing to help compel the British to abandon the seven posts they continued to hold below the boundary with Canada. Besides, he questioned whether the American promise to France covered a struggle that France began with a formal declaration of hostilities against Britain; it could be contended that the pledge was operative only in the event that Britain was the aggressor. There was another question. Should Genêt be acknowledged as the French minister?

Washington pondered over the arguments of his advisers. It was right, he concluded, to face the fact that the Convention ruled France and accordingly to accept Genêt as minister. Since France had not formally asked for American help in accordance with the treaty of 1778, he decided that it was not necessary to decide whether the United States would assist France in defending her West Indian possessions. America must not be drawn into the conflict without good reason. He issued a proclamation of neutrality that forbade American citizens to take part in hostilities on land or sea or to commit any unneutral act against any combatant. He wished that America should have "nothing to do with the political intrigues or the squabbles of European nations" and should "live in peace and amity with all the inhabitants of the earth."

It was much easier to assert neutrality than to maintain it. Passionate partisans of France among the Republicans continued to urge that France be assisted, while equally passionate Federalists denounced the French revolutionists as aggressive and bloodthirsty enemies of order, decency, and Christianity. Genêt at length appeared in Philadelphia. He was received by Washington with cool civility, by Jefferson with cordiality. France was suffering from shortages of food, and Genêt proposed that America should undertake to help feed her fellow champions of liberty. Informed that American citizens had been instructed to avoid privateering, to refrain from committing any unneutral act in behalf of France, he let it be known that he was prepared, in order to get help for his country, to appeal from the president to Congress and if necessary from Congress to the American people.

The behavior of the French diplomat deeply offended the president. Washington was also disturbed that spring by recurrent bouts of fever and by word from Jefferson and Hamilton that they were preparing to leave office. If he was vexed by their quarreling, he was nevertheless well aware that both men were irreplaceable, though not indispensable. He persevered. He checked the would-be American privateers and insisted that French warships must not attack British merchant vessels in American waters. He was much worried for a time about the Democratic and Republican clubs, modeled after similar institutions in Paris that served to drive the French Revolution to extremes. Violent pronouncements in favor of France came from them. He came to suspect that the clubs aimed at "the subversion of the government of these states, even at the expense of plunging this country in the horrors of a disastrous war." Did their members wish to ape the members of the French clubs, to expropriate property, to attack Christian churches, to imprison and slay those who were satisfied with the results of the American upheaval? The clubs proved to be addicted to rhetoric rather than martial pursuits, and they gradually lost vigor and number. The schemes of Genêt for invasions of Florida and Louisiana alarmed him. Were there Americans who would help plant the French tricolor at the mouth of the Mississippi, to the profound injury of their own country? He condemned the ventures. He was prepared to use the army, if necessary, to halt Genêt's expeditions, both to avoid war with Spain and to ward off French dominion over the mouth of the Mississippi. Happily Genêt and his American friends were unable to raise the men and money necessary to mount the attacks upon the Spanish.

The behavior of Genêt was so outrageous that Washington decided, late in the summer of 1793, with the unanimous approval of his cabinet, to demand that the French government recall him to Paris. As it happened, a decision to call the erring minister home was reached in Paris before the receipt of the demand. Genêt was replaced by Joseph Fauchet, who brought with him word that the friends of Genêt at the French capital had lost power and that he could expect to go to the guillotine after returning home. Genêt asked for asylum in America, and Washington mercifully saved the life of the troublesome diplomat by granting the request. Genêt married a daughter of Governor George Clinton, lived on as a gentleman, inventor, and contented resident of the republic he had wantonly sought to injure. The generosity displayed by Washington toward Genêt was the more remarkable in that American

friends of the Frenchman had abused the president in print. Philip
Freneau, that "damned rascal," as Washington called him, had
nastily referred to the president as "king."

In that August of 1793 Washington had other worries. Jefferson
would not remain in office beyond the end of the year, and Hamilton, desiring to resume the practice of law in order to care for a
growing family, would not keep his post much longer. The approaching departures of the two men made Washington feel "like a
man going to the gallows." Yellow fever broke out in Philadelphia.
Hamilton was attacked by the dreaded disease and recovered, but
it carried away hundreds of Philadelphians. It was impossible to
carry on public business, and the president went home in September with Martha for a holiday. He enjoyed it, the more because he
was able to attend a ceremony for the laying of the cornerstone of
the Capitol in the Federal City, now named Washington in his
honor. He bought four lots in it. To be sure, even the building of
the new city was supplying trouble for him. He had chosen Pierre
Charles L'Enfant as architect, but Jefferson, who had been entrusted with overseeing the development of the city, had successfully insisted upon discharging L'Enfant, to the distress of the reluctant president. Still, it was evident that Washington was to have
a mighty monument.

By November, Washington was back in Philadelphia, now free
from yellow fever because the mosquitoes that spread it had been
checked by cold weather. Congress was able to assemble. The nation was faced with new problems arising from the French Revolution, in particular with difficulties caused by the British naval
blockade of European ports under French control and also with
the continuing refusal of Britain to withdraw her garrisons from
the seven posts she held on the American side of the boundary with
Canada. British minister George Hammond was forbidden by his
superiors even to discuss evacuation of the forts, and they had
declined to consider the American grievance with Gouverneur
Morris, sent to London as a special emissary by Washington. Britain steadfastly refused to do anything about it until the Americans
paid delinquent debts to British merchants and did justice to Loyalists who had been deprived of their property by American legislatures. Britain had also placed severe limits upon Americans trading
with British colonials in the Caribbean Sea.

What was even worse, in the eyes of Americans seeking to trade
with France and of men who sympathized with them, was the

stringency of the blockade. According to such international law as existed at the time, the British navy, by stationing warships along the coasts of Europe, could search and seize neutral ships carrying "contraband of war," presumably munitions and other military materials, to the French. The vessels of neutrals carrying their own foodstuffs were entitled to pass through the blockade. Venturesome American sea captains sought to circumvent it profitably by taking to France foodstuffs and other goods that had been produced in the French islands of the Caribbean and loaded in a neutral West Indian port. Vessels breaking the rules, with their cargoes, could be seized and sold, the proceeds being distributed among the captors. Accordingly, British naval captains zealously ignored the American subterfuge and took dozens of American vessels. Moreover, searching neutral merchantmen off the coasts of Europe, British naval officers lengthened the list of contraband so as to justify expropriation. While engaged in such searches, they even began to impress American sailors into royal service. The British navy was chronically short of crewmen, and deserters from it were to be found in American crews. Forcibly carrying off such men, British captains did not always bother to make sure that they were taking British subjects. A sailor born in England who claimed to be an American citizen very likely became a British tar, and even American-born sailors were dragged off into British service. New grievances against Britain mounted in Philadelphia. Besides, the French, contending that the Americans ought to resist the British seizures, assumed that their failure to do so justified French grabbing of American ships and cargoes.

The insults and injuries inflicted by the French offended even passionate Republicans, and the hurts perpetrated by the British angered even devout Federalists. Hence, early in 1794, there was a clamor in Congress for strong measures against the French and for vigorous action against the British. There were Republicans eager for a declaration of war against Britain. What to do? The Federalists urged that preparations be made for war but that a special envoy be sent to London to try to persuade Britain to alter her policy. Washington faced the worrisome situation with a changed and inferior cabinet. Edmund Randolph had replaced Jefferson; William Bradford had become attorney general; and Timothy Pickering had succeeded Knox. Later Oliver Wolcott, Jr., became head of the Treasury. Randolph endorsed both proposals. It was suggested by Federalists that Hamilton be sent to London. Madison offered resolutions in the House of Representatives calling for new and punitive duties upon British and French goods as a mode of compelling the European contestants to moderate their behavior.

Washington moved slowly but surely. He was firmly opposed to any step that would unnecessarily lead to war with either of the European contestants. It was well to indicate American displeasure with both and to make at least some preparation for hostilities. But he was doing everything possible to avoid an armed conflict. He remedied minor and just complaints from George Hammond; to avoid charges of favoritism he declined officially to receive royalist exiles from France. Accordingly, with his consent, Congress imposed a temporary embargo upon American vessels and arranged to build six powerful frigates—warships that eventually brought renown to the American navy. Congress also endorsed the raising of a substantial army, but it was allowed to remain a paper force. The patience of the president was rewarded. Word came that Britain, maintaining her blockade upon the coasts of Europe, would permit Americans to trade with the French islands in the Caribbean. He decided to send a special envoy to London. He sensibly refused to appoint Hamilton, obviously too pro-British for the mission. Any treaty made with the British by Hamilton would almost certainly be rejected by the Republicans in the Senate. Despite protests from many Republicans he tendered the appointment to Chief Justice John Jay, a more moderate Federalist. Jay was also disliked by the Republicans, especially the Virginians—they believed that the New Yorker as secretary for foreign affairs in the time of the Confederation had preferred to strive in behalf of American commerce on the Atlantic rather than to devote himself to the opening of the lower Mississippi to American trade. Washington made other diplomatic appointments that soothed moderate Republicans. Gouverneur Morris, minister to France, was exceedingly offensive to the revolutionists of Paris because of his aristocratic notions and demeanor. The president brought Morris home and replaced him with James Monroe, a disciple of Jefferson who turned out to be much too fond of the revolutionists. Also, Washington sent Thomas Pinckney, a South Carolina Federalist, to Madrid to try to secure opening of the lower Mississippi to American traffic and settlement of the boundary dispute with Spain.

John Jay had a difficult assignment. His chances of successful bargaining were injured by Hamilton, who had fallen into the bad habit of talking to George Hammond regarding American policy. Hammond, fully informed regarding American desires, plans, and expectations, relayed them to his superiors. Sweden and Denmark were trying to form a league of armed neutrals to defend their rights on the seas. Such a combination, with Russia and America, would pose a problem for Britain. Thanks to Hamilton, Hammond was able to assure Lord Grenville, the British foreign secretary, that the Americans were talking about the proposed league but that they would not join it. Confirmation of Hammond's reports was obtained in London by reading American diplomatic dispatches, for the British had broken a code in which they were transmitted. Jay arrived at the British capital after Lord Howe had asserted British mastery of the English Channel by defeating a French fleet in the battle of the Glorious First of June. The British cabinet was consequently in a rather cheerful mood. The prime minister, William Pitt the Younger, was disposed to make a bargain with the Americans, but it did not seem necessary to make great concessions to the former colonials. Lord Grenville dealt with Jay without haste.

Jay did at last secure a treaty, signed on November 19. Washington received a copy of it early in March, 1795. He read it unhappily. Its terms were so favorable to Britain that they displeased even Hamilton. Britain made only trifling concessions with respect to the rights of neutrals. The twelfth article, which stipulated that American vessels trading in the West Indies should be limited to seventy tons, was galling. But Britain did undertake to evacuate by 1796 the seven forts near the Canadian boundary garrisoned by redcoats. America was to pay still unsettled debts of her citizens to British merchants incurred before the War of Independence, and Britain was to compensate Americans who had lost property as the result of illegal seizures of ships and cargoes. No reference was made to impressment, and the British claim that America had violated the treaty of Paris with respect to the Loyalists was silently abandoned. But if the new treaty was far from satisfactory, there was a great gain in it for America—departure of British troops from American soil, which, with the victory of Wayne at Fallen Timbers, opened the way for American occupation of the Old Northwest. To refuse to sign the agreement was to risk increasing conflict with Britain, even war. Secretary of State Randolph advised against acceptance of the treaty, but Washington wisely chose to subject it to close examination and possible revision. He had arranged for a special session of the Senate to consider it, in June. At length, maintaining secrecy regarding its provisions, he sent it to that body.

A drumfire of opposition to the treaty began even before it was submitted to Congress. In view of the fact that it offered little to benefit commerce, one might expect the Federalists to denounce it. But it was the creation of Federalists, and they rallied in support of it. One might expect that the Republicans, concerned for agriculture and westward expansion, would find the document sufficiently pleasing to endorse it; but it was not of their making, and they opened a vigorous campaign against it even before they were entirely familiar with its terms. Benjamin Franklin Bache, a grandson of Franklin and publisher of the newspaper *Aurora,* bizarrely condemned Washington's secrecy as unconstitutional—an early and striking instance of the tendency among Americans to conclude that any measure they find to be distasteful violates their fundamental rights. Bache not only assailed the treaty before he was fully informed regarding its contents, but came forward as a rather nasty critic of the president. When the provisions of the treaty became known, fusillades of condemnation came from the Republicans. There were twenty Federalists and ten Republicans in the Senate—barely enough Federalists to meet the two-thirds vote required for ratification. Setting aside the obnoxious twelfth article, they closed ranks. After secret debate the agreement was confirmed by a strict party vote of twenty to ten.

Struggle over the revised Jay Treaty continued, for it could not go into effect without the approval of the House of Representatives, since money was needed to execute it. Its terms were made public, and were hotly condemned. Jay was burned in effigy; Hamilton, speaking in defense of the treaty at a public meeting in New York, was struck in the head and bloodied by a stone. In Philadelphia an enthusiastically angry crowd heard Irish orator Blair McClenachan shout, "What a damned treaty! I make a motion that every good citizen in this assembly kick this damned treaty to hell!" The crowd paraded to the house of Pierre Adet, recently appointed as successor to Fauchet, and tried to persuade him to join in the festivities. He prudently refused. The angry citizens then burned a copy of the treaty on the doorstep of George Hammond and broke windows in his house.

In the summer of 1795 Washington himself momentarily turned against the treaty. He learned that Britain had undertaken to seize any and all ships carrying foodstuffs to European ports under French control. He agreed in confidential discussion with Randolph that the British demanded too much. Events changed his mind. While he was on a brief vacation at home, he received a letter from Pickering urging him to return to Philadelphia as soon as possible for a "special reason" that could be communicated to the president only in person. Washington set out as soon as possible to find out why Pickering had sent the mysterious message. In Philadelphia he was informed by Pickering that it had been sent after consultation among Pickering, Wolcott, and Bradford. They had seen evidence that Randolph might be in the pay of France—a letter from Fauchet to his superiors in Paris that seemed to indicate that the secretary of state had asked for money from Fauchet in 1794 in return for political favor, a letter intercepted by the British and conveyed to Wolcott by George Hammond. Washington was shocked. He knew that Randolph had money troubles, and he was now given reason to believe that the advice of Randolph with respect to the treaty was tainted by a desire to please the French, who were eager to prevent an accommodation between the Americans and the British. Besides, his sound judgment told him that it was of the first importance to get the British troops out of the forts along the boundary with Canada, that commercial grievances and hurts to national pride were minor and transitory. The withdrawal of the redcoats, with Anthony Wayne's victory at Fallen Timbers, would open much of the Old Northwest to early settlement and would place American hegemony over the region almost beyond doubt.

After a meeting of the cabinet on August 21 in which Randolph repeated his advice, in which the other members counseled Washington to sign the treaty, the president announced that he would do so. Shortly afterward he asked the secretary of state to explain the contents of the letter. Randolph declared that he was innocent and resigned his post. He wrote a series of protests to the president. In the following December, having obtained from Fauchet a statement that he had not accepted French money, Randolph published a *Vindication* in which he asserted that he had been abused by the president. Washington never commented upon the *Vindication*. Presumably he continued to believe that his former friend was guilty. It may be that Randolph was indeed innocent. But the charge made against him does not fall because Fauchet tried to exonerate him. The demeanor of Randolph may have been conclusive for the president.

The hullabaloo concerning the treaty went on and on. Approval of it by Washington made him a target of censure that reached a crescendo after he returned to Philadelphia in the autumn from a brief vacation in Virginia. Addresses against it came to the president from several towns and cities, and Republican editors assailed him as never before. They asserted that the American people wished the treaty to be rejected, that he was trying to thwart their will, that he was behaving like a dictator. Benjamin Franklin Bache declared that Washington had been carried by "false ambition" to "the precipice of destruction." He had become "the omnipotent director of a seraglio instead of the first magistrate of a free people." He was accused by writers in Bache's *Aurora* of "political degeneracy," denounced as a "usurper," and stigmatized as a man who had fought in the War of Independence only for personal aggrandizement. He had been born with little ability, and it had not been developed by a good education. At that time, embarrassed for lack of money, he was raising it by selling land and was drawing his salary three months before it was due. Obviously, he was cheating his fellow citizens.

The president, aging and weary of politics, carried on. Not surprisingly, he encountered great difficulty when he sought a replacement for Randolph. Five men, including Patrick Henry, who had become a Federalist, refused appointment as secretary of state. At last Washington was forced to place a reluctant Pickering in the office and to put James McHenry of Maryland in the Department of War. All the original members of the cabinet were gone; all had been succeeded by inferior men. Washington did not bend under the storm of abuse. Believing that execution of the treaty would benefit the nation, he insisted that he must use his own judgment regarding it. He was not a glorified clerk registering the will of the people; besides, he estimated that the considered opinion of the "yeomen," of plain folk, would be the same as his own.

The newspaper censure of the president continued after Congress reconvened in November. Republicans greeted the appearance of Randolph's *Vindication* with pleasure, not because they admired Randolph, who had been a lone wolf in politics, but because it embarrassed Washington and the Federalists. But would the Republicans use an easy majority that they possessed in the House of Representatives to crush the treaty by refusing to vote the money necessary to execute it? They were greatly tempted, and there was hot debate in the House for many weeks. However, Washington received a splendid birthday present on February 22, 1796—news that Thomas Pinckney had been almost amazingly successful in negotiations at Madrid. He arrived at the Spanish capital at a time when the dominating Spanish minister, Manuel Godoy, was seeking peace with both France and America. Godoy consented to a treaty that gave America all that could be asked. The American version of the boundary between the Floridas and the United States was accepted; Spain pledged to refrain from stirring up the southern Indians against the United States; the Americans were to enjoy free passage through the lower Mississippi; and they were given a place of deposit for American goods at New Orleans. The Pinckney Treaty was, of course, rapidly approved by Washington and the Senate.

Thoughtful Republicans, pleased by the splendid result of the Spanish mission, so helpful for the development of the republic below the Ohio River, pondered. They knew that the vilification of Washington by the newspaper writers was without foundation. Petitions in favor of the Jay agreement poured into Philadelphia. They had to recognize that America must sometimes make the best of a bad situation. The Senate was about to endorse a treaty whereby the nation paid ransom to North African pirates in return for permission to let American merchant vessels use the Mediterranean—even Britain, with all her sea power, was accustomed to paying such bribes. Was Jay's agreement so bad that the House should refuse to follow the leadership of the president and the Senate? At last ten Republicans in the House set aside party. They joined with the Federalists in Committee of the Whole to supply the money necessary to execute the treaty. The result was a tie, 49 to 49. Then the Speaker, Frederick A. Muhlenberg, altruistically used his vote to break the tie and to bring the appropriation before the House. Offending many fellow Republicans, he sacrificed his career as a Republican politician, but the House undertook to provide the money, by a majority of three on April 30. The Senate, of course, concurred, and the revised treaty was accepted in London. In the late summer and early autumn of 1796 Anthony Wayne proudly accepted the surrender of the British forts at Maumee and Detroit.

XXIII

The Farewell of the President

Like most of the Republican politicians, Jefferson and Madison too violently condemned the Jay Treaty. In retirement at his beloved Monticello, amidst quiet rural scenes that should have cooled his ardors regarding public questions, Jefferson called it "an infamous act which is nothing more than a treaty of alliance between England and the Anglomen of this country against the legislature and people of the United States," an extraordinary judgment. Although Washington had not addressed appeals to the country in behalf of the accord, his view of it was well known. It was obvious that the public and the Congress had at length decided to follow "where Washington leads." Jefferson unhappily commented regarding the victory of the president that "his honesty and his political errors" had very likely served as a curse to his country. Such was not the considered verdict of the mass of American citizens. Republican politicians who went home after the conclusion of the struggle over the treaty with the expectation that they would be praised for their gallantry and patriotism were sometimes given a cool reception.

It was Jefferson, not Washington, who erred. There were indeed Federalists who feared "mobocracy" in America, who were too fond of Britain, who would have stomached almost any pact with the government of George III. Washington was not of them. Friendly to true liberty in France and elsewhere, Washington would not accept domination by France. Looking ahead toward the time when America would be strong enough to demand her rights from any European power, he saw that it would be prudent for the time being not to make too much of slights and injuries inflicted by Britain or France.

Jefferson was carried away by his sympathy for the French revolutionists. While the struggle over the treaty was still in progress, a new French republican government, in which a Directory of five men served as the executive, had sent Pierre Adet to Philadelphia. Forgetting the embarrassment that Genêt had brought to the friends of France, Jefferson effusively welcomed Adet in an extraordinary letter. He said that the American and French republics had interests and principles in common, that they were bound together by fellowship in war, that they could be "easily kept together." He referred to "the general interest which my countrymen take in all the successes of your republic." He continued, "In this no one joins with more enthusiasm than myself, an enthusiasm kindled by my love of liberty, by my gratitude to your nation who helped us to acquire it, by my wishes to see it extended to all men, and first to those whom we love most. . . . Your struggles for liberty keep alive the only sparks of sensation which public affairs now excite in me." Jefferson did not know that the Directory, much less devoted to freedom than he fancied, was embarking upon a campaign to injure the United States and to drive Washington from office. Adet, doing what he could to prevent ratification of the Jay Treaty, recommended to his superiors that they seize Louisiana in order to exert pressure upon the United States.

The American republic was caught between the French devil and the British deep blue sea. Emanations of hostility, even of hatred, came to Washington from Paris while the bargaining with Britain was still in progress. Having left America after the War of Independence, Tom Paine engaged in propaganda against the government in his native Britain, then joined the revolutionaries in the French capital. He was given French citizenship and elected to membership in the Convention. Then, falling into disfavor with the powers that were, he was sent to prison. Washington did not move to secure his release; nor did Gouverneur Morris. Eventually, through the intercession of Monroe, Paine regained his freedom. Quartered for a time in Monroe's house, Paine began to compose attacks upon the president, which culminated in an open letter to Washington of July, 1796. Paine would have it that Washington murdered Jumonville in 1754, encouraged sycophants, and assisted men who defrauded the United States. "As to you, sir, treacherous in private friendship (for so you have been to me, and that in the day of danger) and a hypocrite in public life, the world will be puzzled to decide, whether you are an apostate or an impostor; whether you have abandoned good principles, or whether you ever had any."

Paine's effusions came at a time when Washington was doing what he could to avoid antagonizing extremist American partisans of France. Thus he refused during many weeks to receive into his household George Washington Lafayette, son of the marquis, sent by the wife of his old friend to America for refuge, until it became clear that nothing could be gained by denying hospitality to the boy. There were limits to the forbearance of the president. It became apparent that the Republican Monroe was misrepresenting the United States in Paris. Consorting privately and publicly with French leaders, he gave the impression that the Americans were not only fond of France but devoted to her interests. Washington therefore recalled Monroe, sending Federalist Charles Cotesworth Pinckney to Paris to replace him. Moreover, Washington quietly pursued long-continued efforts to secure the freedom of Lafayette, whatever impassioned American friends of France might think. He could not achieve his purpose, but the Directory, turning away from terrorism at home, at last took advantage of the overwhelming victories of young General Napoleon Bonaparte over the forces of the Austrian emperor in Italy in 1796 and 1797 to compel the release of the marquis.

Subscribing to the principle that those who are not for us are against us, the Directory concluded that the American government that turned toward peace with Britain was an enemy of France, and that Washington was its archenemy. Aware that American sentiment rather preferred France to Britain, the Directory was encouraged by Monroe, Fauchet, and Adet to believe that French influence in America was far greater than it was in reality. The recommendation by Adet that France secure Louisiana from Spain in order to exert pressure upon the United States had appeal in Paris, and Adet even sent General George Victor Collot to the Mississippi Valley to lay the groundwork for a French occupation. Nothing came of that enterprise, for Spain clung to her colony. But the Directory did undertake to drive Washington from office and bring America to heel. "Washington must go!" declared the French foreign minister, Charles Delacroix de Constant. "A friend of France must succeed him." In March, 1796, Gouverneur Morris sent word from London that the Directory was about to send a special emissary to America with a fleet. Washington was informed that the envoy would demand cancellation of the Jay Treaty within fifteen days. Failing such action, France would declare war. The report was unfounded—even the Directory was not so foolish as to follow such a course. But its reaction was sufficiently drastic. In July, 1796, the Directory set aside the Franco-American alliance and announced that the French would thereafter treat American maritime commerce exactly as the British did. Moreover, adopting a suggestion from Adet, the Directory made it clear through a letter published by the French minister in American newspapers that France desired the defeat of Washington in the approaching election. A third term for him might well lead to war with France. The Directory desired replacement of Washington by Jefferson. To emphasize its wishes, the Directory threatened to break diplomatic relations in the event that Jefferson was not chosen. Adet sent that menace to Timothy Pickering on November 15 and also arranged to publish it in Republican newspapers. John Adams, rather than Jefferson, was elected president, and the Directory executed its threat.

The French attempt to browbeat American voters probably came too late to affect the results of the election. It may have injured rather than strengthened the Republicans. They rallied behind Jefferson as a candidate for the presidency. The Federalists would have supported Washington, but he had formally and unequivocally announced that he would retire to private life at the end of his second term. Most of them stood forth for John Adams. Hamilton strove to secure the election of Federalist Thomas Pinckney, who was popular because he had secured the good treaty with Spain, who might as a member of the planter aristocracy of South Carolina receive the electoral votes of that state. Hamilton urged that some Federalist electors cast one of their two ballots for Pinckney, the other for some person other than Adams. New England friends of Adams then decided not to vote for Pinckney. The result was a victory for Adams, who received the blessing of seventy-one electors; but Pinckney ran behind Jefferson, who was the choice of sixty-eight electors. Two of them, disregarding the an-

nouncement of Washington that he was retiring, cast ballots for
him. The Northeast voted Federalist; the Southwest, Republican.
Federalist candidates for the Senate and House of Representatives
formed majorities in both chambers. Adet was not at all sure that
the defeat of Jefferson really made much difference. He wrote to
Paris, "Jefferson is an American, and as such he cannot sincerely
be our friend. An American is an enemy of all the peoples of
Europe." Certainly Jefferson did not wish to see the tricolor raised
over New Orleans.

There can be no doubt that Washington would easily have won
the presidency a third time had he desired it. Many of the Republican electors would have cast a ballot for him. When the furor over
the Jay Treaty died down, it was evident that he had done well to
put it into force. Whatever scurrilous Republican editors might
write about him, whatever carping Republican politicians might
say about him, he remained the idol of the common folk and a
trusted leader both to them and to more sophisticated men
unblinded by partisan rancor. He might even have been once more
the unanimous choice of the electors. Only a very passionate Republican would have dared to name two men of his party and
ignore the national hero.

By March, 1796, Washington had definitely decided that one
more year in the presidency was more than enough for him. He
was very tired at times, although he seemed commonly to enjoy
good health. Observers noticed that occasionally he remained silent in company for two or three minutes, perhaps the result of
weariness as well as denture difficulty. Not that he had aged remarkably. He remained an impressive figure. An English visitor,
Thomas Twining, who was entertained by the president in May of
that year, commented upon his "tall, upright, venerable figure," his
"impressive dignity . . . the benevolence of his countenance and
the kindness of his address." To Twining, Washington looked like
"the great and good man he really was. . . . His deportment was
that of a general, the expression of his features had rather the calm
dignity of a legislator than the severity of a soldier." Twining perceived the statesman, the gracious gentleman. The soldier had not
vanished, but he could believe that he was not desperately needed
to guide the republic. He fretted under the attacks of Republican
editors. Benjamin Bache even revived and circulated a forgery concocted by the British during the War of Independence to discredit
him. Why must they find, why must they invent grievous faults in

a man who was doing his best for his country? The passions of his earlier years had abated; he had had enough of the adulation and vexation of the presidency. As early as 1795 he had pretty well made up his mind to quit office at the end of his second term, and by the spring of 1796 he was committed to retirement. He wished to go back to his beloved Mount Vernon for the rest of his days. "I am attacked," he wrote, "for a steady opposition to every measure which has a tendency to disturb the peace and tranquility." There would be in consequence "no change in my conduct," but his "anxious desire" was increased "to enjoy in the shades of retirement the consolation of having rendered my country every service" he could. He had not been guilty of "a *wilful* error." He began to prepare his Farewell Address, in which he would both announce his approaching departure from the presidency and advise his fellow countrymen about the course they should follow in the future.

Washington was hard at work upon that famous paper in May, 1796. Using ten paragraphs written by Madison in 1792 when Washington was thinking of leaving the presidency, he drafted a long valedictory and sent it to Hamilton for revision. Never confident of his use of language in public documents, he asked his friend to revise it in its entirety if necessary, in any event to make sure that it was neither verbose nor repetitive. Hamilton was not to make any change in thought. "My wish is," Washington said, "that the whole may appear in a plain style and be handed to the public in an honest, unaffected, simple garb." He particularly desired to include the Madison materials, and even to announce that they were prepared by Madison in 1792, as an indication that he had not lusted to continue in office and that he was not leaving it because he feared that he would be defeated in the election of 1796. Accordingly, Hamilton prepared two drafts, one using the language of the president, the other that of Hamilton. Employing the latter, the two friends proceeded to make a final version, which was not ready for submission to the public for several months. Hamilton improved the paper in form; it would have been better phrased by Jefferson, for Hamilton, logical in thought, tended to be verbose in expression. Its content was that of Washington. He gave it to a friendly Philadelphia newspaper editor in mid-September, and it circulated in time to warn the nation that Washington was not available for a third term.

Informing the public that he had resolved "to decline being considered among the number of those out of whom a choice" had to be made for the presidency, Washington proceeded to offer his testament to the nation. The Americans must give utter loyalty to the union; they should "seek its preservation with jealous anxiety," indignantly frowning upon "the first dawning of every attempt to alienate any portion of our country from the rest or to enfeeble the sacred ties which now link together the several parts." He continued, "Citizens by birth or choice of a common country . . . must always exalt the just pride of patriotism more than any appellation derived from local discriminations. With slight shades of difference, you have the same religion, manners, habits, and political principles. You have in a common cause fought and triumphed together." From devotion to the union would come peace at home, avoidance of "overgrown military establishments . . . particularly hostile to republican liberty," and greater security against foreign attack. The republic, so extensive, must have a central government as strong as liberty would permit. He deprecated the spirit of party, which had its "greatest rankness" in nations having a popular form of government. Partisan passions should be moderated by "the more general diffusion of knowledge." The Americans should cultivate peace and harmony with all nations. "Religion and morality enjoin this conduct. And can it be that good policy does not equally enjoin it? It will be worthy of a free, enlightened, and at no distant period a great nation to give to mankind the magnanimous and too novel example of a people always guided by an exalted justice and benevolence. . . . The experiment, at least, is recommended by every sentiment which ennobles human nature. Alas! is it rendered impossible by its vices?" In any event, the Americans should avoid "permanent, inveterate antipathies against particular nations and passionate attachments for others," a warning to Republicans to withhold their affection from France, to Federalists to refrain from giving their hearts to Britain.

Above all, Washington went on, America must not create "artificial ties" that would involve her in the vicissitudes and collisions of European powers. "Our detached and distant situation invites and enables us to pursue a different course. If we remain one people, under an efficient government, the period is not far off when we may defy material injury from external annoyance." Then, foreign belligerents could be compelled to respect the rights of American neutrals. "Why forego the advantages of so peculiar a situation? Why quit our own to stand upon foreign ground? Why, by interweaving our destiny with that of any part of Europe, entangle our peace and prosperity in the toils of European ambition, rivalship, interest, humor, or caprice? . . . It is our true policy to steer clear of permanent alliances with any portion of the foreign world." There should not be another alliance like that of 1778 with France. Its provisions should be observed "in their genuine sense." For the future, "taking care to keep ourselves by suitable establishments on a respectable defensive posture, we may safely trust to temporary alliances for extraordinary emergencies." He did not, could not, of course, foresee a distant time when the world had shrunk so far militarily that NATO seemed essential to American safety.

The president ended on a personal note. "Though in reviewing the incidents of my administration I am unconscious of intentional error, I am nevertheless too sensible of my defects not to think it probable that I may have committed many errors." He hoped that "my country will never cease to view" his mistakes "with indulgence, and that, after forty-five years of my life dedicated to its service with an upright zeal, the faults of incompetent abilities will be consigned to oblivion, as myself must soon be to the mansions of rest." The forty-five years was an exaggeration, but no thoughtful person could deny him in retirement "the sweet enjoyment of partaking in the midst of my fellow-citizens of the benign influence of good laws under a free government—the ever-favorite object of my heart, and the happy reward, as I trust, of our mutual cares, labors, and dangers."

Washington offered further advice in his last annual address to Congress. He was able to report that the nation was doing well. The British had retreated into Canada; the Spanish were causing no trouble on the southern boundary of the republic; it was at peace with all the Indians; American sailors held by Algerian pirates for ransom had been freed. The nation was prosperous. Congress ought to encourage its economic advance by assisting manufacturing and agriculture. Federal salaries should be increased; they were so low that able and poorer men could not afford to serve their country. He urged the gradual creation of a navy and the founding of a military academy. Once more he recommended the establishment of a national university. He summed up the eight years he had spent in office:

> The situation in which I now stand for the last time, in the midst of the representatives of the people of the United States, naturally recalls the period when the administration of the

present form of government commenced; and I cannot omit
the occasion to congratulate you and my country on the success of the experiment; nor to repeat my fervent supplications
to the Supreme Ruler of the universe, and Sovereign Arbiter
of nations, that His providential care may be extended to the
United States; that the virtue and happiness of the people may
be preserved, and that the government, which they have insti-
tuted for the protection of their liberties, may be perpetual.

Some Republicans in Congress could not let the president depart
without aiming a parting shot at him. The Senate graciously responded to the message, but passionate Republicans in the House
of Representatives, led by William B. Giles of Virginia—so often it
was the Republicans of his home state that assailed Washington—
sought to delete references in the response of the House to his
achievements, wisdom, and courage, together with expression of
regret that he was retiring. Giles was able to muster only twelve
votes out of a total of seventy-nine.

The president made ready to deal with the developing crisis with
respect to France. He arranged to collect a batch of documents
concerning its background and to send them to Congress. They
would be of use when a report came from Charles Cotesworth
Pinckney regarding his reception in Paris. In an accompanying
statement he declared that French "upbraidings" because America
had entered into a treaty with Britain were unwarranted. It was an
earnest American wish to be on the most friendly terms with
France. It was to be hoped that the Directory would reconsider its
policy, cease to interfere illegally with American vessels, and pay
damages already sustained by American shipping. As it happened,
no report came from Pinckney until March 7. Accordingly, Washington bequeathed the French trouble to Adams.

Still one more announcement went to the public from Washington. He now felt free to say that forgeries published by Benjamin
Bache and other Republican editors were such. He had not hitherto publicly responded to the attacks of Bache and his like. Perhaps he was provoked by an assault from Bache in which he was
given credit for saving the nation by retiring. Washington privately
commented regarding that editor that he had "celebrity in a certain way, for his calumnies are to be exceeded only by his impudence, and both stand unrivalled."

There remained arrangements for removal to Mount Vernon,

farewell festivities, and participation in the induction of Adams
and Jefferson into office. The president arranged for repairs to his
teeth, which had become "uneasy in the mouth" and which caused
his lips to protrude—a good dentist must have been a rarity in
northern Virginia.* The Washingtons entertained frequently as the
winter wore on. Moderate Republicans joined with the Federalists
in a splendid celebration of the president's birthday. People
thronged to catch a last glimpse of the Washingtons in public
places and at their receptions at home. On March 3 they entertained at dinner the members of the cabinet, the ministers from
abroad, and other persons. The gathering was gay until the
thought spread through it that there would not be another like it.
Abandoning office, Washington wrote to his old friends Governor
Jonathan Trumbull of Connecticut and Henry Knox that his only
regret was "parting with (perhaps never more to meet) the few
intimates whom I love."

The next day he put on a handsome black suit and a military hat
to attend the inaugural ceremony for Adams and Jefferson. Wearing a long blue coat for protection against the weather, he walked
to the chamber of the House of Representatives. There he was
greeted by a vast outburst of applause. Sitting beside Jefferson, he
watched Adams assume office, Adams handsomely dressed and
wearing a sword. Was Adams carrying a Sword of State, copying
British ceremony? Was he indicating that he was prepared to use
force to defend the United States, if necessary? Or had the vanity
of the new president overcome his good sense? Before the end of
the ceremony tears began to flow, betokening sorrow for the departure of Washington. Afterward he insisted upon leaving the hall
behind Adams and Jefferson and walked home in the company of
Timothy Pickering. Later in the day there was a great dinner in his
honor. On March 8 he called upon the new president to say good-
bye. Before the day was over, he was en route home with Martha.
A week later they were once more at Mount Vernon. Farmer Washington had replaced President Washington.

---

* Martha was also having trouble with artificial teeth.

XXIV

The Farewell of the Hero

A*ssessing the joys* and sorrows of Washington in the light of his own Yankee emotions, John Adams believed that his predecessor in the presidency left it with pangs of regret. But the Virginian gave no sign that he was unhappy as he resumed life at Mount Vernon. He loved the place. Certainly his mind was much occupied. There was the problem of furnishing the mansion with household goods brought from Philadelphia by sea. Another arose from decay of timbers in the house; it was necessary to replace beams to prevent its collapse. He and Martha, with her grandchildren, were well established once more within a few months. But difficulties persisted. His fields and local investments, including lots and houses in the city of Washington, did not bring in much profit. His salary as president had, of course, ceased. He received no pension from government—the republic did not provide, generously or otherwise, for the retirement of presidents and members of Congress until the twentieth century. He was collecting something like five thousand dollars per annum by selling distant lands, and he managed to live in the liberal and gracious way to which he had become accustomed. One problem beyond his powers was posed by George Washington Parke Custis, Martha's grandson. Striving to secure the benefits of formal education for him, Washington sent him to Princeton, then to St. John's College in Annapolis. The young man, to the distress of Washington, proved to be as hostile to formal learning as his father had been. There were other duties to perform—entertainment of guests, who came almost every day, and care of correspondence. He spent much time supervising his farms.

We have an account of a typical day from Washington. He rose with the sun. If "my hirelings are not in their places at that time I send them messages expressive of my sorrow for their indisposition," stirring them to action. He breakfasted soon after seven o'clock, bade farewell to guests who were departing, then mounted his horse and rode about his lands until it was time to dress for dinner, in the afternoon. A walk followed dinner, then tea. He finished his tea at dusk. When the candles were lit, he went to his writing table to reply to letters, but was often disinclined to use the pen. He and Martha commonly went to bed not long after dark, consigning entertainment of guests to her offspring. He had not time to read a book. He fancied that he might not have leisure to peruse a human literary production before "looking into doomsday book."

Conscious that his days might be short, Washington turned to thoughts of his youth. In May, 1798, his old friend Bryan Fairfax, a neighbor and half brother of George William Fairfax, prepared to travel to England. George William was dead, but Sally was still alive. Both Washington and Martha sent letters to her in the care of the clergyman. He wrote in a melancholy mood, in almost pathetic language. His effort to win her love was forty years in the past. There had been many important changes after he settled at Mount Vernon. "None of which events, however," he wrote, "nor all of them together, have been able to eradicate from my mind, the recollection of those happy moments, the happiest in my life, which I have enjoyed in your company." It was a "matter of sore regret, when I cast my eyes toward Belvoir, which I often do, to reflect that the former inhabitants of it, with whom we lived in such harmony and friendship, no longer reside there; and that the ruins can only be viewed as the memento of former pleasures." He had "wondered often" that she did not "prefer the spending of the evening of your life" in Virginia, among her near relatives, rather than in England. In view of the fact that the letter might miscarry, that its contents might become public, he had managed to say more than met a curious eye. So far as it is known, he did not receive a reply.

If his thoughts strayed to the distant past, Washington could not escape the present or ignore the future. He carefully refrained from offering advice to his successor in the presidency, but he could not abandon the great world of affairs. The rupture with France deepened. Three days after Adams took office, word came from Charles Cotesworth Pinckney that the Directory refused to receive him, indeed that he had been denied ordinary courtesy. Thanks to the prowess of Napoleon, the military fortunes of France were at a peak. The Directory put forth new decrees that declared an open season for seizure of American merchant vessels, and scores of them were eventually taken by the French. Adams, desiring to put an end to the crisis, momentarily considered sending Jefferson or Madison across the ocean as a special emissary, but partisan feeling intervened. He had retained all the members of Washington's cabinet. Taking their advice, he sent a commission of three men to the French capital, two Federalists, Pinckney and John Marshall, and Elbridge Gerry, a Republican but a personal friend of the president. Arriving in Paris in the autumn of 1797, they were insulted. They met with three men known to them only as X, Y, and Z, intermediaries of the French foreign minister, Charles Maurice de Talleyrand-Périgord, and were told that they must pay him a bribe of $250,000 in order to see him. They were also informed that America must lend a large sum of money to France—much of which would have been a gift—in order to secure any sort of agreement with the Directory. At that time France had overcome all her enemies on the Continent and was at war only with Britain, which was carrying on the conflict with difficulty. Talleyrand perceived no need to bargain with a feeble government beyond the ocean that was disliked by a large part of the American population friendly to France. Was it useless to try to negotiate?

The contemptuous treatment given the three envoys, together with the continued depredations of the French upon American commerce, created a war fever in the United States. Men formed military units and announced in the newspapers their willingness to fight against the French. In the summer of 1798 Adams and the Federalists in Congress struck at the French, establishing the Department of the Navy and authorizing the navy and armed merchantmen to capture French warships; they also arranged for a provisional army of ten thousand men, which was to take the field when a French invasion seemed imminent. Furthermore, the Federalists put into effect the Alien Act and the Sedition Act. The former empowered the president to expel dangerous foreigners—presumably French or Francophil—even in time of peace. The Sedition Act, aimed particularly at Republican editors and writers presumably addicted to disloyalty, provided for the punishment of any person who undertook to engage in a seditious conspiracy against the United States or to "write, print, utter or publish" lies or scandal intended to defame its government or arouse hatred among the people against it. The law opened the way for incarceration of Republican editors and others who continued to condemn the national government, its policies, and its Federalist leaders. The result was a serious interference with freedom of speech and of the press. One response of the Republicans was contained in the Virginia and Kentucky Resolutions, passed by the legislatures of the two states. The lawmakers of Virginia perceived danger that the national government would turn into "an absolute, or at best, a mixed monarchy." Those of Kentucky, using language supplied by Jefferson, ventured to suggest that the states might be compelled to resort to nullification in order to check federal tyranny.

Washington endorsed all of the new Federalist measures. Deploring factions and parties, he had tried to act only for his country in the early years of his presidency. He believed as late as 1794 that he had favored neither the Federalists nor the Republicans. He was certainly a Federalist in thought and feeling after the struggle over the Jay Treaty. At last he turned almost violently against Jefferson and the Republican party; he came forward as a devout and active Federalist. He had not held it against his Virginia friend that Jefferson had helped Philip Freneau begin his attacks on him while he was still president by giving Freneau an appointment as translator of French in the Department of State. Nor did Washington give heed to a report from Light Horse Harry Lee that Jefferson had described the president as pro-British at a private dinner party in 1794. Jefferson explained that he had merely referred to Hamilton and his like as pro-British. Lee was a "miserable tergiversator," he said. Washington accepted the clarification. He wrote generously to Jefferson, "I have never discovered any thing in the conduct of Mr. Jefferson to raise suspicions, in my mind, of his insincerity." Certainly Jefferson knew very well, Washington added, that he had followed the advice of Jefferson as often as he had adopted that of Hamilton.

However, in May, 1797, American newspapers printed a private letter written by Jefferson to his Italian friend Philip Mazzei, who had indiscreetly published it in Italian. It had been translated into French and thence back into English. But it was clear enough that in the letter he had condemned Washington. He had said that the object of the Federalists, the "Anglican, monarchical, and aristocratical party," was to import the form as well as substance of the British government. The form included "the birthdays, levees, processions to parliament, inauguration pomposities, etc." Jefferson had repeated the charge of monarchical display so often leveled against Washington by Freneau and Bache. It would have been of no avail for Jefferson to claim that the letter had been garbled in translation; he kept silent.

Early in the fall of 1797 there was a bizarre incident that began with a letter to Washington from Peter Carr, a nephew of Jefferson's. Using the name John Langhorne, Carr claimed to feel sympathy with Washington, whom he described as the target of "unmerited calumny" and "villainous machinations." Was Carr sincere? Was the letter an attempt to induce Washington to respond with statements injurious to himself? Was Carr merely engaging in a prank? No answer can be given to those questions. In any event, Washington did not fall into the trap, if there was one. He merely answered the letter politely. Then he learned from a Federalist friend, John Nicholas, that John Langhorne was Peter Carr. Nicholas reminded Washington of the Mazzei letter. Washington wondered whether the murky affair proceeded from an effort by Jefferson to injure him; it crystallized his growing distrust of his old friend. He wrote to Nicholas, "Nothing short of the evidence you have adduced, corroborative of intimations which I have received long before, through another channel, could have shaken my belief in the sincerity of a friendship, which I had *conceived* was possessed by me, *by the person* to whom you allude." Jefferson became *"that man"* to Washington. The rupture was final.

Washington approved, of course, the Federalist preparations for war with France—his devotion to the republic would not permit him to do otherwise. He was at first opposed to the Sedition Act. In May, 1798, he expressed the opinion that it was "better to submit" to "chastisement" by Republican writers "than to hazard greater evils by futile resentment." He changed his mind. After the passage of the law, after the federal courts began to deal rather roughly with outspoken Republicans, he came to believe that it was not without justification. He saw no rampant wickedness in muzzling Republicans who had so long used him for a target, who constantly excused French misbehavior, who invariably condemned Federalist measures. Had they not abused the freedom of the press? He did not believe that it was absolute under the Constitution. He condemned the Virginia and Kentucky Resolutions, so hostile to the exertion of national authority. He believed that "the opposers of government will stick at nothing to injure it." At last he began to urge Federalists in Virginia to come forward, to seek office, to use their political power for the welfare of their country.

He would not spare himself when the nation was endangered. Inevitably he was asked to lead the land forces that were to repel French invaders. On July 2, 1798, he was nominated by President Adams as commander in chief, with the rank of lieutenant general, of all the armies raised or to be raised of the United States. The appointment was unanimously approved by the Senate on the following day, and Adams signed the general's commission, suitably, on July 4. Washington did not hesitate. He would have preferred to sit quietly "under my vine and fig tree." He was aware that the stunning victories of the French revolutionists had been won by young commanders, and he was conscious of his age. However, he was in good health, and he would not refuse to do what he could for his country. He agreed to serve, without pay except for his expenses, provided that he was not asked to take the field unless invasion was imminent and provided that he could choose the high officers who would be immediately under him. He wished to have three major generals, in order of rank Alexander Hamilton, Charles Cotesworth Pinckney, and Henry Knox. If invasion came, which was not very likely in view of British superiority at sea, he assumed that it would be directed at the southern states, the weaker part of the union, the area where sentiment in favor of France was strongest. He calculated that such an invasion might be accompanied by a French occupation of New Orleans. He proposed to entrust command in the states south of Virginia to Pinckney, to employ Hamilton in Virginia. Hamilton would lead the Legion as well as the newly raised troops in his area. All three major generals were, of course, Federalists. Moreover, Washington did what he could to confine all commissions in the new army to Federalists as well as gentlemen. He wanted no extreme partisan of France as an officer under him. Indeed, he was averse to appointment of any Republican, no matter how vigorously that Republican protested his eagerness to fight the French. Recommending men to the president for commissions under the rank of major general—he was flooded with applications—he endorsed Federalists who were healthy veterans of the War of Independence or promising young gentlemen. He especially sought to secure the services of officers who had proved their value in the War of Independence, such as Light Horse Harry Lee, Edward Carrington, and Benjamin Tallmadge. He would not knowingly recommend a man of dubious character for a commission. Colonel William S. Smith, a son-in-law of President Adams, otherwise qualified for an appointment, had unscrupulously twice borrowed money on the same security. Washington would not employ him.

Placing Hamilton above Pinckney and Knox, the new lieutenant general became enmeshed in troubles. Hamilton had been no more than a colonel in the war, well below both Pinckney and Knox. Pinckney was willing to accept placement under Hamilton, but Knox protested. He was still under fifty years of age; he had been a major general when Hamilton was only a colonel; he had been head of the War Department both during the Confederation and the early years of Washington's presidency. He was eager to take the field, but not as a junior to Pinckney and Hamilton. He wrote to Washington. Had he not served well? Had he not gained the esteem and affection of Washington? President Adams supported the claims of Knox. He deserved to be second only to Washington; New England would supply a large fraction of the new army; New England wanted Knox; the major generals ought to have the seniority they possessed during the War of Independence. Looking upon Hamilton as a personal enemy, Adams contended that Hamilton was ambitious, that it would not do to have him in a position to succeed to the supreme command in the event that it was vacated by Washington. The lieutenant general refused to listen. He could not change the arrangement he had made. "I can say with truth," he wrote to the president regarding Knox, "there is no man in the United States with whom I have been in habits of greater intimacy; no one whom I have loved more sincerely, nor any for whom I have had a greater friendship." But it was necessary to make the best possible appointments "when, possibly, our all is at stake." Hamilton must be preferred. "By some he is considered as an ambitious man, and therefore a dangerous one. That he is ambitious I shall readily grant, but it is of that laudable kind which prompts a man to excel in whatever he takes in hand. He is enterprising, quick in his perceptions, and his judgment instinctively great: qualities essential to a military character, and therefore I repeat, that his loss will be irrepairable." Washington undoubtedly had it in mind that Hamilton could not be a menace to the state while Washington was alive. Adams at length gave way. Offered only the third rank below Washington, Knox declined the appointment.

Transports carrying French troops did not appear at the mouth of the Chesapeake or at the entrance to Charleston harbor. Undeclared war between America and France broke out on the seas. The new American navy attacked armed French vessels, capturing about eighty-five of them. Particularly pleasing was the battering administered to the French frigate *L'Insurgente* by the *Constellation* in a battle in the Caribbean. But the Directory drew back. In November, Washington went to Philadelphia to confer with James McHenry, Hamilton, and Pinckney regarding arrangements for the new army. It was reported that "the good old chief looks in fine health" and that his mind seemed to be as "alert as ever." There he met Dr. James Logan, a Pennsylvania Republican who had taken it upon himself to go to Paris in order to plumb the intentions of the Directory. Logan claimed that the Directory desired, despite threats it made against the United States, to reach an accommodation. On December 8 Washington heard President Adams inform Congress that he had received information to the same effect.

Leaving Philadelphia for the last time, Washington was not at all sure that full-scale war could be avoided. On January 31, 1799, he received a letter from Joel Barlow, dated October 2, in which that poet and Republican reported from France that the Directory did indeed desire to put an end to the crisis. The French were softening the decrees that injured American commerce. Washington, having hitherto refrained from offering counsel regarding foreign policy to Adams, relayed the letter to the president. If Adams believed that the letter was intended "to bring on negociation upon open, fair and honorable ground and merits a reply, and will instruct me as to the tenor of it; I shall, with pleasure and alacrity obey your orders; more especially if there is reason to believe that it would become a mean, however small, of restoring peace and tranquillity to the United States upon just, honorable and dignified terms: which I am persuaded is the ardent desire of all the friends of this rising empire." Adams advised the general not to answer Barlow, merely a troublemaking Republican in the eyes of the president.

However, Adams, under pressure from extreme Federalists, including the majority of his cabinet, to deal sternly with France, was encouraged by Washington's letter to resist the pressure. He had had word from William Vans Murray, minister to the Netherlands, that Talleyrand had changed his ways and was disposed to bargain. Given reason to believe that Washington would support him against Federalists eager for war on land and sea, Adams undertook to reopen formal negotiations, to the dismay and anger of hotheads in his own party. The French were indeed disposed to conciliate rather than to widen the fighting, for they were now threatened by a great coalition, including Russia and Austria, that had been created by Britain. Eventually the French did enter into a treaty, in 1800, that brought the undeclared war to a close. The army that Washington was to lead againt them turned out to be only a paper army.

Before the menace of war with France vanished, Washington was urged to return to the political world. As the presidential election of 1800 approached, Federalist Governor Jonathan Trumbull of Connecticut, meditating about politics, concluded that John Adams was neglecting his duties and, what was much worse, that he had created division among the Federalists and was likely to lose his office to Jefferson. Trumbull had an inspiration. The Federalists could set aside Adams in favor of Washington. Trumbull wrote to Washington in the summer of 1799. Would he be willing to come forth as a candidate for the presidency? The letter reached Mount Vernon not long after Washington had drawn up his final will. He gave the suggestion serious consideration. He was in good health, but he wished "to pass through the vale of life . . . undisturbed in the remnant of the days I have to spend here, unless called upon to defend my country." He felt that the burdens of office would be too great for his declining abilities. There was also the fact that he had said farewell to political life; he would be accused of "irresolution" or "concealed ambition" were he to return to it. The election would be settled, he believed, entirely upon the basis of party. If the Republicans "set up a broom-stick" and called it "a true son of Liberty" or "a Democrat," it would "command their votes in toto!" Accordingly, he said, he would do no better in the election than would Adams. He firmly rejected the suggestion, declaring that "nothing short of a serious invasion of our country . . . will ever draw me from my present retirement." Adams was narrowly defeated, and one estimates that Washington would indeed have been chosen, had he offered to serve, had he lived.

Washington gave much more thought to other matters in the summer of 1799 than he did to the proposal from Trumbull. He was worried about money. He now owned 277 slaves, far more than could be usefully employed at Mount Vernon. It was possible for him, by selling many that he did not need, both to secure cash and to reduce his expenses, but he could not bring himself to resort to such a sale, certain to bring unhappiness to the slaves. He even considered the possibility of developing another plantation where the blacks not needed at Mount Vernon could be located. He also was concerned with arrangements for property when he should die. In the late summer of 1798 he had been seriously ill with a fever and had lost twenty pounds. He had rapidly regained weight and was to all appearances in very good health. Nevertheless, he was conscious that his death would come at no distant time. He drew up his will. Martha was to enjoy the use of the bulk of his estate. After her death Bushrod Washington was to have Mount Vernon, and the remainder of the estate except for special bequests was to be divided among his relatives and those of Martha, with one most important exception. He was determined to free his slaves. His personal servant, Billy Lee, was to be freed immediately upon Washington's death. His blacks and those belonging to Martha had intermarried, and he could not legally set loose her blacks during her lifetime. Accordingly, he arranged for all of their slaves to be freed at her death. His executors must provide for the aged blacks, and the young were to be supported and taught to read and write. He stipulated that certain shares of stock should be used to help finance schools and to support a national university, an institution that never appeared.

In the later summer of 1799 Martha was very ill for several weeks with the ague. Before she was fully recovered, in September, Washington was reminded even more emphatically of human mortality by the death of his brother Charles. The general became the last surviving child of his father's second marriage. Then, suddenly, he was himself stricken. On December 12 he went for his customary ride over his lands. It was alternately raining and snowing, a most unpleasant day. He seemed to be as well as usual in the evening, but his throat was sore the following morning. He refrained from taking his usual journey, but he felt well enough later in the day to go out to mark some trees he wished to be removed from the front lawn. He was cheerful and animated as darkness approached. However, he became very ill during the early hours of the fourteenth. He could hardly breathe. At dawn he asked that Albin Rawlins, one of his overseers, come to administer the standard remedy of the time, bleeding.* The general left his bed and sat by a fire, but his condition did not improve. His personal physician and longtime friend, Dr. James Craik, sent for in haste, came. His diagnosis was "inflammatory quinsy." Two other physicians, Dr. Elisha Cullen Dick and Dr. Gustavus Richard Brown, responded to calls for help. The sick man was bled twice more by the doctors. During the afternoon he sat up once more, briefly, but it had become apparent that he would not recover. Efforts to clear his throat were in vain, for he had a streptococcus infection. It could easily have been treated in the twentieth century, after the discovery of penicillin. Bleeding neither helped nor harmed. Washington patiently bore his sickness and the efforts of the physicians to help him. Aware that the end was coming, he asked Tobias Lear, who was doing everything possible to assist him, not to permit burial of his body until two days had passed—he feared that he might come alive in his coffin. A little after ten o'clock at night he quietly entered eternity. He was interred at Mount Vernon on the nineteenth after a funeral attended by numerous local people and punctuated by cannon fire in farewell. Martha lived on until 1802.

As the sad news spread that Washington was no more, the nation went into mourning. Newspapers reported his death in black headlines. There was an outpouring of grief that would not be repeated until the murder of Abraham Lincoln. Republicans joined with Federalists in praise of the departed hero. In an address in Congress his loyal friend Light Horse Harry Lee declared that Washington was "first in war, first in peace, and first in the hearts of his countrymen." In retrospect, Jefferson, perhaps unaware that he had fallen low in the opinion of Washington, paid handsome tribute. Washington, he said, was seriously deficient in no way, indifferent with regard to a few minor qualities, splendid with respect to all the major ones. He observed that Washington did not think rapidly but that his thinking was remarkably sound. King William IV, son of George III, declining to qualify his judgment, afterward declared that Washington was "the greatest man who ever lived."

---

* At that time even sick horses were bled.

Washington was not made of the stone that enshrines his memory. He was quite human. He had a sense of humor. He enjoyed a racy anecdote, and he perceived the ironies of men and things. In thoughtless youth he was sometimes ungracious, sometimes too demanding of preferment; increasingly sure of himself, he became more modest as his merits were recognized. In early maturity he sought property almost too eagerly. Paying his just debts, he insisted that others meet their obligations to him. Happy in his marriage of convenience and gaining wealth, he became increasingly benevolent with the years, dealing gently with honest men who were unable to give him his due, making presents of money to relatives, friends, and worthy causes. He did not abuse his slaves. Renowned for generous hospitality, he acquired superb manners. With little formal education, he learned to express himself very well, although he never achieved excellence in grammar or superiority in syntax. Impressive in appearance even in youth, he was in full maturity a majestic figure, even an awe-inspiring one, except, of course, to Martha.

First in the hearts of his countrymen? In his own time, certainly. But folk knowledge and memory of him faded, and Abraham Lincoln replaced him in popular affection, seizing half of his birthday celebration.

First in war? He was not a battlefield genius, no Caesar, no Napoleon, but he did acquire proficiency in the military art as the War of Independence continued. The progressively more favorable outcome of his major combats is instructive—a great defeat at New York, a less serious one at Brandywine, a narrow defeat at Germantown, a drawn battle at Monmouth, overwhelming triumph at Yorktown. The flaming courage that he had exhibited in Braddock's defeat, that he displayed in the battle of Princeton, was inspiring. His stubborn refusal to give up the struggle, even to consider less than victory, supplied an example of the first importance to his fellow Patriots. No American could have matched his performance. The splendor of his character far outweighed his deficiencies in tactics and strategy.

First in peace? We cannot know precisely what record Lincoln would have made in peace, under far different circumstances. Many will acclaim the behavior of Franklin Roosevelt in the Great Depression. It is difficult to find any grave fault in the political history of Washington. He lacked the gifts of the orator; he was not a gifted philosopher; he was no propagandist; he could not talk glibly about the science of government; he was not very remarkable as a social reformer. The Sedition Act was not anathema to him. But in general he accepted the healthy changes that came with independence. Without him it is likely that there would have been neither those changes nor the independent American republic that made them possible. His great contribution arose from the devotion that he gave to the American cause, to the republic. Unswerving against British monarchy, he sought to be neither a king nor a dictator. Struggling for freedom from Britain in association with Carolinians, Pennsylvanians, and men of Massachusetts, he became utterly an American. There must be only one American republic, one with a magnificent future. Except for his influence, the Constitution might never have been. He would not defend the interests of Virginia or of the South as against those of the nation. Rather, he insisted that the welfare of the nation was fundamental, that all local, state, and regional loyalties must yield to it. As a whole-souled Patriot he gave strength and solidity to the republic during his eight years in the presidency. Before he died, the American "empire of liberty" was sturdily emerging from infancy. It is fitting that the capital of the republic, a state, institutions of learning, innumerable streets, and countless individuals have borne and will bear his name.

Bibliographical Essay

A list of all the materials that the author of a life of Washington might consult would fill a large book. My principal intention in this essay is to point out the more important writings concerning him, together with valuable works concerning his times that throw light upon his personality, problems, and decisions. The references offered herein are highly selective. It is not to be expected that my choices will please everyone familiar with Washington and the eighteenth century. I have doubtless omitted writings that other scholars consider both germane and important; I have very likely recommended publications that another biographer framing such a list would set aside.

The Washington papers, principally in the Library of Congress, supply the foundations for all the worthy biographies of their original owner. The letters and other documents in that collection emanating from Washington, along with Washington items from many other collections, have been most recently and most reliably published in John C. Fitzpatrick, ed., *The Writings of George Washington* (39 vols., Washington, D.C., 1931–44). Donald Jackson *et al.*, *The Diaries of George Washington* (6 vols.; Charlottesville, 1976–79), is the best edition of the diaries. *The Papers of George Washington,* a massive edition that will include writings sent to him as well as those he emitted, is currently under way at Charlottesville. Its first general editor, Donald Jackson, has been succeeded by William C. Abbot. Thus far only the first two volumes (Charlottesville, 1983), have been published.

Until that splendid project is completed, two published collections of letters written to Washington will retain important value, Stanislaus M. Hamilton, ed., *Letters to Washington and Accompanying Papers* (5 vols.; Boston, 1898–1902), covering the period before 1775, and Jared Sparks, ed., *Correspondence of the American Revolution; Being Letters of Eminent Men to Washington, 1775–1789* (4 vols.; Boston, 1853). Letters and reports to Washington are also available in the published papers of his contemporaries in collections such as Charles Francis Adams, ed., *The Works of John Adams* (10 vols.; Boston, 1850–56); Lyman Butterfield *et al.,* eds., *Adams Family Correspondence* (4 vols. to date; Cambridge, Mass., 1963–); Lyman Butterfield *et al.,* eds., *Diary and Autobiography of John Adams* (4 vols.; Cambridge, Mass., 1961); *The Lee Papers,* Collections of the New-York Historical Society (4 vols.; New York, 1872–75); Henry P. Johnston, ed., *The Correspondence and Public Papers of John Jay* (4 vols.; New York, 1890–93); Stanislaus M. Hamilton, ed., *The Writings of James Monroe* (7 vols.; New York, 1898–99); Otis G. Hammond, ed., *Letters and Papers of Major-General John Sullivan,* Collections of the New Hampshire Historical Society (3 vols.; Concord, N.H., 1930–39); Stanley J. Idzerda *et al.,* eds., *Lafayette in the Age of the American Revolution: Selected Letters and Papers, 1776–1790* (Ithaca, N.Y., 1977); Julian P. Boyd *et al.,* eds., *The Papers of Thomas Jefferson* (20 vols. to date; Princeton, 1950–); William T. Hutchinson *et al.,* eds., *The Papers of James Madison* (10 vols.; Chicago, 1962–77); and Harold C. Syrett *et al.,* eds., *The Papers of Alexander Hamilton* (26 vols.; New York, 1961–78). Projects for the publication of the papers of Nathanael Greene, John Marshall, and other worthies of Washington's time are also under way. Edmund C. Burnett, ed., *Letters of Members of the Continental Congress* (8 vols.; Washington, 1921–36), is similarly useful. It is in the process of replacement by a much more complete collection by Paul H. Smith *et al.,* eds., *Letters of Delegates to Congress, 1774–1789* (5 vols. to date; Washington, D.C., 1976–).

Many biographies of Washington have been published, the first being that by "Cherry Tree" Mason Locke Weems, *The Life of George Washington; With Curious Anecdotes . . .* (Philadelphia,

1918, for example), a popular work that has been reprinted many times. Chief Justice John Marshall produced *The Life of George Washington* . . . (5 vols.; London, 1804–1807), without exhausting research or use of his personal knowledge of the subject. Washington Irving, *The Life of George Washington* (5 vols.; New York, 1856–59), was a superior biography in its time and still possesses some of the Irving charm. Henry Cabot Lodge put forth *George Washington* (2 vols.; Boston, 1889), without adding much to the Washington canon. A better study was Paul Leicester Ford's *The True George Washington* (Philadelphia, 1896). Woodrow Wilson's *George Washington* (New York, 1897) broke no new ground, and Owen Wister will be remembered for his excellent Western, *The Virginian*, rather than for his study of an actual Virginian in *The Seven Ages of Washington* (New York, 1907). The year 1926 was marked by the appearance of W[illiam] E. Woodward, *George Washington: The Image and the Man* (New York, 1926), and of part of Rupert Hughes, *George Washington* (3 vols.; New York, 1926–30). Woodward, a leader of the debunking school of biographers, combined slender research and bias against his subject to limn an unreal and unfavorable image. Hughes, in an unfinished biography that terminated in the midst of the War of Independence, eschewed Washington worship and added to our knowledge of the Virginian by a skeptical approach. The bicentennial of Washington's birth stimulated other writers, including William Roscoe Thayer, *George Washington* (Boston, 1931). Bernard Faÿ, a French scholar, published *George Washington: Republican Aristocrat* (Boston, 1931), a shallow book. The *George Washington* of Louis Martin Sears (New York, 1932), was laudatory, and John C. Fitzpatrick came forth with *George Washington Himself: A Common-Sense Biography Written from His Manuscripts* (Indianapolis, 1933), a respectable study based upon extensive research. Seven years later came Nathaniel W. Stephenson and Waldo H. Dunn, *George Washington* (2 vols.; New York, 1940), scholarly but marred by the inability of the authors to perceive faults in their subject, including Washington's approach to Sally Fairfax.

A major advance in Washington studies came at the middle of the twentieth century with the appearance of Douglas S. Freeman, J. A. Carroll, and M. W. Ashworth, *George Washington: A Biography* (7 vols.; New York, 1948–57), the first six volumes being written by Freeman, the concluding one by his collaborators. The Freeman opus, containing a storehouse of information gleaned from many sources, is remarkably detailed. Its approach is too strictly temporal. It mingles trivia with matters of great importance in such a way that materials regarding particular issues are sometimes unnecessarily scattered. Moreover, relating only what Washington knew at the moment of making a decision, the narrative is sometimes rather limited in scope. Freeman knew less about the eighteenth century than he did about Robert E. Lee. Even so, the Freeman-Carroll-Ashworth opus is a remarkable achievement. That massive work was followed by another, James Thomas Flexner, *George Washington* (4 vols.; Boston, 1965–72), which is both scholarly and readable. A condensed version of it, *Washington: The Indispensable Man* (Boston, 1969), is available in paperback. Flexner's approach is temperate and sophisticated. Shorter lives of Washington continue to appear. Howard Swiggett's *The Great Man: George Washington as a Human Being* (Garden City, N.Y., 1953), is shallow but witty. Other, more recent biographies have been put forth—Marcus Cunliffe, *George Washington: Man and Monument* (London, 1959); North Callaghan, *George Washington: Soldier and Man* (New York, 1972); and Robert F. Jones, *George Washington* (Boston, 1979).

A number of special studies regarding phases of Washington's life deserve attention. William S. Spohn's *Itinerary of George Washington, from June 15, 1775, to December 23, 1783* (Philadelphia, 1892), retains usefulness. Paul Leland Haworth, *George Washington: Country Gentleman* (Indianapolis, 1925), is interesting. Eugene E. Prussing, *The Estate of George Washington* (Boston, 1927), is enlightening. John C. Fitzpatrick disposed of several canards in "George Washington Scandals," *Scribner's*, LXXXI (1927), 389–95. Thomas C. Frothingham put forth *Washington: Commander in Chief* (Boston, 1930). In the following year appeared David M. Matteson, *Washington and the Constitution* (Washington, D.C.), and Everett E. Edwards, *George Washington and Agriculture* (Washington, D.C.). Charles Arthur Hoppin, *The Washington Ancestry . . .* (3 vols.; Greenfield, Ohio, 1932), traced the Washington line through various persons back to Sulgrave Manor. In 1932 Leonard C. Helderman contributed *George Washington: Patron of Learning* (New York). Charles Henry Ambler, *George Washington and the West* (Chapel Hill, 1936), dealt usefully with its important subject and did not find serious fault in Washington as a land speculator. Bernhard Knollenberg, *Washington and the Revolution* (New York, 1940), contains a number of essays that coolly and cogently examine the behavior of Washington in response to the so-called Conway Cabal and in affairs of the War of Independence. Curtis P. Nettels, *George Washington and American Independence* (New York, 1951), offers close argument to the effect that Washington was steadily in the forefront among the defenders of American rights before the War of Independence. William Bell Clark, *George Washington's Navy: Being an Account of His Excellency's Fleet in the New England Waters* (Baton Rouge, 1960), is interesting regarding the ships Washington sent to sea early in that struggle. Louis Martin Sears, *George Washington and the French Revolution* (Detroit, 1960), is very friendly to Washington. Bernhard Knollenberg wrote valuably and astringently about the younger Washington in *George Washington: The Virginia Period, 1732–1775* (Durham, N.C., 1964). John Powell, *General Washington and the Jack Ass, and Other American Characters in Portrait* (Cranbury, N.J., 1969), has for its principal essay an amusing chronicle of Washington's efforts to breed mules. General George Washington and Marvin Kitman, *George Washington's Expense Account* (New York, 1970), reprints the account the general submitted at the end of the War of Independence and rather amusingly compares it to that of a twentieth-century American man of business. Forrest McDonald, *The Presidency of George Washington* (Lawrence, Kan., 1974), has relatively too much to say about Alexander Hamilton and Thomas Jefferson, too little about Washington.

There is a plethora of historical writings concerning the eighteenth century, of which only a few works can be mentioned, that supply background for Washington's remarkable career. For the French and Indian War one may consult Louis K. Koontz, *The Virginia Frontier, 1754–1763* (Baltimore, 1925); Hays Baker-Crothers, *Virginia and the French and Indian War* (Chicago, 1928); and Kenneth P. Bailey, *The Ohio Company of Virginia and the Westward Movement, 1748–1792: A Chapter in the History of the Colonial Frontier* (Glendale, Calif., 1939). One may learn somewhat about the Indian problem of Virginia and her southern neighbors in the Seven Years' War and afterward in John R. Alden, *John Stuart and the Southern Colonial Frontier: A Study of Indian Relations, War, Trade, and Land Problems in the Southern Wilderness, 1754–1775* (Ann Arbor, 1944). The same author has produced, I think, the best general history of the period 1763–1789 in *A History of the American Revolution* (New York, 1969). For the approach of the War of Independence one may go to John C. Miller, *Origins of the American Revolution* (Boston, 1943), a colorful account, and the analytical studies of Bernhard Knollenberg, *Origin of the American Revolution, 1759–1766* (New York, 1960), and *Growth of the American Revolution, 1766–1775* (New York, 1975). Pauline Maier, *From Resistance to Revolution: Colonial Radicals and the Development of American Opposition to Britain, 1765–1776* (New York, 1972), has comment on American political notions. R. Don Higginbotham has contributed an excellent large-scale military history, *The War of American Independence: Military Attitudes, Policies, and Practice, 1763–1789* (New York, 1971). Willard M. Wallace, *Appeal to Arms* (New York, 1951), is a brief and readable history of the war. Charles A. Royster offers *A Revolutionary People at War: The Continental Army and the American Character, 1775–1783* (New York, 1980). Howard H. Peckham, *The War for Independence: A Military History* (Chicago, 1958), stresses the difficulties faced by the Patriots. A British view of the struggle is to be found in Piers Mackesy, *The War for America, 1775–1783* (Cambridge, Mass., 1964), largely based upon British sources. Valuable and novel information regarding casualties has been brought forward in Howard H. Peckham, *The Toll of Independence: Engagements and Battle Casualties of the American Revolution* (Chicago, 1974). The modern studies of the Loyalists are the best ones—William A. Nelson, *The American Tory* (New York, 1961); Paul H. Smith, *Loyalists and Redcoats: A Study in British Revolutionary Policy* (Chapel Hill, 1964); and Robert M. Calhoon, *The Loyalists in Revolutionary America, 1760–1781* (New York, 1973).

For the development of the national government and the states during and immediately after the War of Independence, the works of Merrill Jensen, including *The Articles of Confederation: An Interpretation of the Social-Constitutional History of the American Revolution, 1774–1781* (Madison, Wis., 1940), and *The New Nation: A History of the United States During the Confederation, 1781–1789* (New York, 1950), have been seminal. The student may also go for such matters to Forrest McDonald, *E. Pluribus Unum: The Formation of the American Republic, 1776–1790* (Boston, 1965), and Gordon S. Wood, *The Creation of the American Republic, 1776–1787* (Chapel Hill, 1969). Edmund C. Burnett, *The Continental Congress* (New York, 1941), and Jacob N. Rakove, *The Beginnings of National Politics* (New York, 1979), cast light upon the early Congresses. Jackson T. Main, *The Sovereign States, 1775–1783* (New York, 1973), is useful. Of great and enduring quality is

Allen Nevins, *The American States During and After the Revolution* (New York, 1924), which chronicles the social and intellectual changes that came with independence. For understanding the emerging South and the attitude of Washington toward it, one should examine John R. Alden, *The South in the Revolution, 1763–1789* (Baton Rouge, 1957), and *The First South* (Baton Rouge, 1961). The making and adoption of the Constitution are covered in Clinton Rossiter, *1787: The Grand Convention* (New York, 1966); Carl Van Doren, *The Great Rehearsal: The Story of the Making and Ratifying of the Constitution of the United States* (New York, 1948), which is readable; Robert A. Rutland, *The Ordeal of the Constitution: The Antifederalists and the Ratification of the Constitution of 1787–1788* (Norman, Okla., 1966); and Jackson T. Main, *The Anti-Federalists: Critics of the Constitution, 1781–1788* (Chapel Hill, 1961).

John C. Miller, *The Federalist Era* (New York, 1952), supplies a general account of the presidencies of Washington and John Adams. Noble E. Cunningham, Jr., offers *The Jefferson Republicans* (Chapel Hill, 1957), which can be supplemented by Lance Banning, *The Jeffersonian Persuasion: Evolution of a Party Ideology* (Ithaca, N.Y., 1980). Richard Buell, Jr., has somewhat to say regarding philosophical differences between the Federalists and Republicans in *Securing the Revolution: Ideology in American Politics, 1789–1815* (Ithaca, N.Y., 1972). We are reminded by Louise B. Dunbar, *A Study of Monarchical Tendencies in the United States from 1776 to 1801* (Urbana, Ill., 1923), that all Americans did not become devout republicans in 1776. Alexander De Conde, *Entangling Alliance: Politics and Diplomacy Under George Washington* (Durham, N.C., 1958), deals with the continuing role of the Franco-American alliance of 1778. Richard B. Morris, *The Peacemakers: The Great Powers and American Independence* (New York, 1965), is useful for the background of international relations after 1783. The two important treaties of 1795 are covered in the standard works by Samuel F. Bemis, *Jay's Treaty* (New York, 1923), and *Pinckney's Treaty: America's Advantage from Europe's Distress, 1783–1800* (Rev. ed.; New Haven, 1960). William Stinchcombe, *The XYZ Affair* (Westport, Conn., 1981), carefully analyzes the affair. For the Alien and Sedition acts and consequent struggle, one should go to James Morton Smith, *Freedom's Fetters: The Alien and Sedition Laws and American Civil Liberties* (Chapel Hill, 1956). There is a good account of the rebellion in western

Pennsylvania in Leland Baldwin, *Whiskey Rebels: The Story of a Frontier Uprising* (Pittsburgh, 1939).

Biographical studies of the friends and enemies of Washington also help us to see him in a clearer light. J. H. Hutson, *John Adams and the Diplomacy of the American Revolution* (Lexington, Ky., 1980), deals sternly with John Adams. The best and most readable biography of Benedict Arnold is that by Willard Wallace, *Traitorous Hero: The Life and Fortunes of Benedict Arnold* (New York, 1954). Carl Van Doren, *Secret History of the American Revolution* (New York, 1941), is principally devoted to the treason of Arnold. That subject is also covered in James T. Flexner, *The Traitor and the Spy: Benedict Arnold and John André* (New York, 1953). William B. Willcox, *Portrait of a General: Sir Henry Clinton* (New York, 1964), is a thorough study of a remarkable officer. John R. Alden, *Robert Dinwiddie: Servant of the Crown* (Charlottesville, 1974), is a brief biography of the Virginia governor. Lewis Leary, *That Rascal Freneau: A Study in Literary Failure* (New Brunswick, N.J., 1941), is helpful about Freneau. John R. Alden, *General Gage in America* (Baton Rouge, 1948), helps to understand Washington's problems at Boston in 1775–1776. Paul David Nelson, *General Horatio Gates* (Baton Rouge, 1976), is a good biography. Charles Lewis has contributed *Admiral de Grasse and American Independence* (Annapolis, 1945). Theodore Thayer, *Nathanael Greene: Strategist of the American Revolution* (New York, 1960), is the best study of Greene that has been published. Ira D. Gruber, *The Howe Brothers and the American Revolution* (New York, 1975), is scholarly and standard. For Alexander Hamilton one may consult James T. Flexner, *The Young Hamilton* (Boston, 1978); Forrest McDonald, *Alexander Hamilton: A Biography* (New York, 1979); and the fuller life by Broadus Mitchell, *Alexander Hamilton* (2 vols.; New York, 1957). Robert D. Meade deals sympathetically with his subject in *Patrick Henry* (2 vols.; Philadelphia, 1957, 1969). Thomas Jefferson is lucidly and compendiously presented in Dumas Malone, *Jefferson and His Time* (6 vols.; Boston, 1948–82). There is a sound one-volume study of that Virginian by Merrill D. Peterson, *Thomas Jefferson and the New Nation: A Biography* (New York, 1970). Louis Gottschalk, *Lafayette* (4 vols.; Chicago, 1935–50), is a work of thorough scholarship covering the early life of Lafayette that supersedes all earlier writings. For Arthur Lee, see Louis W. Potts, *Arthur Lee: A Virtuous Revolutionary* (Baton Rouge, 1981). Charles Royster, *Light-Horse Harry Lee and the*

Legacy of the American Revolution (New York, 1981), is important. Irving Brant's *James Madison* (6 vols.; New York, 1941–61) is learned and exhaustive regarding an American leader who had received insufficient attention. R. Don Higginbotham offers superior biography in *Daniel Morgan, Revolutionary Rifleman* (Chapel Hill, 1961). Don R. Gerlach's *Philip Schuyler and the American Revolution in New York, 1733–1777* (Lincoln, 1964), is thorough. The brief biographies in George Billias, ed., *George Washington's Generals* (New York, 1964), and *George Washington's Opponents: British Generals and Admirals* (New York, 1969), offer a number of valuable interpretations. Richard C. Knopf, *Anthony Wayne, a Name in Arms: Soldier, Diplomat, Defender of Expansion Westward of a Nation* (Pittsburgh, 1960), is the best biography of that general.

Index